QUÉBEC: THE UNFINISHED REVOLUTION

By the same author

"Opinions publiques et systèmes idéologiques," *Ecrits du Canada français,* Montréal, 1962.

Les groupes et le pouvoir aux Etats-Unis (Québec: Presses de l'Université Laval and Paris: Armand Colin, 1965).

Société et politiques. La vie des groupes. Volume 1: *Fondement de la société libérale.* Volume 2: *Dynamique de la société libérale* (Québec: Presses de l'Université Laval, 1971, 1972).
English translation forthcoming, University of Toronto Press.

La prochaine révolution ou le Québec en crise (Montréal: Leméac, 1973).

Nationalismes et politique au Québec (Montréal: HMH, 1975).

Québec

The Unfinished Revolution

Léon Dion

FOREWORD BY Hugh Thorburn

McGill-Queen's University Press   MONTREAL AND LONDON 1976

This translation by Thérèse Romer is a revised
and enlarged edition of *La prochaine révolution*
Copyright Ottawa 1973 par
les Editions Leméac Inc.

Translation © 1976 McGill-Queen's University Press

International Standard Book Number 0-7735-0242-4 (cloth)
0-7735-0279-3 (paper)

Legal Deposit 3rd quarter 1976
Bibliothèque nationale du Québec

Printed in Canada by John Deyell Company

In memory of André Laurendeau

CONTENTS

Preface   *ix*

Foreword   *xi*

1. Tradition and Progress   1

     From the Old Regime to the New   1
     The Polarities of Ideologies: Conservatism and Progressivism   11
     Towards a Self-Determined Consciousness   20

2. National Identity: Hopes and Disappointments   31

     Origins and Characteristics of a Nationalism of Growth   32
     Québec and Canada's Future   41

3. Economic Aspects: Emancipation and Constraints   53

     Industrial Society and Political Action   54
     Business and Québec Society   62

4. Political Life: Hopes and Disappointments   73

     The Liberal Party and the Choice of a Leader   74
       for the Post-Quiet Revolution Era
     Political Action and Political Parties   84
     Politics Between Culture and Economics   92

5.   Politics and Nationalism in Québec   105

The Political Dimensions of Québec's Nationalisms   108

   1. Conservative Nationalism   113
   2. Liberal Nationalism   125
   3. Social Democratic and Socialist Nationalisms   141

Hypothesis and Conclusion   162

   1. Nationalisms and Politics   163
   2. The Role of the Elite and the Masses   169
   3. The Development of Nationalisms   171

6.   The Coming Revolution   177

The Crisis of the Political Community   180
The Crisis of the Regime   187
The Crisis of Political Institutions   190
The Crisis of Values   192
Developmental Trends   197
Epilogue   201

Notes   *209*

PREFACE

This book is a collection of papers and articles that have previously appeared in various newspapers, journals, and books. Although the topics deal with virtually every aspect of society—technology, economics, social structure, culture, political strategy, and goals—the underlying concern is constant.

The English edition is appreciably different from the earlier French version. Some of the material published in La prochaine révolution *is not reproduced here, either because it seemed of little interest to the English reader or because it lacks current relevance.*

For the English edition, I have written a new chapter entitled, "Politics and Nationalism in Québec." Although this piece has already been published in French (H.M.H. 1975) it was conceived for the English reader. In working upon it, I kept in mind the many Anglophone groups, of academics and students, professionals, businessmen, the RCMP, military men, politicians, union leaders, and others, whom I have had occasion to address over the last fifteen years. I tried to go back, in my mind's eye, to these varied audiences and to take up, more systematically than had then been possible, the ideas exchanged with my listeners. As compared with the other chapters, all of which were written in the heat of the moment, under the spur of concrete events, this chapter and the concluding part of the book entitled "The Coming Revolution" systematically present my views on Québec, seen as an entity on its own, in its relations with the whole country, and with the rest of the world. None of the papers collected here claim to be the last word on the highly complex subjects dealt with. They will be seen, I hope, as the views of an academic who has long taken an active interest in the present and in the future of his country. Guided by one motive, that of being sincere with myself, it is my hope that these pages will evoke interest and response among non-Francophone readers.

My own views and my way of thinking have of course evolved over the last ten years. Like all my contemporaries, I have felt the impact of changing times and circumstances. I have shared the fears and hopes of my countrymen, and have not side-stepped commitment whenever it seemed necessary to take a stand; but I have nevertheless always been careful to express my views with moderation, to temper ideas with common sense. Words need to be handled with as much caution as weapons. Throughout these papers, then, I have attempted to weigh my words, to present balanced judgements.

Another and more important aspect is common to all these papers: they are devoted to or reflect one society, that of Québec. They describe and record a critical time in that society's history, in its growth. They show the extent to which its fate is intimately bound to that of the Western world, on the one hand; and on the other, the extent to which Québec society is engaged in defining and reshaping itself.

Serious crises have assailed Québec in the last few years. They will be very much in evidence in this book. Such a close-up view is no distortion of reality, but a sober effort at analysing the significant upheavals, cultural, social, and political that Québec society has undergone. While poorly resolved crises may irreparably damage the future, this can be prevented if the dialectical components of a crisis are perceived in time and allowed to promote new syntheses, leading to a new shaping of ideas and institutions.

"The Unfinished Revolution" arises out of the past, yet it is firmly bound to the present. The current forces tugging at the fabric of society impose a series of ever quicker, ever rougher tugs upon the thread of historical continuity. We hold this thread in our hands. More than on anything else, the unity of this book rests upon one concern: how, while allowing for necessary change, we may keep the thread from breaking.

FOREWORD

The time is past when English Canadians went around asking, "what does Québec want?", while separatist alarums were being heard from *la belle province*. Now it seems that the storm has passed, and we are back to worrying about economic problems. But wait, Québec has not gone back to sleep in the vanished world of Maria Chapdelaine. It continues to change at an accelerating pace; and while a less theatrical scene than in the period of the late sixties culminating in the crisis of October 1970, it is profoundly altering its structures and changing its perceptions of itself and its situation. It is preparing to make a new and dramatic impact on a distracted English Canada. To help the English Canadians to comprehend the depth of the ongoing crisis, and to appreciate the way the people of Québec see the situation, this translated and expanded version of *La prochaine révolution* has been prepared. It presents an analysis by one of the best French-Canadian social scientists of the condition of present-day Québec in the modern world, in which scholarly depth and objectivity are combined with the intimate knowledge and feeling of a committed member of the Québec community.

Léon Dion is the right man to do this job. He is widely respected in Québec as one of her leading social scientists, who invariably commands attention when offering his analysis of political issues. Also he has an international standing as a scholar, specializing in political science. His words therefore have a dual authority as those of a thinker on the problems of modern society in crisis, and of a French-Canadian specialist in modern Québec's political and social life. He has served as special adviser to the Royal Commission on Bilingualism and Biculturalism, as co-editor of the *Canadian Journal of Political Science,* and as editor of *Recherches sociographiques.* He is a member of the Royal Society of Canada, and is past president of the Canadian Political Science Association. He is the author of an internationally acclaimed, two-volume study of interest groups *(Société et politique: La vie des groupes),* and several other books in the field. His contributions to scholarly journals, as well as to popular reviews and newspapers are legion. *La prochaine révolution* appeared in 1973. This translation includes more recent material, notably Chapter 5, which was especially written for his English-language audience.

Why has the earnest concern in English Canada about the imminent separation of Québec seemingly passed away since the October crisis of 1970? A superficial answer would refer to the election of the Trudeau government, and the implementation of some of the recommendations of the Royal Commission on Bilingualism and Biculturalism, such as the enactment of the Official Languages Act, and the opening of opportunities for French-speaking people in the federal civil service. Also one thinks of the election and re-election of the Bourassa government in Québec, inaugurating better relations with Ottawa; but the most important is the traumatic effect of the October crisis, and the powerful response of Ottawa, which served to stamp out terrorism, and shake the separatist cause, albeit temporarily.

Such simplistic and superficial explanations are shown up for what they are by Léon Dion's analysis. If English Canada was lulled into complacency by the end of terrorism and the electoral success of the Liberals, it should not have been. The continuing thrust of the separatist appeal has proceeded apace—as revealed by the 30 percent of the vote cast for the Parti Québecois in the 1973 provincial election (masked by the Liberal near-sweep of the seats in the National Assembly).

Léon Dion analyses the problems of Québec on two levels: the social, economic, and political problems peculiar to that province inasmuch as they have grown out of its past; and the profound crisis of self-confidence and meaning through which the whole western world is passing, and which has had such a destabilizing effect in Québec, still uneasy on its feet under the impact of over-rapid modernization and demystification.

The book traces the changing values of French Canada from the Church-oriented eighteenth- and nineteenth-century ideal of the simple, rural community guided by traditional religious values, eschewing the corrupting influences of the city and of commerce, to the modern situation where these ideals are rejected but the community is divided in its choice of possible new ones. The old doctrine was nationalistic, but in a way that offered no threat to the prevailing Confederation, because it respected established authority as legitimate, and accepted the domination of economic and commercial life by English Canadians and Americans. The new perspectives involve an urban and competitive role for French Canadians, leading them to challenge this domination, and the system of which it is a part. The result has been more strident nationalisms: liberal, social democratic, and socialist; a rejection of the old paternalism in favour of demands (sometimes unconscious) for participation in the political process; and a growing disenchantment with the old regime. The new self-assertiveness of the Québecois has resulted in a nationalist, and for some a separatist, stance. It has led to an expanded role for the provincial government, including the taking over of Québec Hydro, and the rapid growth of education and social services. These changes provided jobs for the new graduates of Québec's educational institutions, and thereby kept their loyalty, and prepared them to claim their place in the business world. There were others, however, who turned to the marxist critique, especially in the labour and teachers' unions. The ground was prepared, therefore, for a radical doctrinal conflict in Québec society, at a time of a generalized crisis of authority.

The liberal nationalism of *Cité libre* and the rejuvenated Liberal party of Jean Lesage reacted against the traditional nationalism as practiced by Duplessis. It championed free speech and political realism, the modernization of society, economic development, and the welfare state. Victorious in 1960, the Liberals secularized the educational system and undertook a crash program of economic development, that benefited the middle class most of all. The dislocations that accompanied this rapid change brought disenchantment for some, and prepared the way for more radical ideas.

The most important of these was the combination of separatism and social democracy that formed the Parti Québecois. Beyond this was the more ideological marxism of the group around the review *Parti pris,* which favoured an independent, socialist Québec, drawing its leaders from the masses rather than the bourgeoisie. It accused the Parti Québecois of seeking merely to replace one group of middle-class leaders with another, without sufficiently changing the structures of society. However, the more moderate position of the PQ is winning popular support under the shrewd and engaging leadership of René Lévesque, who has skilfully exploited the growing nationalism, both liberal and socialist, of the Québecois. As PQ support grows so does the momentum of nationalism, and its consequent separatism. In reaction to this the Liberal government has fought back with an emphasis on economic priorities ("100,000 jobs" and "profitable federalism") and a defence of the status quo. Clearly this is a confrontation course.

Unfortunately these developments are not sufficiently perceived and understood in English Canada, where the Québec concept of a Canada of two nations, English and French, stands discredited and forgotten. There is no appreciation of the French-Canadian felt need for protective constitutional structures, to make up for their minority status. If this unawareness and indifference persist in English Canada, the situation is bound to deteriorate and lead at last to a dramatic confrontation.

All this corresponds in time with the weakening of legitimate authority that the western world is currently experiencing. The decline of religion and tradition means the end of belief and reverence. In its place must come legal power based on the recognized competence of the leaders, and with the means of participation in government extended to the people. This concertation or organic cooperation of all the elements of the population could lead society through its crisis; otherwise it will fall victim to either anarchy or rule by expert civil servants working behind the façade of a pseudo-charismatic leader. For Québec the problem is to find a synthesis uniting her traditions with progress, making possible a government that takes into account the poor as well as the prosperous.

This is the kind of trenchant analysis that Léon Dion develops, both provocatively and profoundly, in this book, which presents issues that must be confronted in the future politics of Canada. It is better that they be recognized and thought through while there is still time for policies to be implemented to meet the many-faceted crisis that he sees inexorably approaching. This book will serve to awaken English Canadians to the continued existence of a challenge to the national accommodation that they thought had been secured with the election of the Trudeau government. Léon Dion provides a stimulating and informative basis for thinking through the problem anew, and, it is hoped, finding a lasting solution.

HUGH THORBURN
QUEEN'S UNIVERSITY

Tradition and progress

In the ordinary course of events—that is during historical periods extending over decades or centuries—societies may evolve within the rather narrow limits set, on the one hand, by tradition as it affects human minds; and, on the other, by the pressures of need and by the impact of specific factors, spurring men on to the acceptance of sporadic change. These long episodes of apparent calm may be called the latent periods of history. Then all of a sudden, often unaccountably, change snowballs in rate and extent; individuals and groups are ready, within a few years, to accept more change than in past decades or even centuries. These are the periods called "revolutions," either by contemporary or by succeeding generations.

Thus in the early sixties, after an unsigned article in *The Globe and Mail* had talked of the "Quiet Revolution" to describe the changes then occurring in Québec, Quebeckers themselves started speaking of the "révolution tranquille." Two of my papers, different in form but close to each other in spirit—the first written in the spring of 1961 on the eve of the "new era," and the other in January 1966 when it was clearly losing momentum—attempt to explain these years when so many dreams, often rooted in the past, took the shape of plans and projects, led to a number of definite achievements, or remained glittering promises, stillborn.

A. FROM THE OLD REGIME TO THE NEW

Right now we in Québec are in a transitional phase between two political

Section A of this chapter is an abridged and somewhat rearranged version of an article that originally appeared in *Cité libre*, no. 38 (June-July 1961)

regimes, and shall be for some time to come, just as we are in a phase of transition between two types of society. This convergence of political, social, and cultural conditions is more than random, passing chance. The former Union Nationale government corrupted and degraded a number of the values and mores of our traditional society by putting them to self-serving uses. Some of this debased behaviour has come to inspire revulsion, as did the government, and will not survive its downfall. The new Liberal government, on the other hand, if it follows the path it has set for itself, will be a forerunner and catalyser of values and patterns attuned to modern society.

The time is opportune to appraise our problems, which are fascinating as those posed by any society. I shall first attempt a short assessment of the climate since the Liberal victory in the provincial election of 22 June 1960; and shall then try to gauge the extent to which the current government will promote the emergence of new elites.

1. The Social Climate

The Paul Sauvé interregnum (September 1959-January 1960) cushioned some of the impact of the Liberal victory that followed on June 22. For it is a fact that Québec's political emancipation did not follow the Lesage team's coming to power; it had already begun under the Union Nationale government. It is under the Union Nationale that my generation first tasted some of the fruits of political freedom. We were grateful to the man who surprised us by establishing, as rapidly and decisively as if these moves had long been ripening, the basic conditions for our political emancipation (above all by demystifying the concept, so far wholly negative, of provincial autonomy). Many people extended this gratitude to the party led by Paul Sauvé. And so, despite his sudden death on 2 January 1960, and despite obvious dissension and disenchantment within the Union Nationale led by the weak Antonio Barrette, Lesage's Liberal team barely made it to power.

The brief Sauvé episode blurred party issues, and will prevent the Liberals from ever garnering full credit for Québec's political emancipation. Is this good or bad? Surely it is never desirable for governments to lay claim to too much credit. The path to arrogance is short and may often lead right back into the abuses that were initially in need of correcting. Power has long been known to corrupt, and vice comes more easily to rulers than does virtue. Jean Lesage therefore does well to emphasize that his government is "a friend of the people." This is true at the moment and will continue to be so for some time to come—so long as the people succeed in keeping a sufficiently tight rein over the men in power. The winning party claims to be eager to govern with and for the people and would be horrified at any suggestion of wielding power without the active involvement of the people or regardless of their interest. Is this mere cant on the part of our new leaders? I think not, and am inclined to give them every benefit of the doubt. Indeed there is hardly any other choice. Nearly all those who have no particular personal interests to defend tend to feel optimistic about the future. There is some complaining and revolt among the old tenants of the entrenched patronage system. Still, it is just as well never to expect too much of any government, even the best. As the Chinese proverb says: Do not ask that a snake have legs.

It is common knowledge that governments tend to be allergic to criticism. During their early months in office, several of our new ministers repeatedly asked for straightforward, rough and ready criticism, claiming they needed it to get their heavy legislative program under way. They did not even bother to call for "positive" criticism, as the consecrated expression goes. Everyone knows what government spokesmen mean when they talk about "positive" criticism. Are our new political leaders engaging in a masochistic exercise? I rather tend to believe that their wish to be criticized reflected both a measure of political inexperience and a desire to do a good job of running the government.

Can such enlightened broad-mindedness survive real criticism, criticism fresh off the presses? That is another matter. It is particularly difficult for anyone in power to admit he may be exercising it ineptly. Power is legitimate to the extent to which it is being properly used. That is why rulers, especially those who have just been through the electoral process, are extremely conscious of this basis for legitimacy; and that is also why they may sincerely believe that the only "proper criticism" is the kind that justifies their actions. On the other hand, a young government still short on experience may promote what we can view as "preventive" criticism, prior to legislation. Such criticism helps a government to assess public opinion on this or that topic and to overcome the new leaders' hesitancy about this or that course of action. This I believe is the type of "preventive" criticism the new government expects of the people, and it would indeed be a pity if such criticism were not forthcoming.

In a parliamentary system such as ours, criticism initially comes—on a partisan basis, but nevertheless usefully and regularly—from opposition parties in the legislature. In our case, unfortunately, there is no real opposition facing the government. Seldom have we seen so large and so fatuous a parliamentary opposition. Its weakness lies in its failure to grasp the fact that autocratic political methods can only work in the hands of a party in power. Save in an electoral period, no opposition party can afford to exercise "bossism" when the "boss" is no longer there or when potential "bosses" lack the means to have their schemes put into effect. Otherwise such a party will discredit itself and attract the wrath of the public. A number of voices in *Cité libre, Le Devoir, Situations,* and elsewhere have deplored the absence of effective opposition in the Legislative Assembly. But, having decried this serious shortcoming, they at once slip into abstract speculations about the stance the opposition party "should adopt": to the "right" or to the "left" of the Liberals. Yet the hard, practical fact is this: there is no organized opposition to temper the purely obstructionist tactics of MLAs, and it is doubtful whether the election of a new leader during the Union Nationale's next convention will appreciably improve matters. In a system such as ours, only one remedy would work: a general election called by the government. This would in all likelihood encourage the Union Nationale to hold its leadership convention promptly, after which a politically promising figure such as Jean-Jacques Bertrand could launch the big house-cleaning required within the party. And if in the meantime the people were to make judicious choices, they would return to the Legislative Assembly a batch of Union Nationale MLAs better qualified than the last. As to whether the next government or the next parliamentary opposition might be "left," "right," or "centre," that will be for the parties to campaign upon and for the people to decide.

Not only are we deprived of a functioning parliamentary opposition, but worse still, there is no viable criticism forthcoming from "partisan" intellectuals. This is, without any doubt, the most poisoned part of the legacy handed down to the Union Nationale by Maurice Duplessis.

Duplessism, like McCarthyism, was basically allergic to anything smacking of "ideas." Duplessis never did anything to attract intellectuals, because he knew instinctively that such a step would be suicidal. Not only did he not seek to win them over, he deliberately set them aside, preferring to neutralize their influence by discrediting them in the eyes of the people. A few intellectuals had to be used in producing the Union Nationale's publications, campaign platforms, and so on; but they always stayed firmly in the background and were kept muzzled. As long as Duplessis held the reins of power, not only did the absence of intellectuals in the party not reduce his influence upon the population, but on the contrary it gave him more strength by allowing a little group of opportunists to exercise their power unchecked.

Now that the safety brake has been applied (and our parliamentary system still manages, despite wilful tampering, to act as such a brake), now that the Union Nationale has become a simple opposition party, the absence of intellectuals in its ranks has become painfully obvious. The party has no spokesman with sufficient prestige to be read or heard by any but fanatical supporters or willing sheep. More serious still, this lack of a high-calibre opposition party deprives the new government of objective and reasoned, though partisan, criticism—which it wants and needs—instead of the mindless parliamentary obstruction it is now getting. It may be claimed that, though worthwhile partisan criticism may be strikingly absent, "independent" criticism survives and is all the more useful for being devoid of factionalism. But let us look at the facts: no such criticism has yet emerged on any appreciable scale. One may doubt whether it is at all likely to do so, given the temperament, the training, and the interests of intellectuals, even beyond current unfavourable circumstances. Glance through Le Devoir, La Presse, Cité libre. Listen to random television or radio public-affairs shows. You will be surprised to note how very few commentators talk about provincial politics (and also, perhaps, how many of them pass as omniscient pundits, knowledgeable about every aspect of Canadian, international, or provincial relations). Another fact may strike you: the uniformity and mediocrity of the views expressed. And yet they represent a vast range of backgrounds: former apostles of Catholic Action, laymen, fascists, socialists, marxists . . . Most of them now sing the same tune. Nor are they averse to a little currying for favour. It is their past experience, of all things, that has led them to this. These are people who have for years been outspokenly critical of the party in power, while remaining outside the ranks of the official opposition. They persisted, despite risks to their families and themselves. For years they fought and struggled for "change" regardless of utterly bleak prospects. Now, most if not all are in their forties—in this middle period of life when it is important to "settle down" for the next twenty or thirty years of one's existence.

And now, all of a sudden, the political situation has spun around. On the one hand, the Union Nationale has fallen apart, and on the other, the provincial Liberals have become a fashionable party for our intellectuals, so far deprived of a backdrop able to give political weight to their ideas. Finished is the sterile and wordy milling around the Rassemblement and the Union des forces démocratiques (founded after 1956 on the initiative of the editors of *Cité libre,* Pierre Elliott Trudeau and Gérard Pelletier) whose constitutions also sounded their death-knell. Everybody has now fallen into line behind Jean Lesage's attempts at reform (save, of course, for a brief period under Sauvé when there were Liberal desertions and attempts—cautious, I must admit—to place the province's fate in the hands of a new saviour). Now, the intellectuals need no longer see themselves as a lost generation.

Since efforts are no longer vain, and since ideas for the first time are finding some echo in establishment circles, social, clerical, and political, it is high time to realize that apart from "preventive" criticism—itself limited in time and scope—the government is no longer faced with any vigorous criticism, therapeutic or diagnostic. For the time being therefore (and for how much longer?) the government is operating without the braking mechanism which is perhaps the most effective tool for safeguarding and preserving democracy. It is a great pity that there are no signs of serious and long-range criticism on the horizon. It is all very well to claim that the men of the present government are young and full of good intentions and that they should be given the benefit of the doubt; but in ten years' time they will be the elders of another age. I should be sad to see them then thinking as Nietsche did, prematurely aged and on the threshhold of insanity, when he said: "The person I am greets with regret the person I might have been."

When gauged against the variety and vigour that criticism generates, the intellectual climate that prevails in these, the early days of the new regime, is dull, colourless, mediocre. In large measure this is because the values which the government lives by, like it or not, have not been sufficiently spelled out. We know that we must each contribute the best of our effort to building the new society, stone by stone. But we must first have a clear idea of the kind of society we wish to have for ourselves and for our children. Politically—as in so many other fields—we are now in a period of transition. Pray God we shall know how to avoid yet another shipwreck.

2. The new regime and the intellectuals

The new regime is more than just the new government. It is also a new society in which elite groups are trying to find their place.

Yet it is also quite clear that the government's key men are the artisans of the new society. Intellectuals largely react to the stimuli provided by the men in power. It is therefore important to discover how political men view the new society and to understand how they intend to play their role.

The growing convergence of the public and the private sectors is evidence of the overwhelming influence of government, with its tremendous long-term effects, especially in these early days of a welfare state era. Conditions in both sectors will in the long run be evaluated on the basis of common standards, the standards of a human consciousness at last in harmony with its environment. Let me simply mention the wave of inquiries recently launched into hospital administration. It is clear that the new Hospital Insurance Act has perhaps not set off, but at any rate has vastly promoted, the holding of such inquiries; and it should be noted that such private institutions as hospitals are now, under the spur of the new conditions, becoming part of the public sector.

Another facet of the same situation appears in the easygoing if not immature behaviour of some of the men now in power. While widespread corruption in the former government dragged its reputation in the mud, I sometimes get the feeling that a few of the members of the new government are trying to build their castles on the moon. Perhaps a little drunk on the power which the people have for a time given them, and politically inexperienced, they seem to think that nothing has been done before, that theirs is the job of starting from scratch.

Yet another sign: the use by some political figures of the expression "the State of Québec" when referring to the government of the province of Québec.[1] I have heard people claim that this is an echo of an earlier nationalistic background, whether *Laurentien* or *Jeunes-Canada,* still very fresh in some of their minds; but the very simplicity of this explanation seems to leave it wanting. I rather tend to believe that our political figures are so fascinated by the role that the government will be called upon to play in the wake of the economic and welfare policies they are designing or drafting, that the traditional term "the provincial government" seems to them a wholly inadequate reflection of today's dream and tomorrow's reality. Given this outlook, only the prestigious word "State" appears suitable in their eyes.

All these signs and interactions affect the thinking and the action of the intellectuals.

But first, who are these intellectuals? In a numerically small and relatively unsophisticated society such as ours, practically anyone can list all their names from memory. Of course, I am particularly referring to the upper reaches of our intelligentsia, the little group spotlighted by the mass media through which it has an impact on the whole community. They are no more than a hundred or so, and nearly all of them live in Montréal.[2]

The formative period for members of this group occurred in the rather unusual and difficult circumstances between 1930 and 1945. Events had then kept these young people on the sidelines. But now, in the transition period between two regimes, they are putting down deep roots into the new society.

Three factors are especially favourable to them. First of all, their ideas now tend to be well received by political authorities, by the clergy, and by the social establishment.[3] It would be very interesting to determine accurately how far the current government platform reflects the ideas and ideals which this group expressed in earlier years. Second, their ideas, taken up and conveyed by powerful mass media, thereby get adopted by the middle-reach intellectuals all the more easily as these views have lost (or very nearly lost) their unorthodox avant-garde flavour. Third, as the intellectual elite learns to enjoy power, its appetite becomes more ordered, its attitudes more "proper" and less shocking to the man-in-the-street; the elite now has a mass audience, and one may pick up echoes of its ideas at a bus stop or in the corner store.

This new situation creates a problem. In the months following the government change-over, those who had promoted the change and had formerly ranked as non-conformists must now take a stand vis-à-vis the freshly emerging reality. What are they to do? A number of the old battle themes have lost their vigour. So, either one imperceptibly moves into conformism (current model), or else the search is on for a new identity, for new battle cries.

But finding a new battle cry means singling out some of the social shortcomings that the government changeover failed to correct. Delicate business, at best. Whoever ventures upon this path may find himself alone, out in the cold, without the support of his former companions at arms. Most of those who formerly ranked as non-conformists, through force of circumstance rather than by temperament, will find it fairly easy to co-operate with the men of the new government. They will accept key jobs as civil servants or as public-relations men; or they will engage in preventive criticism in the press, radio, or television and will contribute to creating a favourable public climate towards the new men in power.

During the last six years of the former government, "Duplessism" had become the dominant theme of every debate. Over the last four years, it was practically the only subject of discussion. Nationalism and clericalism were generally only broached as sub-themes of that broader topic.

Both supporters and adversaries of nationalism and clericalism would have much to learn from John Milton's essay on "Toleration." Even the

Chinese *Ancient Books* counselled indulgence in battle: always leave your enemies a face-saving exit, they admonished. In the heat of the struggle, both sides should beware of mistaking molehills for mountains. It is legitimate to favour tradition, whose time-tested values it would be foolish to abandon indiscriminately; but it is also legitimate to promote the appearance of new values, better suited to some of the features of a rapidly and profoundly changing society. It is important to realize that, in any evolutionary process, ancient values mingle with the new. Strains and breaks do occur, to be sure, but they are an essential condition of progress.

Most of the intellectuals would like to work in the framework of the new possibilities created by the present government, while carefully maintaining their independence towards the powers that be. This attitude flows from the logic of their present position and doubtless also from their temperament. André Laurendeau is the one who best succeeds in expressing the views and attitudes now emerging among the opinion-makers. Over and above his outstanding personal qualities and talents as a journalist, he is one of the few who has shown concern over the shabby treatment accorded by our society to its scientists and researchers.

However, the new paths that seem to attract intellectuals provoke shifts in centres of interest and lead to new definitions of changed situations, and so cannot fail to have repercussions on both the present and the future of certain social movements. An example: formerly, socialism was a rallying point for a number of these people; today it is all but ignored. The New Democratic Party, desperately trying to channel various left-of-centre currents and seeking to entice intellectuals in every imaginable way, falls short of rallying any serious support at a time when critical choices confront it. The NDP leaders will have to realize that the current cross-roads are not favourable to their movement, and will need to find a solution to the deep-seated ambiguity underlying its very existence in Québec. How can this be achieved without the concerted help of some first-rate minds?

An additional factor affects the intellectual elite: the mass media, particularly television, are wide open to them. Through very hard work, in the past eight or ten years a number of them have acquired considerable mastery of the media and have gained a wide audience. At the same time, they are, willy-nilly, subject to the constraints of the media, flowing from both the democratic aspirations and the capitalistic structure of our society. It is well known that the content of the media in socialist and communist societies is qualitatively superior to what we see in a capitalistic system.[4] In societies governed both by democratic aspirations and by a capitalistic outlook, we see the mass media underestimating the mental capacity and the expectations of the public while at the same time underrating artists, researchers and scientists. All too often, the lowest motivations prevail. The CBC's budget is in large part underwritten by the federal government, which should free the Corporation from basic commercial constraints; yet this is not the case. Two kinds of examples may serve: we have reason to be proud of some of our symphony broadcasts and radio or television plays, most of which happen to be government financed. Putting such shows on the air takes months of the authors' and artists' time, yet their annual earnings, compared to those for commercially-sponsored soap-opera productions, are insignificant. The quality of symphony concerts and especially of television drama is thus likely to deteriorate; indeed, they may disappear altogether. Playwright Marcel Dubé bluntly stated, some months ago, why he had turned to writing television serials such as *Côte de sable*. He had worked for six months, he said in substance, to write a play for television, and had been paid $1,500; surely food for thought. Professionals who appear on television—doctors, lawyers, engineers, researchers, and scientists, are similarly slighted. We might well benefit from the USSR example instead of slavishly following the United States model. Much better advantage might be taken of the experience and knowledge of our qualified people in developing the content of our programs, with less emphasis on off-the-cuff shows whose moderators often lead our experts beyond the field of their specialty or give them inadequate time to answer questions.

If the Lesage government wants to initiate a new era, it must find ways of giving scientists, researchers, and philosophers a place in our society. This is a small group of course, and it has more than its fair share of eccentrics. Moreover, apart from those who are lucky or enterprising enough to have friends in the United States, Europe, and perhaps even in Toronto, most of these people have few if any colleagues, and are thus an easily overlooked group.

Yet a society that claims to be civilized should by definition secure an adequate physical and mental environment for its men of learning. It should provide them with the necessary working tools, and enable them to be published and read in their own language. Above all, they should not be asked to become popularizers, but valued as original researchers, creative in their respective disciplines. It would also be a gross mistake for Québec to publicize and encourage only work dealing with the French-Canadian community. Research, like science, must have no set boundaries. The advancement of knowledge among us requires windows thrown wide open to the contemporary world; and the work of our researchers must not be perceived, as it all too often is, as just a matter of promoting the local product. Their work is, above all, a contribution to knowledge. It may, of course, also have a practical or topical aspect, but this can only be secondary and incidental.

Why, you may well ask, attach so much importance to so small a group? Well, precisely because they are so few at this stage, and because their presence and contribution are essential and irreplaceable.

Which brings me to the most serious problem facing us right now: the problem of goals. The new government cannot long hope to meet the needs and desires of our emergent society if the long-term objectives that guide today's actions and projects are not soon defined. The government can no longer be a simple afterthought of capitalism, as were its predecessors, the

Duplessis and Taschereau administrations. The repercussions on our social and economic system of the social welfare legislation already in force and of the legislation to come in the next few years will unquestionably be tremendous, if one may judge by the effects similar legislation has had on the people of Western Europe, particularly Scandinavia. North America is at present the only part of the world where capitalism still seems secure. However, economists have in the last few years detected a number of chinks in the system. Of course it reacts and adapts itself, and thereby it also changes, if imperceptibly. Indeed, perhaps the forecasts of Joseph Schumpeter will come to pass, even in North America. The great economist foretold that the end of capitalism would not be caused by catastrophic revolutions as Marx had believed, but by a shift in human attitudes, when people ceased to see the system as worth-while. Capitalism would slowly wither away, claimed Schumpeter, as most people came to lose interest in it. It would disappear gradually, as do all values and institutions in a democracy, in the light of successive electoral results. Hence, neither government legislation nor even the election of a so-called socialist government would bring about any permanent institutional transformation of the North-American economic system. Rather, as a result of the new social welfare programs, people would come to prefer seeing things run by public servants instead of by the managers of private enterprise; they would learn to experience a more pressing need for public goods such as social benefits that assure personal and family security, rather than for consumer goods and luxuries, produced by private enterprise whose advertising often stimulates an artificial demand, even among low-income groups; the people would come to appreciate education open to all, health services free of charge—indeed all the facilities not offered by private enterprise, but which governments may and do make available.

It may be worth repeating that changes in the collective outlook result from a great many factors. One of these factors is the political and partisan orientation of governments; but its action is not divorced from that of the other great trends that bestir societies. In fact, the influence of the political factor is not always overriding, even though it is both more basic and more autonomous than marxists believe. Also decisive is the influence of non-political elites who are undergoing substantial changes in their view of the great variety of economic, religious, and occupational components of their lives.

In the transition period Québec is undergoing, projects, legislation, political decisions, and feedbacks, will enhance each other and will contribute to shaping society's views, the cumulative effects further expanding as the various programs are implemented. This in no way amounts to tagging any ideological label on the Lesage government. Indeed not! It is rather a matter of staying abreast of changes in our society's outlook, which is likely to undergo some radical if gradual shifts in the coming years, and of trying to foresee, as much as possible, the emergence of new forms of behaviour.

Traditional attitudes and behaviour will inescapably be questioned, though not necessarily rejected. This re-examination will of course be performed by real-life men—but men working in a given context, their thoughts and actions governed by the spirit of the times. It is neither in one fell swoop nor overnight, but inch by inch and over the years, that the economic system and other institutions will be weighed and judged. Their reshaping will depend upon what is in the minds of the people and upon the wisdom of their leaders.

Are we really witnessing the dawn of a new era, or did the June election merely switch the parties in power? Will we see a repeat performance of the events of 1936, or will we have a government which will at long last give birth to the new society? In a moving letter sent to *Le Soleil* last fall, René Chaloult recalled the hopes that he and other leading figures of the time had placed in Duplessis and his *nouveau régime*. He admitted the deep disillusionment which soon marked the best men in the Union Nationale party—those who had contributed so much to Duplessis' victory over the thoroughly corrupt Taschereau administration. A whole generation was thus wasted, and our society's growth considerably retarded. If we really want a new regime to take root, our attention and watchful concern should primarily centre on our political figures. They cannot but fail in their task if they are abandoned or betrayed by the new elites. No man, no limited group of men alone, can shoulder the whole burden of change. The effort has to be shared by many. No group is unnecessary or superfluous. Society must learn to use all of its resources—each having a role to play according to his capacity. Then, perhaps, in ten years' time, we will be able to say that June 22 really marked the beginning of a new era.

B.   THE POLARITY OF IDEOLOGIES: CONSERVATISM AND PROGRESSIVISM

Less than ten years ago, intellectuals believed Québec society to have reached a critical point in its existence. Many had joined the Rassemblement des forces démocratiques. Their diagnosis was despondent: "sterility" of minds, "monolithic" thinking, "ubiquity" of the right—the social fabric seemed to them worn out. And yet today, intellectuals define the situation in very different terms. They tend to speak of "dynamism," "growth," and "revolution." How does one explain so surprising a reversal in so short a span?

A brief review of the facts leads us to conclude that social conditions, even though they have improved in this short interval, are not as radically different as the contrast between the above sets of labels would suggest. The different outlook therefore mainly seems related to psychological factors. Ten years ago, Québec was reaching the end of a long period of political conservatism: the impression of social and intellectual immobility was

Section B of this chapter was published in *Recherches sociographiques* 7, nos. 1 and 2 (January-August 1966).

thereby amplified. Today, we are in a period of political progressivism: awareness of social and cultural change is thereby enhanced. Conversely, the extent of change in certain areas was then ignored whereas today we tend to underestimate the importance of conservatist residue.

A fairly detailed survey carried out in 1958 by the Institut d'éducation des adultes in various levels of society revealed, among members of a great variety of associations, both a sharp awareness of the power of traditionalism, and a firm attachment to democratic processes and to the values characteristic of modern civilization.[5]

On the other hand, debate on Bill 60—a critical point in our recent history, as a consequence of which a Department of Education was at last established—has shown the strength with which many associations and individuals still abide by the old values and institutions.[6] They can thus be termed change resisters, while others, who wish to promote new values and institutions, can be called change agents.

Appearances notwithstanding, today as ten years ago, the divergence of outlook and aspiration between individuals and groups is intense. But in both instances, a particular state of mind leads people to magnify one of the two main ideological currents to the detriment of the other. Why this strange behaviour? Can one go beyond the simple psychological explanation put forward earlier in this chapter?

The problem may be expressed as follows: how is it that the stock of ideologies available to a society (ideology being defined as a more or less elaborate system of representations reflecting group interests and aimed at promoting action) is clearly far more diversified than the protagonists seem to realize? How is it that in a given society a whole set of ideologies tends to lie fallow, while at the same time another set, which seems to engender action, centres around a single way of viewing the world?

Everything happens as if there existed, within society, polarizing forces that affect social ideologies as soon as they acquire a general function and meaning, drawing them into the orbit of the two dominant ideological constellations which I shall call ''conservatism'' and ''progressivism.'' I shall use the two expressions to denote two contrary outlooks, one, conservatism, centring around the consolidation and defence of existing values and institutions; the other, progressivism, aiming at introducing new or renewed values and institutions. I shall use these two concepts as abbreviations to denote two different and opposed processes underlying the polarization of ideologies.[7]

In this section, I intend to identify these polarization mechanisms, having assumed they exist, and to examine the effects of this polarity upon the influence and the fate of ideologies. The polarizing mechanisms will be sought out, on the one hand, by studying the very nature of the underlying social web within which influence is exercised, and on the other hand, by examining the analytical methods generally applied to ideologies— methods which centre around the outlook of political authorities rather than that of social agents. After this inevitably abstract outline, I shall briefly describe how the polarization of ideologies affects Québec.

1. The polarity of ideologies and the interests of the political authorities

Political authorities,[8] whose main goal is to stay in power, have a natural interest in promoting conditions favourable to social harmony and conversely, in playing down or hiding outbreaks of social conflict or conditions leading to these. The interests of political authorities are, I believe, the first factor behind the polarization of ideologies.

It would be tempting to analyse conditions conducive to polarization along conservative-progressive lines: the convergence of parties towards the right or the left; the alternation of weak and strong governments; the shift from new regimes into old; the turnover of old and young bureaucracies; the cycle of preparing and implementing new projects, and so forth.

It is in the nature of political systems to want to perpetuate themselves. Governments control ideas and manipulate values to maintain and, if necessary, to justify their control over people. Political platforms become political formulae and these more or less accurately reflect the conservative or progressive leanings of the regime. In some cases these formulae are enshrined in an official ideological creed. The conservative or progressive tendency is of course magnified where there is more or less spontaneous collusion or overlapping between various social oligarchies and political authorities. In extreme cases, as in totalitarian societies, the movement of ideas is legally restricted by a pseudo-philosophical super-system which leaves social agents a very narrow margin of spontaneous adaptation to social situations.

This conservative or progressive syncretism, attuned to the interests of political authorities, produces a convergence of social ideologies in two extreme constellations. Hence the ideological polarization of a society. One of the two constellations is necessarily favoured at the expense of the other. The underprivileged ideological constellation is thus prevented, in many ways, from acquiring any tangible political punch. It is relegated to marginal political and social groups or institutions. Hence the impression that counter-ideologies are absent or weak. But this impression is misleading, because, at the edges of the authorities' areas of influence, for instance in opposition groups—or, in their absence, in study groups and secret societies—the opponents of the regime are busily forging weapons, that is gathering alternative social ideologies into an ideological constellation at the pole opposite to the officially favoured conservative or progressive doctrines. But such a counter-constellation, when presented as an alternative platform to rally those who are opposed to the regime, may carry little weight or exercise little influence upon the political formulae guiding the rulers in elaborating policies and in taking decisions. Hence the impression of ideological monolithism gained when observing the situation only from the point of view of the existing power system.

To the extent to which democracy prevails in a society, the tendency for one of the two sets of ideological constellations to be thus pushed into oblivion wanes. Democracy makes political systems more permeable to the ideas and the feelings generated by consensus and conflict within the social system. Democratization brings to light how ideologies are distributed among associations and groups, and reveals alignments between social leaders through the inevitable confrontations that arise when political power is exercised. But even in democratic governments, political authorities have their interests to preserve, and so tend to be guided by conservative or progressive notions of culture and of society when elaborating or implementing policies. The ideological counter-constellation is thus more or less down-played. Moreover, when democracy has taken strong root, its state of health is not necessarily constant. It has its own ups and downs. It will act as a filter, more or less porous according to circumstances, more or less permeable to the size and the shape of ideologies born of social pressures and of human temperament.

2.   The polarizing effect of the analytical approach to the study of ideologies

The polarization of ideologies produced by political authorities, especially when they are not democratic, is amplified by the nature of the perceptions often arising from the analytical methods used to study ideologies. These analytical methods concentrate upon the impressive systems of ideas reinforced by political authorities. In other words, there is a tendency to consider as significant only those ideological aspects that are "dominant."

I must quickly emphasize that the study of dominant ideologies is altogether legitimate in itself, and teaching curricula quite properly include these. In fact some such ideologies have reached a high level of formal expression and amount to quasi-philosophical systems. Others, like marxism and democracy, rest upon highly elaborate philosophies.

But those who only consider leading or dominant ideologies run the risk of falling into a couple of traps.

A number of people—and this is the first trap—arrive at their ideological choices in the name of "superior" knowledge or even of "science." In fact, the science whose blessing is sought is not epistemology, logic, or even the sociology of knowledge. It is rather the belief, reached by more or less valid means, that a particular ideology is best designed, or least well designed, to serve the common good. Such people end up by declaring that a given ideology being the best, it is the only true one. They overlook the alternative ideologies produced by the social fabric, thus incorrectly fostering an impression of ideological single-mindedness in society. Such beliefs of course have nothing scientific about them. Rather, they show the attraction exercised by political power upon the minds of men. Of course, students of ideology, like everyone else, have a right to their own ideological preferences and may defend or promote the ideology of their choice. But they should be alert to what they are doing. Scholars, like everyone else, are subject to social pressures and follow their own temperament and inclinations when making ideological choices, even though in their instance the process is likely to be relatively sophisticated.

Still others fall into the second trap: they imperceptibly become advocates or critics of an ideology, even while imagining that they are producing an objective analysis. In fact the attraction exercised by political authorities is so persuasive and forceful that in the very process of study it is easy to slip from ideological analysis into political choice. Instead of probing actual facts and conditions, the analyst may succumb to the rationalizations which governments work out in support of their power and actions. Ideologies may thus be taken to be synonymous with the formulae used to describe a given political regime. In this way, the ideologies come to be practically identified, by the analysts themselves, with the choices favoured or denounced by governments. The intellectual path ultimately no longer lies in analysing or studying ideologies themselves, that is searching for their sources and examining their internal structures; it merely consists of showing why such or such a political approach has been chosen by the men in power, and in cases where the choices are not yet final, why this or that tendency should prevail.

In other words, either an ideological choice is justified by claiming it to be scientific, or else, while claiming objectivity, a given political alternative is praised or decried. In either instance (and this is the significant point) the supposedly objective analyst approaches his task from the point of view of the political authorities. And this contributes, as I have just indicated, to further amplifying the ideological polarization produced by the action of the political authorities themselves.

So it is all too often the case that even analysts do not manage to grasp the spontaneous and complex world of collective representations which arise out of the multiple and varied range of social experience. Often unawares, they help to spread the illusion that ideological possibilities are limited to the dominant doctrines. This illusion can only be dispelled by adopting another analytical approach. Instead of examining ideologies from the point of view of political authorities, one should start with the point of view of social agents—associations, groups, individuals—who are attempting to define their relationship towards political authorities. Such an approach will permit detachment from the polarizing influences of political power and will bring into view the full range of ideologies stemming from social situations and individual temperaments.

3. The polarity of ideologies in Québec

Much has already been written about the endogenous and exogenous factors which have unduly delayed the democratization of the political regime in Québec. The smallness and the relative isolation of our society have long promoted collusion and confusion between the two dominant powers, Church and State. Hence, the development and the lasting influence of a "conservatist" outlook based on near-feudal clericalism and paternalism. This ideology, offering both practical and ethical guidelines, has long given the holders of the two allied powers both a "good conscience" and a high degree of control over the people.

Québec's conservatism had several features in common with traditionalism. The electoral distribution of legislative seats gave tremendous relative weight to the rural vote as compared to the urban, so that political authorities could, with impunity, denounce urban and industrial values and ignore the new social groups produced by urbanization and industrialization, particularly by the working classes and the intellectuals. The political formulae embodying this conservatism enhanced traditional values and institutions, particularly those born of a rural setting. Instead of moving towards the values and institutions of an urban and industrial society, Québec staunchly stood by the great North-American laisser-faire dogmas.[9]

The most serious consequences of this conservatism lay in Québec's economic occupation by alien industry, business, and finance, non-French in language and culture; and in the development among French Canadians of a political culture strikingly similar to that of colonized peoples: the rise of *rois nègres,* kinglets who bow to the will of economic rulers while publicly treating them with consummate contempt; armies of profiteers of every description, serving the Chief and sharing the spoils of financiers' largesse; the invention of institutional mechanisms aimed at preventing the emergence of an enlightened and free public opinion; the development of electoral methods designed to ensure popular support for governments whose social, economic, and cultural measures systematically go against the basic interests of the people. In brief, the governments which have succeeded each other in Québec have long applied policies that merely enshrined Québec's backwardness; and they justified this by conservatist, clerical, and paternalistic formulae long discarded in most other Western societies.

In different periods, the combined weight of Church and State rested more or less heavily upon the people. But this weight was always more than ample to perpetuate conservatism in spite of widely varying historical and social conditions. On public occasions, at historic events, within social movements, at religious ceremonies or political celebrations, conservatism set the tone and provided the theme. The reference points being always the same, there resulted a strong impression of near-perfect ideological consensus covering practically all social groups and associations.

In actual fact, the social and intellectual synchronization produced by vigilant, conservatist leaders provided a heavy screen of prejudice, of stereotype, and of official lies, to mask the surprising diversity of social situations and of collective and individual leanings.

The intellectuals' position became especially difficult. For a long time, some of them had publicly denounced the prevailing clerico-political conservatism. But the ruling authorities had prevented the intellectuals' message from reaching the people. For a long time Québec's intellectuals were kept from power and rendered harmless. When they started trying to make their views heard, especially from 1950 on, they were made the targets of a wave of falsehoods and denunciations, designed to discredit them. Thus, barely ten years ago, for anyone to proclaim Québec's urban and industrial goals was still tantamount to his being described as "rootless," or as a dangerous revolutionary, even by those who were directly wrestling with the problems of an urban and industrial society.

Social science began to be taught in Québec relatively late, preceding by some fifteen years the democratization of public institutions, and, without any doubt, powerfully contributing to this democratization process, by damping down the influence of clerico-political conservatism.

These two processes, namely the development of social studies and the democratization of society are now well underway and they have begun, not without difficulty, to converge upon specific projects both within the Church and State and among social institutions and groups.

However, historical roots are so strong that even social-scientists have a great deal of trouble in undertaking a study of ideologies not so much from the point of view of political authorities as from that of the forces active in society. Thus we are barely beginning to see a start to the unveiling of the real content of the religious ideologies disseminated by religious groups and churches.[10]

There are as yet very few studies of political ideologies as experienced within parties and political and para-political movements. Even among specialists, there is still a tendency in practice to liken political ideologies to electoral slogans, and to confuse ideological approaches with political choices. Emphasis upon the truth or falseness of ideologies rather than upon their internal structure and the modes of their social existence has almost exclusively attracted attention to the great political options open to Québec within the Canadian context: the list of possible options constantly lengthens and their respective merits are endlessly debated.[11] As a result, no serious study has as yet been published upon the ideologies formulated within the Separatist movements; the surprising recent ascent of Social Credit has only so far given rise to a few articles;[12] and no one has yet studied the exceptional opportunity offered for ideological confrontation within administrative advisory committees.

Moreover, the tendency of intellectuals and specialists to define situations in the light of political authorities' view-points gives undue importance to the formulae aimed at creating an attractive image of the government of the day. Current expressions such as *maîtres chez nous, politique de grandeur, nationalisme positif, Etat, ami du peuple, valorisation de la fonction publique, dynamisme de l'Etat,* are all slogans rather than concepts expressing the realities of the current political regime.[13]

These formulae, designed to enhance the progressive attitudes and actions of the present government, which have at times caught the public eye, are of course vastly different from the formulae used by the former government; traditionalism, ruralism, and catholicism were then the order of the day. But to determine the extent of real contrast, we must remember that ten years ago the intellectuals were opponents of the former regime, whereas today they have become the propagandists of the new regime. It is true that this change of outlook is linked to the radical change in the rulers' attitudes towards intellectuals. It is also true that the justifications claimed by political authorities themselves have greatly changed: ten years ago the motto was respect for "traditions"; today it is "the challenge of progress."

However, to the extent to which all these formulae lead us to believe that ten years ago the hold of conservatism encompassed the whole of society whereas today progressivism has won out everywhere, to that extent the formulae produce a limited and misleading vision of the ideological reality at the grass-roots level.

There has of course been an acceleration in the rate of social change over the last ten years. The most remarkable aspect of this evolution has perhaps been the ideological thaw in ruling circles. But we must avoid confusing the social order with the political order. Each of these orders follows its own logic. No doubt it is not immaterial whether the political principles upon which a society is based are conservative or progressive. Indeed it is in the light of such principles and on their behalf that the rulers elaborate and defend their policies and programs for the whole of society. But the overthrow of conservatism as a political formula and its replacement by progressivism does not mean, as is sometimes assumed, that society has abruptly gone over from the traditional type to the post-industrial type of civilization. The reversal of political formulae means rather that the future course of society becomes subject to different political dynamics. Societies develop at a rate linked to the nature of their institutions and to the temperament of men. This rate of development slows down or accelerates according to whether the impulses propelling political action are conservative or progressive. If the political principles underlying society are conservative, social development is not arrested despite an impression of immobility; conversely, when the political principles are progressive, social development, even though encouraged, may occur less rapidly than would seem. Society is not unlike an iceberg whose tip occasionally swings around showing either a static or a changing face; but the rate of real change under the water line varies appreciably less than appears on the surface, on either of the two visible faces.

The decisive phenomenon in Québec's contemporary situation is not an acceleration in the rate of change, nor the extent of current shifts; it is rather the suddenness with which conservatism has been replaced by progressivism as the dominant political formula. This phenomenon accounts for the impression, ten years ago, that there was an absence of social ideologies corresponding to the wish for change among social associations and groups; it also accounts for the weakness, today, of ideologies expressing the will to perpetuate traditional values and institutions. The surface impression is a false one, in both instances. It survives because, instead of devoting their attention to the aspirations and pursuits of social agents, analysts concentrate upon the political authorities.

The debate on Bill 60 showed an image of Québec society far different from that built up in the slogans that reflect the interests of political authorities. Instead of the now-stereotyped vision of a resolutely progressive Québec, it showed a society torn by contradictory strains and stresses, hesitant about the road to be followed.

The debate on Bill 60 in fact represents far more than the sum of briefs presented by associations and individuals concerning the need for a Department of Education. The unique importance of this debate, as I see it, is that it promotes a clear identification of the main strengths and weaknesses of Québec society. The positions taken regarding Bill 60 exemplify the images, the representations, that Québec society holds of itself on an issue whose stakes it perceives as basic. Therefore during the debate, society significantly revealed its real-life ideologies. In sorting out their views on Bill 60, associations and individuals did far more than participate, with varying degrees of success, in a decision-making process. They at the same time brought to the fore entire sets of attitudes which determine their view of society in relation to its past and to its current condition, as well as to its future.

The debate on Bill 60 has shown that ideological cleavages among groups and individuals are very marked. It has brought to light deep divergences between generations. It has shown up the opposition between political philosophies and has provoked the inevitable confrontation between the affluent and the underprivileged. It has brought to the surface the fears of the English-speaking minority. More basically, under the influence of the action of political authorities, the positions taken on Bill 60 clearly fall into two categories, one tending toward the conservative pole, the other toward the progressive. In both numbers and influence, the partisans of free enterprise, corporatism, and clericalism were by no means overwhelmed by the supporters of economic planning, democratic process, and secularization. Those who believe that conservatism in Québec is no more than a vestige that will disappear with the passage of time are greatly mistaken. It would be enough for conservatism to become once again the dominant political formula for the ideological situation to be reversed.[14]

The debate on Bill 60, finally, showed that the united front of the two dominant authorities, Church and State, even though perhaps less complete than formerly, is still very significant. But at the same time, the climate of negotiations between State and Church leaders showed that clerico-political conservatism had lost a great deal of its impact. The still-recent democratization of political authorities has already caused a shift in their relative weights. During the debate, both took a public stand, and were at least attentive to the views put forward by social agents. Yet the legislation establishing the Department of Education and the Conseil supérieur de l'education (Higher Council of Education), while clearly a tool adapted to current needs, was nevertheless, in the view of the minister himself, Paul Gérin-Lajoie, the result of a compromise between opposed ideological tendencies which had clashed during the debate.

When we stop looking at ideologies from the point of view of political authorities and approach them from that of social agents, the impression of uniformity is quickly replaced by the realization of intense conflict between opposed ideologies, even though recent political developments brought about a complete reversal in the two camps. It is no longer the progressives who are struggling for political recognition as of old, but the adepts of conservatism who are staunchly defending their threatened positions.

Today, as yesterday, the stock of ideologies available to society is more diversified than is generally believed.[15] In both instances, the course of events shows the existence of a great variety of ideologies. In the overall view, these may be attracted into the orbits of the two dominant constellations; and if one of these ideological constellations is more privileged than the other, this will be due to the polarizing effect of political power. Recent democratization has toned down but not abolished this polarizing effect altogether. Hence the persistent impression of a certain ideological uniformity, in spite of the conclusive evidence, accruing every day and strengthened by the political stakes at issue, that there is intense ideological conflict among social agents and among political authorities themselves.

C. TOWARDS A SELF-DETERMINED CONSCIOUSNESS

The number and size of the rifts occurring in the fabric of our societies are daily making more incongruous any explanations attempting to account for them. It is no longer possible simply to blame the incompetence on the malice of men, or the momentary shortcomings of institutions. Instead, we are up against very far-reaching changes both in society and in human outlooks. Twilight is falling upon a social order whose main pillars were erected in the nineteenth century. But already looming out of the shadows is a new civilized order. The introduction of television and the development of the first computers in the early 1950s were events whose effects are comparable to the invention of printing around 1450. Like the end of the fifteenth century, the second half of the twentieth marks the beginnings of a radical cultural revolution which, by demystifying age-old orthodoxies, destroys both the web of human relationships and man's interrelation with his environment. Ideas, organizations, things, men themselves,

The final section of this chapter first appeared under the title: "Vers une conscience autodéterminée," *Revue de l'Association canadienne d'éducation de langue française. Pour un Canada français autodéterminé* 1, no. 1 (December 1971): 4-11.

everything today changes or is replaced so swiftly that there are practically no stable reference-points left. From now on, the only possible way of adaption is continuous adaptation.

The shock of the current revolution upon human beings is so intense that a number of people cannot contend with it. In every area of activity there are changes in the nature of the knowledge necessary for coping with life, and in the bases of decision-making. These are challenges not easy to meet—even for, or particularly for, leaders. The root of the problem lies neither in machines, nor in institutions, but in the minds of men. Some, probably the majority, are engaging in a last-ditch attempt to stop the tide by seeking refuge in conservatism, or by becoming ultra reactionary, sometimes under the mantle of liberalism. Others, on the contrary, want things to "swing" and are in favour of radical reforms in institutions and in the rules of the game. The leaders, confronted with such contrary pressures, hesitate, look for a middle way, and in its absence adopt ambiguous or contradictory positions which make the situation still worse. Messages of distress flow in from every side, from countless people who are dreading shipwreck on the rocks of uncharted change; powerless to decipher the messages, the leaders become unwitting accomplices of both reaction and radicalism.

In elaborating projects and taking decisions, it is of course important to bear in mind those who for one reason or another would like to stop or to slow down change. An effort should be made to hear their views, to relieve them of their anxiety. But it is even more important to understand those who have reason to complain of the way in which they are treated by society. Their aspirations may well be in tune with history. Some go so far as to describe themselves as "dissenters" and they are often perceived as revolutionaries. What do these protest groups, multiplying so rapidly in every society, represent—young people, students, intellectuals, various minorities, the urban and rural poor? Why are they blaming established institutions—family, school, church, labor unions, industry, the media, political parties, the judicial and penal systems, the government? It is urgent that we re-examine these protest movements according to a different set of premises from those used so far. Like the new technology, only even more so, these movements are forcing institutions into major shifts which can no longer be side-stepped. They are neither "aberrations" nor simple system "malfunctions." On the contrary, they unveil, doubtless imperfectly and inaccurately but nevertheless significantly, some of the features of tomorrow's world.

Contemporary Québec is an excellent example of this rapidly changing world, with the multiple contradictions that divide it and the sometimes tragic unrest that rocks it. Few societies have known changes as profound over a ten-year period as those Québec has gone through. Its population patterns, its educational system, its religious observances, and its political habits have all undergone what amounts to a revolution. The demystification of traditional values, the demoting of elites, the questioning of leaders, have all proceeded at a dizzying pace. Only yesterday, churches, the apparently invincible ramparts of a whole civilization, proudly stood in the middle of villages, some of which had been created for reasons verging on the religious. In cities, churches were lively meeting grounds for whole neighbourhoods. Today, many church buildings are empty and up for sale; or else religious practices have been modified almost out of recognition to entice the faithful into remaining as churchgoers.

By breaking the ties which bound them to their familiar world, Quebeckers suddenly see themselves cut off from ancient certainties, now anachronistic. For the first time they are individually feeling the strain of uncertainty, paying the price of existential freedom. Men and women, long bound by the prescriptions of the past (traditions, the old techniques in every field) and the mirages of the future (joys of salvation, electoral promises), are plunging headlong into the present, without trustworthy guidance, a present they have to build by themselves. They must take over the shaping of their own lives in particularly trying economic and social circumstances.

Thus, a great many Quebeckers, chiefly among the least privileged social groups, have awakened to a new consciousness of themselves and of their destiny. Whether we think of citizen committees in our inner-cities, or of various attempts at forms of organizations such as the *Opérations-dignité* in rural communities, we see people who, despite their low economic and educational status, are determined to influence their current situation and are themselves trying to control the events that affect them. So far, these movements have generally been underrated, and most have been judged not by their own criteria but by outside points of reference. Yet it is as important to get to know what forms this new collective consciousness takes as it is to examine the reforms required if this new consciousness is to contribute to a renewal of society.

1. The signs of the new collective consciousness

Until a few years ago, the paternalism of leaders and elites largely shaped the forms of popular consciousness. Credulity, servility, dependence—but also trust, stability, security—were the basic features of this consciousness. The "revolt" of some people against their parish priest or their member of the Legislative Assembly only represented the side of the coin opposite to that of the filial respect felt by the great majority. Such revolts were perceived as limited and childish by the leaders, who had no trouble in keeping them under control. But today, very clear signs tell us that the "good old" paternalistic times are over. Apathy and a withdrawal from any form of collective commitment are dismaying features of our times. There is growing insensitivity to the old beliefs which not so long ago actively inspired the people and encouraged them to act according to the wishes of officialdom.

Community mobilization and a special new breed of leaders has been instrumental in awakening people—an active few—to the new realities. It is not easy to analyse the new consciousness fully and accurately. It surfaces on many occasions, though fragmentarily. And it swiftly assumes new forms; for instance in the lower St-Lawrence and in the Gaspé Peninsula, a big gap separates—in a short time-span—the BAEQ (1963-1966)[16] from the *Opérations-dignité*[17] (1970 up to now the present time). Nevertheless, in spite of their frequently evanescent nature or perhaps because of it, the "fronts," "citizens' committees," *Maisons du chômeur* [Home of the un-employed], and even terrorist movements give evidence of the inadequacy of official institutions, of crises at the executive and control levels, as well as of ideological realignments among individuals and communities. Certain features of the new mentality are clearly perceptible.

A first and basic feature: those who acquire the new consciousness reject the paternalism which used to provide them with security and a certain form of happiness but denied them justice. They do not feel at one with officialdom or with the politicians in power. They have dispelled the fog that masked government shortcomings and human weaknesses (exaltation of authorities, belief in the special charisma of leaders, etc.); they are beginning to free themselves from the "faith of the humble" and from "the party spirit" which turned them into the docile tools of authority. They are questioning the representative role of powerful interest groups and of political parties. More and more, they wish to choose their own representatives from among the people whom they know to be their friends and in whom they have confidence. Their relations with such representatives are no longer based upon filial respect but upon an evaluation of the representatives' ability to formulate desired goals accurately. This changed relationship has had two effects. On the one hand, it has prompted growing indifference among the population towards religious taboos and towards partisan struggles; the people are ever more clearly realizing that it is the quality of their own lives that is at stake. On the other hand, it has resulted in the growing vulnerability of leaders to the popular will. The concept which best embodies this new interrelationship is participation. Even though politicians and intellectuals have been shockingly indifferent to this great idea, participation will not soon be gotten rid of, for it has taken firm root in the thinking of those among the people who are most deeply concerned.

The new collective consciousness—and this is its second characeristic—is caught up in a vicious circle of growing expectations and mounting frustrations. In fact, it is difficult to imagine how it may ever prove possible to separate the two. For some time now, demands, claims, and counterclaims are coming in so fast that answers must necessarily seem slow in appearing. Reforms are inadequate, and are thus not perceived as reforming anything. Growing pressures indicate that, meantime, conditions have further deteriorated. Radical protest against the "system" 'does not merely come from young people and certain kinds of intellectuals. It is spreading among citizens in impoverished city neighbourhoods and in depressed areas. And since it feeds on the grim misery of the poor, their protest may well prove more intractable than that of the more affluent radicals.

A third feature of the new collective consciousness lies in its unaccustomed approach to rationality. As against the abstract concept of rationality held by scholars and technocrats, a living and human version is gaining growing numbers of followers. Instead of abiding by criteria drawn upon the "objective" laws of nature, including human nature, or upon the efficiency of systems, methods, and technology, the new rationality rests on a review of the motives that prompt men and of the ideals underlying the goals they pursue. This form of rationality may be called "social"; in its context, values become central instead of merely being ranked among other components, to be borne in mind and measured against "objective" criteria, as is the case with scientific and technocratic rationality. So, whereas for scientific and technocratic rationality the value of participation only amounts to a legitimate aspiration which should be allowed for, inasmuch as practicable, within programs based on "objective criteria"—for social rationality, this value of participation is as much of a constraint upon action as the "objective" criteria themselves. In the first case, decent living conditions are seen as depending upon a certain level of education, an adequate standard of living, and so on, without initially taking into account the degree of involvement of individuals and communities in the activities that affect them; while in the second instance it is the extent of participation itself, more than any other factor, upon which the quality of life will be seen to depend.

Pushed to their respective limits, these two concepts are worlds apart. One of our most pressing tasks is to discover the dialectic paths whereby they may be reconciled. Believers in social rationality should be reminded that it is abstract rationality that produced science, technology, innovation, and ultimately, economic prosperity. Nevertheless, it is also quite clear that abstract rationality only poorly lends itself to social organization; and such scientific disciplines as economics, psychology, and sociology every day contribute new evidence of this fact. How many plans seemed brilliant on paper, only to be found totally wanting in practice! When abstract rationality is applied to investigating and controlling men's behaviour, it may turn into rough manipulation and lead to revolt or to abject apathy. In studying institutions, we see that the most serious problems are not caused by institutional or mechanical defects, but by the resistance of men to reason imposed from outside.

Perhaps the most striking feature of the new consciousness is the extent to which it is driven by a powerful wish, not always clearly expressed, for self-determination. Unmistakably, though sometimes awkwardly, people are expressing the desire to move out of the subordinate status which has since time immemorial been the lot of the great majority. Whole groups who have long bent their shoulders under the yoke are lifting up their heads and learning to walk erect. Less and less do people accept having their behaviour dictated from above. There is indignation over the broken promises or the hesitations of leaders. There is anger against situations that force people into begging. They want to earn their living, like everyone else in the twentieth century. Things "have got to change" and had better start changing right away. Weary of pleading and of seeing their pleas unmet by government, or being answered too late or unacceptably, encouraged by the new-style leaders, people are taking the initiative into their own hands, are themselves formulating their projects, and are occasionally turning to specialists or governments for help with the practical application of their programs. In other words, the will of men is being given priority over that of bureaucracies.

Perhaps nothing better points up the nature of a consciousness geared to self-determination than the methods of action beginning to be used by underprivileged groups to make their points of view and their aims clearly known and to obtain justice from the establishment. Every era and every society has had its pool of methods of action upon which individuals and groups draw according to the specific conditions facing them. The fact that groups choose to use a particular method rather than any other at any given point in time provides revealing information about the society. If we claim, quite justifiably, that violence is characteristic of our era and of our society, that is not mainly because of the attitude of the powerful groups which, today as in the past, are trying to keep the upper hand by every means available. Of course they need not, because of their privileged position, use openly disruptive means. The fact that our era and our society are violent is mainly due to the determination of underprivileged social groups, and of those far removed from power, to be heard, and, if need be, to frighten in order to be heard. Unrest among farmers, urban guerillas, "creative destruction" by students, terrorism, all these remind us in more ways than one of the fourteenth and fifteenth century peasant revolts in France, *La Jacquerie*. The protest movements' short-term efficacy should not mask the fact that, unless they turn into organized revolutionary movements, their demonstrations are condemned to failure. The current brushfire revolts should however convince leaders—better than the peasant revolts did the fifteenth-century French lords—of the need for far-reaching reforms.

More and more, the alienated or underprivileged groups realize that politics is a tug-of-war between individuals and groups in the struggle for power. They get to see that in liberal societies conflict very often predominates, and they discover that primary emphasis is devoted to damming up the effects rather than curing the causes of such conflict. On the other hand, they run headlong into the flagrant inequality of the means available to ordinary citizens. The fact that violent methods of action are increasingly being used does not signify that those involved have unsteady temperaments. If, like other groups prompt to voice moral indignation at violent actions, the violent groups felt sure of having the ear of the establishment, they would be equally disinclined to raise their voices. Their violent leanings reflect the paltriness of the dialogue and the inadequacy of channels of communication between them and the establishment.

Engaging in public demonstrations and in systematic obstruction, even going so far as to destroy the means of their own livelihood, whether tools or resources,—all these are ways of drawing attention to their situation and trying to obtain improvement. The weapons of the weak can only be shattering ones. Unlike these people, the favoured groups have a choice between many "peaceful" means: money, specialized knowledge, information, internal cohesion, bargaining power, blackmail, corruption, and so on. The underprivileged only have the advantage of numbers, and the fear that this particular advantage, ruthlessly used, may inspire. And who can blame them for using as best they can the only card they hold? In doing this, are they not following the same rules of the game—based upon conflict, and the precept that right is might—as those followed by the privileged (e.g. professionals or businessmen) and by political leaders? Demonstrations, riots, these are the threats, potential more often than actual, that the underprivileged are ready to hold over the heads of the rest of society as evidence that their intentions are serious.

It would be a serious mistake to confuse the self-determined consciousness with the means, often violent, which men may be forced into adopting to gain recognition. For the underprivileged are in fact only seeking the same ends as the privileged: to get a hearing from the establishment, to draw its attention to their problems, to obtain the elaboration and implementation of specific programs meeting their needs as rapidly as possible, to get some control over the rules of the political game, and finally to take an active part in the decision-making processes when their interests are at stake.

In this way, resorting to extreme methods throws light on basic aspects of the condition of underprivileged groups. It would therefore be singularly short-sighted to condemn out of hand the fact that such methods are used. Indeed, as long as social goals and the rules of the game do not change, it is unrealistic to condemn men, particularly if this condemnation only covers the underprivileged and leaves aside or ignores the stratagems, often reprehensible, of the affluent. Ultimately, it is only the dissenters, who, by convincing the establishment of the pressing need for reform, will manage to introduce progressive elements into liberal systems, thus preventing outright revolution.

2. The conditions of self-determination

The goal of self-determination is without any doubt ingrained in the consciousness of our times. Even though the rapid spread of democratization favours the development of this form of consciousness, many obstacles still lie in the way. To those who learned how to deal with men along the old and well-tried paternalistic lines, the new approach seems singular and untractable. For authorities, it represents a disturbance. It hits at the heart of familiar beliefs and practices which used to lend long life to institutions. No wonder, then, that the new aspirations often leave the establishment deaf, dumb, or disconcerted. However, the trends that give it impetus are irreversible. We must therefore expect serious unrest if circumstances and institutions do not adjust to the movement.

While it is not without reason that the machinery (political parties, pressure groups, the civil service, parliaments, governments) is often blamed, we must also remember the men behind the mechanisms, for it is they who are capable of making these change to fit the needs. These men include, of course, both those who are awakening to the new consciousness and also their immediate leaders, but more particularly the establishment which holds the essential controls.

Without in any way attempting to obstruct the drive towards the broadest possible self-determination, it is essential to recognize the constraints which may otherwise wear down even the hardiest enthusiasm. It would be an unfortunate illusion among underprivileged groups to imagine that they will themselves find, without outside assistance, viable solutions to their many problems. Of course, on the whole, they do not need reminding that they are powerless on their own. In fact, they tend to underestimate themselves, and this in itself is one of the main causes of their destitution. They acknowledge their ignorance and therefore incorrectly conclude that it is impossible for them to learn, and so to overcome their handicap. Fortunately, many of them are enrolled in courses, offered by a variety of organizations, including government agencies, such as the Welfare and the Education departments; and these, in addition to giving people access to practical skills, give them a better sense of their own possibilities and limitations. They can get the help of specialists in reorganizing the setting in which they lead their lives. They are not naturally inclined to subversion or revolution. If they do revolt one day, it will be as a last resort, and because of having been duped for too long.

In formulating their aspirations and giving consistency to their projects, these people rely upon leaders who see things ''clearly'' and who have ''the right contacts.'' These leaders come from the same environment: a parish priest here, a member of the legislature there, or a notary, a forestry engineer, the president of a local association, the manager of the neighbouring radio station. At first sight, this might seem to be a return to the old elite system under a new guise. But nothing is further from the truth. It is precisely among those who are beginning to feel the stirrings of self-determination that the authority of the old elites has worn thinnest. The new leaders are awakeners, animators, guides, and most often, catalyzers. They serve to trigger the amazing transformations occurring among the people. It is because they play an essential role in helping people to achieve maturity and to re-organize the social framework that they are brought into the picture. They are accepted but, at any rate in principle, they are not allowed to dominate. The mission of the new leaders is to bring to the light of day a new humanity, emerging on the campuses of our colleges and universities, in the back streets of slum districts like St. Henri in Montréal or St. Roch in Québec City, and in the woods of poverty-stricken St. Paula of Matapedia, or St. Esprit of Temiscouata.

Even beyond whatever influence the new leaders would admit to wielding, the people who seek self-determination depend on their help in selecting goals and in searching for means of action. This is a source of constant temptation for the leaders. The intentions guiding their activities are sound enough to leave no room for the accusation sometimes launched against them, which charges them with being charlatans, demagogues, or agitators. They know their limitations and are prompt to call for help from experts or public servants when needed. Of course, they are not exempt from human weakness, and the role they play in the renewal movement makes them particularly vulnerable to popular pressure. In order to keep up their reputations, or to maintain consistency in their action, they run the risk of overstepping their capabilities and of taking advantage of the still vast credulity of those who trust them. They are also up against the pressures of those who, in difficult moments, want the leaders to bear the full burden of decision making. This is evidence that self-determined consciousness is still in its infancy. But, as people acquire the pride that comes with self-confidence, they are bound to disown any leaders who might have fallen into the old patterns of playing the good boss or the good father. The new leaders must know that if, for one reason or another, they fail in their praiseworthy goal of contributing to the advancement of the people, they will be the first targets of the anger serving to vent the pent-up frustrations for which they may not themselves bear the primary responsibility.

It is up to the leadership in every sphere of activity—whether government, university, business, or labour union—to lead the way in understanding the awakening now occurring among students, young people, the inhabitants of city slums and depressed areas. This very leadership for so long, up until the 1950s, barred the flow of new ideas. Then, after a sudden realignment, they promoted the expression of new aspirations, and they have even in a number of ways stimulated the current emancipation movement. At this point it is within the reach of their power to channel the movement and to learn the new roles that are theirs, as Cabinet minister, member of the Legislature, parish priest, school principal, director of a research centre, or whatever.

No one denies—at any rate no one should deny—the need for government in one form or another. The very complexity of the problems to be solved makes it more than ever necessary to have an organization able to gather together the people needed to do various jobs, and to give them the means for action and for decision making. It has become fashionable to claim that the people must take over political parties and governments so that these will reflect and serve the people's interests. To the extent to which this means that it is no longer possible to conceive of a good government without the people, this is a valid idea. Government programs only have a chance of success if they reflect the views of the groups affected.

And this presupposes that the groups have been involved in the whole of the decision-making process from the planning stage to execution. We should ensure that a given program is truly the "baby" of the population concerned, rather than the brain-child of bureaucrats. A good example comes to mind: Laval University's Forestry-Research Fund headed by André Lafond; it has given constant support, throughout the various stages of creating forestry farms, to the input of *Opérations-dignité*. That is the true meaning of participatory democracy. If the establishment rejects the new rules of the game, social groups will do without this leadership and will take action into their own hands. Such a development, triggered by the establishment itself, would lead to the setting up of parallel organizations, to frustration, chaos, and finally either to apathy or to revolt.

The barriers which nature, technology, organizations, and men put in the way of the smooth running of human societies are so many and so considerable that it is inconceivable that people should be able to manage on their own, without the systematic and consistent help of co-ordinators and suppliers of resources of every kind. In spite of the astonishing creativity— unfortunately all too seldom put to work—that individuals exhibit when acting on their own or in small groups, it is nevertheless true that large organizations have acquired a quasi-monopoly in the field of technical innovation. Currently at any rate, it is up to government officials to draft most of the contemplated legislation and to develop political programs. Systematic co-operation between public bodies and large private organizations is required if large-scale projects are to succeed, since they involve so many complex variables. For instance, creating stable jobs impinges on a vast array of operations: development, management, leadership, marketing, cost accounting, middle- and long-term planning, and so on. The paths of the new consciousness, geared to self-determination, necessarily crisscross the whole of society. They affect the establishment, as much, if not more than, the immediate grassroots leadership.

To seek self-determination is not to take a solitary stand in the defence of isolated causes. It is the attempt to fulfil one's personal potential while remaining within the social spectrum. Those who have decided to master their environment, and their immediate leaders, know that their projects have no chance of success unless they are also fully supported by the establishment. Otherwise they remain the toys of little isolated groups without much chance of becoming the starting point for great collective undertakings. However, if the establishment disappoints their expectations, they and their leaders are resolved to operate on their own, whatever the immediate or remote consequences of their act may be. This is a new aspect of the situation, which the establishment can no longer afford to ignore.

Individuals and communities will attach little value to any large-scale program that fails to take into account their specific situation, as they perceive it. But they quite understand that the optimum coherent development of a region or of an area of activity must necessarily rest upon the planned use of resources and energies to the benefit of the whole community. They also understand that even the best efforts may be applied wastefully or improperly. It is thus a proper aim to ensure that overall solutions should take into account the concerns of all the parties affected, and that everyone should contribute, to the best of his or her abilities, to solving a community's problems. The fragmentary nature of some of the recent regional development projects, even though they were sometimes supported by reputable research institutes and funded by governments, acutely illustrates the problem of the necessary linking up of local with regional concerns, and ultimately with national concerns—without either snuffing out grass-roots attempts at self-determination, or encouraging communities to venture on paths that can only lead them into failure and frustration. The situation would not have deteriorated so much had proper action been taken in time.

The questions raised by the new circumstances of collective action are many and important. They all of them, in one way or another, touch on the central problem of reorganizing society—a reorganization both basic and radical. How to create communications between individuals, leaders, and establishment, which will permit all the necessary information to circulate so that everyone can fulfil his new responsibilities adequately? How to reorient the interaction mechanisms (interest groups, political parties, advisory bodies, mass media) so as to avoid paralyzing obstructions within society? How to channel towards political action the drive of popular movements without introducing wasteful friction and short-changing the energy of the new leaders? How to ensure that a spirit of renewal shall penetrate governments and that anachronistic hierarchies and the super-bureaucracies, disdainful and arrogant, shall be abolished without jeopardizing the accomplishment of essential collective tasks? In brief, how to allow the necessary protests and questioning to break up obsolete structures for the benefit of men without destroying society itself? Naturally, sooner or later, under the implacable thrust of change, the old anchors will be lifted. Is it asking too much to express the hope that the leadership—and society—will not float adrift? If they do, those who are today clamouring for self-determination will not forgive them.

Self-determined consciousness must be tempered by patience. It is impossible in one day to make up for so many years of procrastination. But the leadership will now have to pave the way for a more accommodating, more equitable world. Absolute justice is of course a pipe dream. But it is also the ultimate goal towards which, through countless tribulations, men have unceasingly striven.

CHAPTER

(2)

National identity: hopes and disappointments

Weary of forever asking themselves the question: "What does it mean to be a French Canadian?" to which no satisfactory answer has ever yet been given, Québec Francophones, in growing numbers since 1961, have begun to ask themselves instead: "What does it mean to be a Québécois?"

The use of the expression "Québécois" to replace "French Canadian" shows how much change has been taking place both in fact and in outlook over the last ten years. It does not necessarily follow that Francophone Quebeckers' age-old search for the significance of their collective identity has now come to an end. On the contrary, it is being pursued more vigorously than ever. It may even have reached a critical point: current debate may in fact soon finally yield a far more specific notion of a Québec "we." Many circumstances favour this process. However, it would be a mistake to underestimate the ambiguities and uncertainties still to be dispelled.

Searching for a sense of collective identity runs into some particularly difficult problems: among the grab-bag of slogans and projects, achievements, and stumblings, how can one sort out which represent the deeply-rooted will of the people and which are simply whims of the moment or the urging of an interest group? Among the jumble of voices of alleged spokesmen for the community, how to distinguish between the genuine and the spurious?

The questions are many, as are the positions taken and the ambiguities. However, one fact emerges clearly: over the last ten years, the middle-of-the-road choices have, one after the other, been set aside, views have become polarized, the content of national consciousness is much closer than formerly to the needs and aspirations of real-life people and groups. At the same time, there is a growing rift between specific political and cultural conditions on the one hand, and the deep-down aspirations of growing numbers of social groups on the other. The rift results largely from the rigidity of federal institutions, whose gross inability to adapt to the expectations of Francophones undoubtedly represents the clearest and least debatable factor in the current condition.

Two papers reproduced here, one written in 1962 and the other in 1971, discuss both the impotence of the federal leadership and the radical changes in context and mentality that have occurred in Québec over the last ten years.

In present circumstances, Quebeckers have no other choice but to continue their heart-searching, however disturbing or fascinating, and whatever the end result may be.

A. ORIGINS AND CHARACTERISTICS OF A NATIONALISM OF GROWTH

For the past three or four years we have witnessed a re-awakening of French-Canadian nationalism in Québec.[1] At first sight, one might be tempted to challenge this statement. Indeed, today's nationalists draw upon the language of earlier generations. The slogans, key formulae, and themes advanced by nationalists of every inclination have not changed. For example, retracing the roots of a phrase such as *l'Etat du Québec* takes us over a full century's history of our social and political thought.

Now, in 1963, in their magazines and periodicals, young people are unknowingly repeating the very ideas and arguments that appeared in the youthful work of l'Abbé Lionel Groulx, a man born in 1878. This recurring subject-matter, this continuity in ways of perceiving the situation, are in themselves revealing. They confirm the survival, beyond generations, of the soul of a people. In the words of Hémon's heroine, Maria Chapdelaine: "nothing has changed, nothing will ever change in the land of Québec." Even though this view, half-a-century old, has lost its surface gloss, it is still in some ways valid today. The men have vanished; minds have become more open, thanks to the spread of literacy; industries and cities have pushed back the forest; books, the press, films, radio, and television have imposed new ways of life and have opened up broader horizons. And yet the extraordinary permanence of the same expressions, of the same collective definitions, seems to indicate that French Canadians, through the changes they have undergone in every area of thought and activity, have not been able to solve the problems experienced in their infancy as a people.

However if, instead of looking at the surface manifestations, we exam-

Section A of this chapter comprises the text of a lecture delivered at the Third Congress on Canadian Affairs in November 1963, and published in the magazine *Les nouveaux Québécois* (Québec: Presses de l'Université Laval, 1964).

ine the underlying meanings, we shall see considerable variations in time, related to the circumstances that marked each period. Thus, the general tone of the nationalist ideology underwent considerable shifts in each of the last four decades. We successively saw a nationalism of depression, a war-time nationalism, a nationalism of prosperity, and now, in the current de-cade, we are witnessing a nationalism of growth. It is therefore more to the style of nationalism, than to its ideological content, that people refer when they talk about the "re-awakening of nationalism" in Québec over the last three or four years.

This nationalist revival fuels the great drive towards development seen in every field of activity and in every segment of the community. What lies at the root of our nationalism of growth? What are its features? These are the two questions I shall endeavour to answer here.

The emergence, over the last few years, of a nationalism which I am calling a nationalism of growth, was made possible by a set of circum-stances whose main elements are well known: on the federal scene, we had the defeat of the Liberal party and the departure of Louis Saint-Laurent, the victory of the Conservatives and the rise of John Diefenbaker. On the pro-vincial scene, there was the death of Maurice Duplessis, the premature death of Paul Sauvé, the defeat of the Union Nationale party, the victory of the Liberals, and the rise to power of Jean Lesage in the provincial elec-tions of 22 June 1960. Finally, on the international scene, we witnessed the accession to independence of many African and Asian nations.

The first consequence of the above events was to bring to an end the di-lemma of what I have called the nationalism of prosperity. For Québec, in every field, the post-war years marked both a high point for the federal government and a decline, accelerating from 1956 on, of the provincial government. Even the most ardent nationalists admit that Québec's rapid development resulted largely from federal activities, whereas the provin-cial government generally remained inactive or even applied backward measures to solving pressing current problems. While, on the one hand, federal authorities were being accused of encroaching upon the jurisdiction of the provinces, on the other hand, the corruption and inefficiency that in-creasingly bogged down the Duplessis regime were being widely deplored. It is perhaps in the field of education that the dilemma of a nationalism of prosperity was most acutely felt. There is, for instance, no question that federal assistance to universities was designed to meet a pressing need in Québec as well as in other provinces. Yet, to accept this aid was tanta-mount to abandoning the sole and direct control which Québec had so far exercised in a field considered essential for the survival and development of our French culture. After having ultimately blocked federal aid to uni-versities, the Duplessis Government granted them at least apparently equivalent assistance by introducing provincial income tax.

At the same time, the presence of a French-Canadian prime minister in Ottawa further exacerbated the dilemma of a nationalism of prosperity. Ca-nadianism, as ideologically defined in the Massey Report, had gained some credence among intellectuals and political figures. In its extreme form, Canadianism held that in practice the development of French culture would best be accomplished by Ottawa rather than by Québec. This topsy-turvy nationalism was in fact only a reflection of the deep political crisis in which French Canadians were plunged at the time. As a rejoinder to Canadianists, who were advancing their case by specific actions and projects, Québec nationalists were mainly using defensive arguments, faithfully echoed in the Duplessis government's purely negative pursuit of provincial autonomy.

Diefenbaker's rise to power in Ottawa marked the waning of federal prestige. Growing fiscal deficits, rising unemployment, declining immigration, mounting administrative difficulties, a series of serious political faux-pas committed by the prime minister himself and by his main lieutenants, the fact that French-Canadian ministers were acquiring a reputation for dullness and inefficiency—all these circumstances triggered the most impressive falling back on the province since Confederation. The Duplessis regime became a target for concerted and virulent attack which shook its very foundations. The death of the *chef* laid open the way to progressive forces. Jean Lesage and his team focused the ideas that had been dawning among intellectuals during their long period in opposition; not without difficulty, hesitation, and sometimes compromise, they went on to spread the new message among the people. In brief, the dilemma of the nationalism of prosperity has been overcome.

In the wake of this initial change came the assertion of a need for a strong Québec and the development of the nationalism of growth that we are witnessing today. New men, or men renewed, have everywhere taken over the command posts and are converting into positive collective action the nationalism which, until a few years ago, drew its main support from a conservative, clerical, and paternalistic class, more nearly feudal than bourgeois. Pushed by the eager impatience of a rising generation that never went through the inhibiting experiences of the depression, the world war, and the Duplessis era, these new men must now act without the time to reflect or to explore the lie of the land ahead. Those who mainly knew politics by its misdeeds and ineptness and who, without direct experience of democracy, had to remain content with dreaming and talking about it, must without any transitional phase, switch to seeing the State as a kind of friendly demiurge or, at any rate, as the main tool available to the people for achieving the marvels expected in every field.

No other Québec government has so closely linked nationalism and politics. The link has in fact become so firm that political failure might strike at the very heart of French-Canadian culture. I believe that the best politicians in both main political parties are aware of the risks created by the closeness of the link. This awareness explains both their eagerness to promote political reform and economic development, and their ambivalence towards federal authority as much as towards separatism. They seem to be adopting a position where they can blame federal authorities for possible political failure while keeping open the doors to possible retreat into separatism. If I correctly understand what is happening in the minds of our political leaders, they are consciously or unconsciously attempting to safeguard the mental constructs of French Canadians, whom a long nationalistic tradition tempered and armed against the risks inherent in the current situations.

Seen in this light, separatism fulfils a useful function. Not only does it seem a logical development of the current situation, but it also offers a possible solution to the ensuing problems. Separatist feeling runs like a thread, sometimes strong and visible, sometimes more tenuous but never broken, through the web of more than a century of French-Canadian nationalism. The example, before our eyes, of many decolonized peoples achieving independence, many of them French-speaking, dramatically supports the possible viability of the separatist formula for Québec.

Yet, when we look at things more closely, we may see, among the "independentists" who are not altogether separatists, the same hesitations about the paths to be followed as I earlier detected among the ruling elite. They too, it strikes me, often hesitate to break off all ties with the rest of the country for fear of being swept aside by the current difficult situation. Between the federalist status quo and full separatism is a whole range of intermediate possibilities which leave the door wide open to negotiations with the federal government. Among these positions, one has for the past six or eight months been attracting a great many active independentists and a number of political figures. According to this intermediate view, the aim is to re-organize the Canadian federal system so that the "two nations" may as such become equally sovereign in Ottawa. That is a very attractive approach in theory, at least for Québec's French Canadians, but it would seem to entail considerable practical difficulty. Canada's geographic layout, its tremendous regional disparities, the geographic distribution of ethnic groups, the absence of a common wave-length in the way French Canadians, Anglophone-Canadians, and Other-Canadians experience their national identity—all these factors will, among others, create serious problems for the promoters of the "two-nations" approach when they get down to the specific task of elaborating a confederative system. It may however also happen that the application of the so called "concurrent majorities" theory, in those specific fields of activity where cultural implications loom large, could help to dispel the major sources of tension and conflict between the country's two main cultural groups.

It may well turn out to be that the "two-nations" approach only represents a stepping-stone in the path toward separatism; or, on the other hand, it may represent a turning back toward the more familiar ranges of federalism. Indeed, a sizeable part of Québec's population appears to entertain the hope that a more or less radical reform of current federalism might be enough to allow French Canadians to live in accordance with their new aspirations. What form should this constitutional re-shaping take? No one, I believe, has so far looked at the practical implications of this question except by putting forward suggestions on points of detail; and it would appear that the imaginations of pro-federalists are runnning short. Some believe that the present Canadian Constitution, subject to amending a number of its more anachronistic provisions, will long remain on the statute books, and that the political instruments available to Québec during the nationalism-of-growth phase will, in legal terms, subsist very much along the same lines as in the past.

Yet it needs to be recognized that in Canada we have neither exhausted the possibilities of federalism as a system of political organization, nor have we yet seriously gotten down to the task of theoretically enumerating its various possibilities within the context of a country such as ours.

At present therefore, none of the choices to which a nationalism of growth theoretically lends itself are excluded. And no one can foretell how Québec will finally react to the situation ahead. We only know one essential fact: Québec must be keenly aware of the risks for the future of the French-Canadian community that stem from the current situation. What then are these risks and difficulties?

The nationalism of growth basically rests on the assumption that Québec lies on the threshold of gigantic development in every sector of thought and activity. Those who educated my generation used to speak to us about "our master, the past." Today, we say to the young: "our hope, the future." But to build the future we are hoping for, we must know how to use the possibilities of the present. The nationalism of growth is pragmatic rather than doctrinaire, both in nature and in intent. Indeed, it is its purpose to channel energies and talents into action.

The exceptionally aggressive and at the same time singularly attractive character of the nationalism of growth reflects an awareness both of the difficulty and of the greatness of the tasks to be accomplished. In an interview granted to Jean-Marc Léger (*Le Devoir,* 5 July 1963), René Lévesque, then minister of Natural Resources, used his colourful language to describe both the scope and the requirements of this newly-emerging nationalism. It comes down to directing collective energies towards specific goals, he said in essence, and to applying all the means available to the earliest possible attainment of these goals. Surfacing throughout, like a bad dream, are the memories of past grand designs, short-changed or betrayed by men's inertia or ineptness. French Canadians must first convince themselves that mere survival is just no longer possible, and then must make sure that they can never again slip back to the take-off point. On the other hand, whatever the international economic situation may turn out to be, and it appears, alas, to be shaping up unfavourably for the coming years, the future that lies ahead for French Canadians must necessarily allow them to move ahead or else they will disappear as a people. When outstanding men are ready to take on such a wager, clearly perceiving the stakes, it is not surprising that they should be demanding, both of themselves and of the people, to a degree well-nigh incomprehensible to someone standing outside and not experiencing the pressures of the situation.

Hence the acute and perhaps exaggerated awareness of our collective weakness in every field, from economics to the mastery of spoken and written French; and hence also the search for solutions by the most varied means, often closer to incantation than to a cold and realistic appraisal of real possibilities. Arising from the same root is the ubiquitous use of nationalistic symbols and mottoes, some perhaps intended to galvanize the people, others to maintain for as long as possible an illusion of grandeur.

It may be that the nationalism of growth, in some of its aspects, artificially produces the impression of a general uniformity of views, by masking an awareness of the ideological diversities and confrontations which have of course been enhanced by the pull between, on the one hand, our deep historical roots, and on the other, the features of the pluralistic society into which we have moved. In this way separatist movements, by converging aims in but a single direction, manage to evade debate on perhaps the most decisive issues now taking shape in the minds of people, political parties, or other groups; issues such as the power of the clergy, educational reform, accession to political maturity, the organization of a professional civil service, the role of the State, the place of values in economics, the advancement of underprivileged groups, the promotion of rural and regional development, unemployment, federal-provincial relations themselves, and so forth. Bill 60, which set up at last a full-fledged Department of Education, has opened our eyes to the extent of the crisis now experienced by Québec, torn between the need to set aside obsolete and yet still-cherished traditions, and to give itself a rejuvenated outlook in line with current conditions. It has been claimed *ad nauseam* that the separatist approach presents an answer to the collective alienation generated by the Conquest, reinforced by subsequent history, and recently made more acute by the swift breakdown of traditional institutions and sheltering values. That may well be. But by omitting to analyze the ideologies which grow out of social institutions and which divide French Canadians, by attempting rather to gloss over them so as to accomplish a separatist triumph, the movement runs the risk of drawing us into deadly misconceptions. At the present time, not only does separatism not contribute any solution to our most palpable problems, but it further tends to divert us from a patient search for the right solutions. As well, internal divisions which continue to emerge among separatist factions strikingly confirm the great diversity of ideologies engendered by social pluralism.

Having said this, I still do not rule out the separatist formula as a solution because, as argued earlier, it is a possible radical choice open to us in this era of a nationalism of growth. I believe, however, that the separatist formula has so far not sufficiently attuned itself to what is happening here for it to permeate both men's minds and social institutions without undue stress or strain. To become a practical proposition, the separatist ideology would need to be sieved and reformulated by a great French-Canadian heart and mind, who would meld it with our dominant idiosyncrasies, adapt it to the values that inspire and govern our daily activities—in brief, help it to take deep root among the people. I shall no doubt be asked: Who is this man? Does he exist? That is not the point. The real question is whether circumstances will so develop that the separatist idea becomes embodied in a political party able to attract the best men in every field and to appeal to vast numbers of people. Among them then, there will surely emerge someone with great authority and prestige who will, by taking the leadership, turn the movement into a powerful force.

Even familiar forms of the nationalism of growth occasionally run into pockets of hardened resistance. This occurs within the government as well as in the two main political parties, and hence also among institutions, groups, and individuals, who oppose this or that project for reform, however concrete and well-defined. When our best politicians were stressing the need for us to become "masters in our own house," to "take over control of our economy," "create a first-rate educational system," and so on, they were trying to stimulate, attractively and in ways leading to action, motivation among those individuals and groups most capable of producing the enormous quantity of energy required by the scope of the tasks to be undertaken. In the same way, when René Lévesque repeatedly emphasized that the State was "one of us, the best of us," he wanted to bring out the fact that in circumstances such as Québec's, the State needed to be exceptionally dynamic so as to orient and channel individual initiatives and fill the obvious gaps still left unattended. But our public figures have nevertheless run afoul of individuals and groups paralyzed by distrust of the State, a distrust arising from a long tradition of unbridled liberalism and of poor government. The desire to calm this quiet understandable distrust and to convert political mottoes into electoral slogans may have led to awakening, among certain kinds of intellectuals and of young people, aspirations altogether out of line with our real possibilities, even assuming a government ten times as good and as efficient as it is, and backed by unwavering popular support.

One thus detects a tendency to ignore objective factors which, beyond formulae and political slogans, have always conditioned, do so today, and will continue to condition our existence as a people. It is all too easy to overlook the fact that persistent effort alone will lead to whatever greatness may be open to us. It is all too easy to overlook the extent of co-operation and help we will need to seek and maintain outside of Québec, if we are to participate fully in the various interrelationships, in the complex and multiple financial, business, and industrial networks that criss-cross each other in every direction, and which whether we wish it or not, for better or for worse, condition our development and surround our daily lives. Finally, there tends to be misunderstanding about the true nature of our ethnic temperament. We are perhaps, to go back to an idea long ago put forward by l'Abbé Groulx, the most European of all American peoples; but we also carry in our minds and bodies the ineradicable influence of the New World; an influence exercised upon all those whom it has for the past four centuries drawn into its enormous spaces with their always moveable boundaries. We, the descendants of a handful among the millions of immigrants from all races and all cultures, have given a French face to a corner of this huge North-American continent, elsewhere largely Anglosaxon. This in turn has modified our original temperament and has made of us, to follow Groulx's idea, the most American of Europeans. So far we have avoided, as a people, total surrender to the charm of this continent, from a fear of losing our identity. But the cost has been an enormous dispersal of energy. The achievements of the Manicouagan hydro-electric development give us very tangible evidence that, in the era of a nationalism of growth, it is not by evading but by meeting the challenge with which this continent confronts men that we will firmly establish on the shores of the St. Lawrence the bases for a viable French civilization.

Unless we start consciously developing a language and sets of attitudes more in tune with our collective condition and our possibilities, we will soon become unfit to cope with the risks inherent in a nationalism of growth. The tasks we must at all costs undertake, the problems we must absolutely resolve, are already complex and demanding enough, for us to refrain from building castles in the air, particularly stemming from roots elsewhere than on the North-American continent.

However we can and certainly must improve our written and spoken French, and our educational system; we can and must increase our participation in business and industry. We can and must establish links with other French-speaking countries. But the real questions that need to be asked today are: Is that what we really want? Are we ready to expend the necessary effort? Might we not be inclined to take the easy way out by claiming that the means available to our people are inadequate, thus explaining away our unreadiness for the industrial society, and masking our passivity? In fact, do we always use the means available fully and efficiently? Do we really attempt to find the best ways of making up for the inadequacy of resources?

These are questions that public men, intellectuals, and group leaders must first ask themselves, subsequently putting them to the people as a whole.

Québec's French Canadians have always tended to blame the federal government for the problems and failures often occasioned by the provincial government. During the period of our nationalism of prosperity, this error led us into apathy and to the brink of dictatorship. But during the nationalism of growth period, the same error may sound the death-knell of our existence as a people. To achieve a measure of effectiveness similar to that of the people who for better or worse surround us, we must first learn to give ourselves a good government in Québec and must learn to maintain it. The current government enjoys the good will and support of the people. Our initial task must be to create a climate in men's minds which will allow it to become a really good government, without its running the risk of rejection by the electorate at the next turning point.

After we have had a good government in Québec for a sufficiently long period of time, the province's relative position within the country and vis-à-vis Ottawa will doubtless have become sufficiently strong to let us benefit from the advantages inherent in a large-scale country.

But the future is not yet ours, even though today's actions are giving it shape. In a period of nationalism of growth, federal-provincial relations are likely to raise countless thorny problems. To fulfil its aims in a variety of fields, Québec will need enormous revenues, and the issue of tax-sharing will become crucial. But it would be misleading to see this as a way of shoring up the Québec government's financial stability. In the past three years Québec has undertaken a number of large-scale programs where return on investment is low or where it will not materialize for some years. On the other hand, in the effort to catch up and launch positive development programs, Québec will have to exercise a degree of initiative that will give its government the image of being far more progressive than that of the federal government.

Unlike the case in the days of the nationalism of prosperity, the federal authorities will no longer be forging ahead of Québec in elaborating and introducing political programs. The reverse is more likely to happen, and we can already see early signs of this, perhaps leading to new federal-provincial conflicts. Only the development of a pre-legislative federal-provincial body, which would integrate and share out the respective functions and responsibilities, could put an end to the unfortunate and hasty round of measure and counter-measure in which both levels of government have begun to engage.

Finally, in this period of a nationalism of growth, if Québec is to give its full support to a federal formula, it must have the opportunity, in line with its aspirations and its capabilities, to make the French component of our national culture flourish throughout the country, within the federal civil service, in crown corporations, and in private enterprise.

This is not a matter of instituting bilingualism for everybody, or of achieving a cocktail-like biculturalism. Bilingualism must be understood not as a knowledge of the two main languages by all Canadians, which would be an absurdity, but rather as the practical acceptance by all Canadians of the equality of both languages, as well as the essential application of bilingualism throughout the country's major institutions. Biculturalism must in the first instance be understood to mean the co-existence of the two different ethnic groups which up to a certain point rely upon the same political, social, and economic institutions for the survival and development of their respective cultures; and in the second instance, it must be taken to cover the multiple links and interrelationships between them, resulting from their association and from the co-operation necessary to fulfil their common responsibilities toward the community as a whole. This, I believe, is the approach that the Laurendeau-Dunton Commission, just set up by the federal government to enquire into the state of bilingualism and biculturalism in Canada, is planning to take.

If we manage to solve the difficulties outlined above, and as we become more conscious of Quebec's strategic position within the country, Quebeckers' understandable mistrust of the federal government will gradually yield to a willingness to play a growing role in the contest. The nationalism of growth cannot, like previous forms of nationalism, be purely ethnocentric. Whatever may otherwise happen, Québec will need allies and clients among English Canadians. Such support may at times be found among the Niagara Peninsula's industrial interests, among Western farmers, among British Columbia's forestry complexes, or among the Maritimes' farmers and fishermen. One day, Québec will realize that it is only by taking advantage of the whole range of possibilities made available by democracy, that it may cease to be a permanent minority, becoming instead a minority which, through associating with other minorities, can achieve majority status on particular issues. When that day comes, it will be apparent whether the tests of the nationalism of growth have been successfully met. In the long run, Québec will get more and will do better through reconciling differences with other provinces and with the federal government than through blackmail, threat or, more especially, through terrorism.

At any rate, whatever political choices we may favour for tomorrow's Québec, it is desirable, if not essential, that we should today work together to fulfil the great potential lying before us as a result of current circumstances. Jointly, we should assume the risks as well as the achievements the future may bring. The nationalism of growth is a basically healthy attitude, with, one hopes, a healthy aftermath. It should allow Québec to undertake sound patterns of development, provided doctrinaire attitudes and conflicts do not paralyze us on the way, and provided we remember to work hard.

B. QUÉBEC AND CANADA'S FUTURE

It was in 1962 that the ''crisis'' of Canadian federalism first became widely discussed. The Royal Commission on Bilingualism and Biculturalism, set up in July 1963 to ''enquire into and report upon the current state of bilingualism and biculturalism in Canada,'' managed, after twenty-three regional encounters throughout the country in 1964, to issue a long Preliminary Report with a view to alerting Canadians about the seriousness of the situation. This Report, made public in February 1965, arrived at the following diagnosis:

All that we have seen and heard has led us to the conviction that Canada is in the most critical period of its history since Confederation. We believe that there is a crisis, in the sense that Canada has come to a time when decisions must be taken and developments must occur leading either to its

The remaining section of this chapter comprises the text of a paper presented to the Special Joint Committee on Canada's Constitution, 30 March 1971, Issue no. 6, Third Session of the 28th Parliament, 1970-1971, 60.79-60-88 (see pages 60: 4-88 for the complete record). The text was also published in *Le Devoir,* 12-13 April 1971.

break-up, or to a new set of conditions for its future existence. We do not know whether the crisis will be short or long. We are convinced that it is here. . . . The crisis has reached a point where there is a danger that the will of people to go on may begin to fail. This is an initial diagnosis, not a prophesy. . . . What is at stake is the very existence of Canada. . . . The chief protagonists, whether they are entirely conscious of it or not, are French-speaking Québec and English-speaking Canada. And it seems to us to be no longer the traditional conflict between a majority and a minority. It is rather a conflict between two majorities: that which is a majority in all Canada, and that which is a majority in the entity of Québec.

At the time, most of the country paid scant attention to the above statements. French-speaking Quebeckers welcomed the report, which they felt accurately reflected their sentiments. But they had reached the point where only specific reform proposals affecting them directly and immediately— proposals which naturally could not be part of a preliminary report—could have fully awakened their attention. Anglophone Canadians, to whom the message was essentially addressed, generally turned a deaf ear for a variety of reasons: scepticism over the validity of the diagnosis; faith in the healing powers of time; confidence in the ability of the Canadian political system to resist any assault; from whatever source. These and similar reactions gave evidence that the Commission had not managed, as it planned, to spur Anglophone Canadians to action.

Six years have now passed since the publication of the Preliminary Report. What stage have Canadians now reached? Are they any more ready to accept the measures that would "develop the Canadian Confederation on the basis of an equal partnership between the two founding races"?

It is of course unfortunate that, on bringing their investigation to an end, the Commissioners were unable to reach agreement on how to deal with the major political and constitutional issues that divide Canadians. This in no way detracts from the merit of the impressive work accomplished by the Commission. Their ultimate inability to agree should not lead to the misleading though plausible argument that, if ten supposedly wise people, working under the most favourable circumstances, and far from the line of fire, proved unable to reconcile their differences, how can it be hoped that all Canadians and their spokesmen, up against the rough and tumble of everyday life, should have any better chance of success? The argument is misleading, for the analysis does not hold. How then is one to account for the Commission's inability to reach agreement upon the means to counter an evil which, by their own account, may prove fatal for Canada?

It was a turn of events, more than anything else, which explains the Commission's inability to complete the program it had set for itself in the two years that followed its creation in 1963. By 1967, the "crisis" had taken on proportions well beyond those envisaged initially by the commissioners, and it spilled over the boundaries of the research plan they had elaborated in 1964. Thus, when they looked for a common ground to deal with the "major" questions they had agreed to keep until the end, the commissioners found both the necessary data and their working criteria bitterly wanting.

Not only do the signs of the crisis, which the Commission diagnosed in 1965 with a lucidity still striking today, persist, but they have further deepened. And further symptoms, particularly disturbing, came to compound the picture. Thus, to report on the new situation and to prescribe appropriate therapy, the Commission's whole approach would have had to be revised. It was, at that point in time, impractical to undertake a new detailed review of the situation. Nor was it feasible to examine constitutional reform without appropriate additional studies. The matter was therefore shelved; but a preliminary task still remains to be completed: defining the specific objectives that may serve as the corner-stones of a new constitutional order.

Courage is needed to look at the situation clearly. We face a difficult choice: either to put forward a series of radical corrective measures and to attempt to convince Canadians that they must be applied, regardless of cost (and also without the absolute certainty that they will prove adequate to save Confederation); or else, to accept as inevitable Québec's separation from the rest of the country and to seek in good faith every means to minimize the damage for all parties concerned. The time for half measures is past.

The situation has indeed greatly changed over the past four years. Any searching diagnosis of the Canadian "crisis" must cover new aspects which are likely to affect its outcome considerably. Ignoring these would be a serious mistake.

Let us first consider the rising wave of protest against the established social and economic order, that began in the fall of 1968. It would in fact be inconceivable to discuss the crisis of Canadian federalism without touching upon this other crisis which, perhaps more radically still, shook the foundations of the country's political order. In Québec, where liberalized institutions and values are relatively recent, where the social and political framework is especially frail, and where its main bastion, the middle class, is weak and ill-organized, the movements of dissent against the liberal regime are gaining broadest support and making most impact. There is no doubt that the two crises are basically different, so that the waning of the one would by no means automatically entail the disappearance of the other. As the events which followed the War Measures Act of October 1970 clearly showed, the syndromes of the two crises may mesh, both in the minds and in the allegiances of those involved. Thus, today, the Canadian "crisis" has yet another dimension. It is no longer just "federalism" which is attacked. It is the social and economic order itself. Not all Québec separatists are opposed to the Liberal regime. Both in Québec and elsewhere a great many non-separatists are against it and, circumstances being favourable, both types of opponents may come to join forces. It is therefore essential that, in attempting to reform the framework and the operation of the Canadian political system, the aim should be as much to establish more equitable social and economic conditions for all regions and all areas of activity and, specifically, to promote a true participatory democracy, as to create the bases for a new modus operandi between the two main cultural groups and between Québec and the rest of the country.

The growth of governmental activities in every field for the past thirty years has led to qualitative changes in our society. Not only do politics now affect people's daily lives, but they are rapidly becoming a leading factor, determining a great many personal, family, or professional decisions. These changes are upsetting traditional beliefs about the role of politics in a liberal society. People require of their governments both flexibility and strength; flexibility so as to be responsive to the great variety of interests and circumstance in the population; and strength so as to be able to meet, rapidly and firmly, the expectations of individuals and communities. These new conditions of everyday life and of political organization are deeply altering the theory and practice of Canadian federalism.

In their desire for both strong and flexible political decision-making centres, Canadians will either turn towards the federal government or towards their own provincial governments. Some of the provinces will doubtless place more reliance on the federal government, and account will have to be taken of this preference. Others may choose to put their faith in their own provincial authorities, and their choice will also have to be respected.

Francophone Quebeckers have long made up their minds. All the available information is crystal clear: the vast majority favours the Québec government, which they consider more sensitive to their needs and aspirations and which they control more directly (its responsibilities being in the fields of education, recreation, social security, labour, regional development, and social and economic incentives).

Thus, in examining the reform of the Canadian federal system, we have to ask ourselves: is it possible, within a single political context, to accommodate both a strong federal government and weak as well as strong provincial governments? And if a province wishes to extend its field of action into key areas of social and economic acitivity, how can this be reconciled with the equally legitimate wish of the federal government to do likewise, and how will other provinces react to the special modus vivendi that will result between the province concerned and the federal government?

The obvious growth of Québec separatism since 1967 is itself a major component of the new situation. The fact that a legitimate political party is seeking to achieve separatist goals by the normal methods of liberal democracy, and that it may well eventually take power in the province by due electoral process, singularly complicates the situation. Now is the time to find the means to reconcile the two different orders of values which might come to clash if the current status quo were rigidly maintained regardless of the costs, namely a normal desire for political stability and a respect for the greatest possible freedom, subject to the necessary constraints of living in a society. It must be remembered that most liberal societies, when gripped by serious internal contradictions, have either collapsed or have scuttled their liberal creed.

These developments, and others which will doubtless occur in the coming years, oblige all of us to make an earnest effort to understand, more accurately than we did in 1962, when the farsightedness and wisdom of Canadians fell somewhat short of the mark. Had we been capable of taking the necessary decisions then, we would doubtless not be at today's crossroads. The range of possibilities has dangerously narrowed since. However, precisely because they are more pressing than formerly, the decisions that need to be taken are that much clearer today. Canadians will have to give up sterile debate on abstract notions such as "the two nations," "a special status for Québec," "associate States," and the like, and deal with concrete problems.

No power in the world can prevent Francophone Quebeckers from perceiving themselves as a society and as a nation, original and distinct from the Canadian whole. Conversely, in spite of their good will, few Anglophone Canadians manage to perceive themselves as a specific nation within the Canadian context. Indeed, Quebeckers understand this very well, and the best-informed of them have abandoned or soon will abandon the "two nations" idea which caused so much useless debate and which met with such poor electoral response. The same may be said about the ideas of a "special status for Québec" and "associate States." If agreement is first reached over the substance, it will subsequently prove easier to identify the ensuing consequences.

But before reaching agreement about the bases of a new constitution, it will be necessary to elaborate a provisional modus vivendi. I only see one principle able to rally Canadians: it is the principle of the right to self-determination, both for Québec and for any other province so inclined. In the general introduction to its Report, the Royal Commission on Bilingualism and Biculturalism considered the degree of self-determination that either society may exercise in relation to the other: no limits were set to the application of the principle since, as the Commission saw it, it might even encompass separate statehood. The principle of self-determination has the advantage of being both normative and functional. The fluidity of the current situation becomes less and less bearable for a growing number of Canadians. On all sides, people want it to be clarified one way or the other. The principle of self-determination neither predetermines the country's sociological make-up and that of its component parts, nor does it prejudge the future of Canadian federalism. It does not rest upon a hypothetical event, but upon a right which it is sufficient to recognize—that is the right of peoples to choose their own path, a right whose content may be defined with accuracy.

The solemn proclamation of the principle of self-determination would not mean Québec's automatic separation from the rest of the country. The possibility cannot of course be ruled out. But it may also happen that, in the light of the new attitudes which would surely emerge in the rest of the country, Québec might of itself, subject to certain conditions, decide to remain in a renewed Confederation. Recognition of the principle of self-determination will, however, at last force a serious and methodical review and a radical reform of the conditions that keep Quebeckers in an irritating and intolerable position of inferiority.

I am not unaware of the measures that the federal government, the Civil Service Commission, and various government departments have been introducing over recent years to improve the situation. I also note that these various measures have borne fruit, and that others still under study may do more. Moreover, I believe that the federal government is on the right track: a functional and practical approach, even though partial, has more chance of success than an impressive program far removed from reality. It is, however, pressingly urgent to rethink the assumptions upon which the reform is based, to accelerate it, and to extend it to other areas. The goal remains the same: rebuild Québec's confidence in federal institutions, without provoking in the rest of the country a backlash of feeling that these measures are harmful. While it is plausible that corrective measures satisfactory to Québec may be unacceptable to the rest of the country, and while the social and political repercussions of the economic slow-down and of other unfavourable factors (notably the growing US control over the Canadian economy and culture), place definite limits on the tolerance and generosity of Anglophone Canadians, their good-will is essential if adequately powerful corrective measures are to be attained. It is no use pretending that the cost of maintaining Confederation will do anything but weigh heavily on the material and moral resources of Canadians. The goal of establishing real equality of opportunity for Francophones within Confederation is every day growing more difficult to achieve; each day that circumstances and outlooks deteriorate further, the signs of impatience grow on every side.

An adequate program of action, geared to current needs, would, I believe, include the following points:

1. Recognition of the need to maintain a strong percentage of French-speaking unilinguals in Québec, as an essential condition to the survival of the French language in Canada. Currently, the percentage is 75 percent. However, in an urban and industrial society it may rapidly dwindle if control of the economy continues to lie outside the Francophone community, and if the weight of Canada's bilingualism rests almost exclusively on Francophones as has been the case so far. Francophones represent 28 percent of the total population of the country, but account for 70 percent of the officially bilingual people (that is, 30 percent of all Francophones are bilingual); whereas Anglophones, who represent 72 percent of the population, only contribute 30 percent of the bilinguals (that is, only some 4 percent of all Anglophones are bilingual). Consequently, more than 80 percent of the whole country's official bilinguals (who are 12 percent of the total population) are French-speaking. In normal circumstances, the ratios would have

been reversed, a majority of bilinguals coming from the numerical majority, as is the case in Switzerland. Québec's Anglophones doubtless already provide, and will increasingly provide, a share of the bilinguals whom Canada will need. Twenty-nine percent of them are bilingual, accounting for more than 50 percent of all Canadian Anglophone bilinguals. We have to devise means of relieving Francophone Quebeckers of the obligation to learn English if they are to lead a normal life within the Québec economy and in federal institutions. For them, as for the Anglophones of other provinces, the decision to learn the second language should be based only upon considerations of mobility and of greater variety in the choice of a career.

2. A choice of institutional bilingualism rather than individual bilingualism, and a continuing analysis of the conditions promoting institutional bilingualism in federal institutions. With the firm and clear introduction of institutional bilingualism, the federal civil service will be perceived as both French and English, rather than as "bilingual" which is now the case and which can only in practice mean the crushing predominance of English.

3. An accurate estimate of the number of middle-range federal civil servants, and a recruitment program for Québec Francophones, so that they may come to occupy 30 percent of these posts within the next ten years. The Royal Commission on Bilingualism and Biculturalism estimates these middle-range posts to number approximately a quarter of the total, that is more than 100,000, and the present ratio of Francophone office-holders at less than 15 percent. Thus, 1500 new Francophones would have to be recruited annually to achieve the 30 percent target in ten years. Indeed, this is the minimum size required to create a French milieu within the federal civil service and to provide an adequate pool of potential Francophone top-echelon civil servants. This would obviate the need to recruit senior Francophone officials outside the service, which entails serious disadvantages. Subsequently, the aim should be to increase the share of mid-level Francophones to 35 percent and even 40 percent. In this way, it would become possible for Québec Francophones to identify with the federal civil service and to place more trust in the federal government's ability to represent their interest and aspirations. However, I admit the enormous practical difficulty of implementing such a program. An analysis of mid-level posts will doubtless help to reduce to below 100,000 the number of key positions and thus reduce the number of new Francophones to be recruited each year. But this will certainly remain on the order of several hundred a year. We are being called upon to pay a high price to offset the effect of many year's neglect.

4. The setting up of French-language administrative sections in the civil service, so that government employees may work and pursue their careers unhindered in their mother tongue if they so wish. If such units are to achieve their goal, there must be sufficient Francophone unilinguals in the

service to forestall the temptation of turning them all into bilinguals. At the same time, a certain number of bilingual civil servants will be necessary to fill co-ordinating posts and to accede to top-level posts. A sufficiently high number of Anglophones and Francophones may want to learn the second language to become eligible for these high-prestige posts, in which bilingualism will be a prerequisite. The federal civil service will have to adapt its language-training programs to these requirements. Only then will Anglophone officials, who have gone to the trouble of learning French, no longer be "forced" to continue working almost solely in English, as has nearly invariably been the case.

5. Offering separate advanced training programs to civil servants both in French and in English. So far most of these programs have been offered in English, only a few courses being available in French. Hence considerable frustration for Québec Francophones, who may develop a two or three-year lag in their careers as a result of the need to learn English, and who, by training, become so acculturated to English as a working language that they are incapable of pursuing their careers in French, even if this is required of them. It will be necessary to watch that the prerequisites and conditions for admission to these programs are identical for both the French and the English groups, and that the content is equivalent. It is high time that staff training courses should correct a situation both unfair and untenable for Francophone civil servants.

6. Administration deconcentration aimed at keeping exclusively French-speaking units in Montréal. There are already a good many federal offices in Montréal, but I understand they are not seen as a way of increasing the French-speaking capacity of the federal civil service. Not only should such federal offices in Montréal be more numerous, but they should operate more widely than they do now. The decision to establish them in Montréal might flow from a general deconcentration policy, aimed at every part of the country; or else it might be geared to the strengthening of French within the civil service. Without prejudice to efficiency, the establishment of deconcentrated administrative units in Montréal would have the double advantage of giving them a cultural environment more favourable to French than are Ottawa or Hull, and reinforcing the Francophone work bases in Montréal itself.

7. Improving the communications network between Ottawa and Québec, and more particularly between federal civil servants on the one hand, and Québec civil servants and academics on the other. What seems most lacking, on both sides, is adequate information on a variety of subjects. Few holders of key posts in Québec are well acquainted with their opposite numbers in Ottawa, and few Ottawa people know their counterparts in Québec well enough to call them up on the telephone and really involve them in developing federal policies. Many empty regrets and pious hopes are expressed by federal ministers and officials, as is frustration by

Québec's civil servants and the university community, with suspicion mounting on both sides. Only by accelerating the increase in Francophone Quebeckers among middle-range civil servants, and promoting the best of them to the upper echelons, will the communications network between Ottawa and Québec be improved. People who know and respect each other tend to keep in touch spontaneously.

8. An improved alignment of federal and provincial policies so as to ensure co-ordinated social and economic development. In key areas, notably in the field of fiscal and financial policies, consultation between different levels of government should not only be optional but mandatory, and even in some cases enforced. Thus, without necessarily revising jurisdictional prerogatives and running the risk of weakening the state machinery at a time when it needs to be strengthened, working methods more conducive to co-operation may be encouraged, and a mutual climate of confidence built up. The present situation is intolerable. How many projects, carefully prepared by Québec, have in the recent past been stymied by the appearance of reports independently prepared by the federal government in the same field? How many initiatives, undertaken unilaterally by one side or the other, have been aborted by the ill-will of the party who took umbrage at not having been consulted? The ill-feeling arising from a lack of official and genuine consultation between the different levels of government is not limited to Québec. It exists in other provinces. But in Québec it is compounded by other frustrations, and so tends to be magnified. The feeling of having one's hands bound, of being the toy of Ottawa which abuses its power to tax and to spend, is exasperating to Québec's ministers and civil servants. The lack of co-ordination between practical programs also seriously contributes to reducing the Canadian political system's ability to cope with the grave problems it faces. Alas, by contrast with Great Britain and Sweden, administrative and political consultations are not held in high esteem here. Many prejudices born of ignorance, inhibit such exchanges which could, when properly and judiciously used, be an immense advantage in a political context such as Canada's.

9. Direct federal support to Québec in its efforts at promoting the French language and culture. The federal government will have to ensure that French is the main working language in federal offices and agencies in Québec so as to serve the Francophone population in French, and to project a French image both in Québec and in French-speaking countries. Praiseworthy efforts have been made along these lines in recent years and results are already perceptible but not yet sufficient. Moreover the federal government, in consultation with the Québec government of course, should do its part to encourage Ontario and foreign firms (mainly American) who do business in Québec to accept French as the main language of work.

10. An attempt to rally all Canadians around a great common project

capable of galvanizing collective energies and channelling them towards constructive achievements. It is by attempting to give a practical content to the phrase "participatory democracy" that it may best prove possible to meet the dreams and hopes of a people who are turning cynical and unruly. In Québec as much as in the rest of the country, the leaders seem in no way inclined to take the necessary steps to introduce true participatory democracy. The hopes and projects promoted by spreading the ideal of participation among the urban and rural under-privileged groups, will end up by turning them against public authorities, and against liberal values and institutions, if they continue to encounter indifference, lack of understanding, or even active opposition among the establishment. It is important to invent the nuts and bolts of a true participatory democracy and to undertake the necessary reforms in the social and political mechanisms. Economic circumstances and the temper of the people require action without vacillation. Large-scale reforms, whether undertaken federally or provincially, will doubtless have profound repercussions on the nature and the operation of Canadian federalism, which it is still too early to foresee.

The above proposals, and other similar practical measures which could surely be imagined, can be adopted and implemented without the need for a prior reform of Canada's legal and constitutional framework. Doubtless, as their effects become felt, a new political style and language will develop, new interest patterns and alignments will emerge, new relationships will appear, Québec's relative position vis à vis the federal government and the other provinces will crystallize. Thus, gradually, the main lines of a new modus vivendi for Canada's two majorities will take shape and will need to become reflected in constitutional arrangements.

What is the nature of the modus vivendi the future will bring? This is where the unforeseeable dynamics of the principle of self-determination come in.

I must be content to formulate the diagnosis: the Canadian "crisis" has reached its most critical stage. Conditions cannot get worse without precipitating the breakdown of Confederation. Palliatives, aimed at correcting the symptoms rather than removing the causes, can only make matters worse by contributing to the escalation of disappointment and exasperation. That is why the cure must be radical. It is likely that the remedy will taste bitter to the federal government and to English-speaking Canada. But they should seriously pause before rejecting it as excessive or unworkable. The medicine is, after all, aimed at redressing a longstanding situation of discrimination. Anglophone Canadians, if they really accept, beyond lip service, the principle of equal opportunity for Canada's two founding peoples, must learn to measure the practical implications of their attitude and must accept the inevitably high cost of restoring balance.

As to Francophone Quebeckers, even should the best assumptions materialize, it is impossible to foretell their final choice. A number have cast their vote in favour of separation. Others are undecided. Still others fear for the future. An economic upswing, a more extensive share in the country's economic activities, radical changes in Québec's place within Confederation, any of these factors might well cause them to shift attitudes. No one knows whether, tomorrow, a real desire for coexistence will win out over the wish to separate. Perhaps, in spite of every effort, even within a new Confederation, it will prove impossible to establish a climate of confidence between Canadian Anglophones and Québec Francophones. Attempts to prevent the polarization of the two camps may fail, as may the attempts to prevent terrorism which would undoubtedly entail the loss, for all Canadians, of their civil liberties. No one wishes to maintain Québec in Confederation at any cost, especially that of virtually permanent military occupation.

Those who do not desire Québec's separation from the rest of the country must use all legitimate means to prevent it, but they must also be realistic about such a possibility. Should it come to pass, it would be wise to maximize for all parties the advantages of separation and to reduce to a minimum the cost which may well be very high—almost certainly higher than the cost of building a new Confederation—not only for Québec but also for the rest of the country, particularly for Ontario. It is to be hoped that Canadians will have the good sense to forestall a violent and unplanned separation with its aftermath of incalculable human and material loss. If separation must occur, is it too much to hope that both in French and in English Canada men will be found, sufficiently clear-headed to negotiate in advance the general conditions of separation, and to provide for the links both parties may wish to maintain? The weaker party would, otherwise, bear the brunt of an un-negotiated confrontation.

The reforms required to give Francophone Quebeckers full renewed confidence in the Canadian Confederation will weigh heavily upon Canada's resources. Many people nevertheless hope that such reforms can be put into effect, well and soon. But even they understand English Canada's reluctance to accept the heavy cost, considered exorbitant by many, and the attendant hesitations. On the other side of the coin, it is to be hoped that numerous Anglophones will understand and support the choice that Quebeckers feel bound to make, whatever it may eventually be. So, whatever the outcome, the destiny of the "two founding peoples" leads them to an ever-deepening experience of their divergences and convergences.

CHAPTER

3

Economic aspects: emancipation and constraints

French Canadians have never taken any overwhelming interest in business, perhaps not surprisingly. Their share of the economy, even in the part of the North-American continent where they constitute the great majority, has always been and still is insignificant. Most French-Canadian businesses are technologically old-fashioned, producing the least added value. Control over the most productive areas of industry and over the world of finance lies outside Francophone hands, save for a few outstanding exceptions like the Bombardier industries and the Desjardins savings and credit unions. In business and industry, the French language barely manages to hold its own in the lower and middle echelons.

Achievements such as the Manicouagan hydroelectric development, the nationalization of electric power companies, the creation of public industrial and financial corporations during the Quiet Revolution, produced a groundswell of collective pride and, at last, helped to convince many people that no authentic, viable civilization is possible without a sound economic base. At the same time, a general rise in educational levels did much to raise vocational qualifications among young Francophones. There are few people left who continue to believe that Francophones are destined to be eternal "hewers of wood and drawers of water," born for a humble and self-effacing life.

For the past ten years, Quebeckers have tried to meet the challenges of modernization. Considerable progress has already been made in modernizing institutions and even more in acquiring expertise. However, a number of obstacles remain to be overcome and it would be rash to underestimate them. How can Québec make sure of entering the post-industrial age without breaking off the thread of cultural continuity? How can the Francophones communities' age-old economic subjugation be shaken off, how can business become an integral part of Québec while remaining in line with the economy of the whole North-American continent, perhaps through entirely new approaches? How may it prove possible to work in French and *à la française* while at the same time meeting the necessary language and cultural constraints of the environment? How are we to continue raising the quality of our universities and research institutes despite their high cost and the many mistakes made in the process of educational reform—mistakes largely the result of the tremendous amount of catching up that was needed and is still needed—while at the same time ensuring that the contributions to knowledge, the growing expertise, and capacity for innovation help to promote the collective well-being of Quebeckers? How can the State act to stimulate the economy, while at the same time encouraging the spirit of initiative among the people? How are the operation of the economy's key mechanisms and institutions to be co-ordinated—private and public corporations, educational institutions, labour unions, the government—without creating a technostructure that alienates the people or lulls their awareness? How are we to reconcile the requirements of economic efficiency and of social values? How can we make sure that taxes imposed on the wealthy are not used for the temporaty relief of poverty only, but above all for the eradication of its causes? How can we ensure that economic growth will contribute to the quality of life and make a difference in poverty-stricken urban and rural areas without jeopardizing the dignity of the people who live there?

These are all questions which a rational, cool analysis of the situation must seek to answer, and concerning which it would be useless to seek ready-made solutions in preconceived doctrines or formulas.

A. INDUSTRIAL SOCIETY AND POLITICAL ACTION

The problems of Western industrial society are inseparable from those of the so-called liberal society. The crucial questions of our time unfortunately do not lend themselves to instant solutions. We can only attempt to see clearly among the maze of difficulties springing up everywhere throughout society, while at the same time trying to keep a sense of proportion in the reform projects we advocate.

Western civilization, in many of its facets, may well qualify as history's greatest civilization. But it often happens that, when a social order has reached the phase of its greatest maturity, its inherent flaws begin to appear.

In all Western liberal socieities, a tremendous increase in productivity occurred during the last fifty years. There was also a parallel rise in education and affluence in all layers of our society. Nevertheless, two-thirds of

Section A of this chapter is based on the text of the tape-recording of an address given at a symposium organized by L'Ecole Polytechnique de Montréal on 18 February 1971. It appeared in the periodical *L'ingénieur* in May 1971, no. 266.

humanity are continuing to stagnate in underdevelopment, and it would appear that the means to correct this shocking disparity within a foreseeable future are unattainable. Regional and social disparities (poverty, widespread ignorance) persist, even in allegedly prosperous countries such as the United States and Canada. In many instances, advertising agencies promote a shoddy culture that entraps us; Madison Avenue pulls the strings that make puppets of human beings. Rates of consumption are set to meet the needs of production lines. And ideologies that seemed outdated in the 1950s—their demise having been loudly proclaimed—are re-emerging and refuse to be dammed up, despite their highly disruptive effect on dominant values and mores, and hence on established leadership.

The crisis of contemporary society stems from these mounting pressures, as much the result of states of consciousness as of reaction to the existing forms of social organization. An ever growing number of people are unhappy or dissatisfied, and the leaders vainly search for remedies.

1. The complexity of the social order

The main challenge of the decade ahead is one of social goals: how best to put the tremendous possibilities offered by modern organizations to the service of men? It would seem that in the years to come the problems of goals will arise as much at the level of social organization as at that of human values. What type of social organization should be maintained or created so that individuals and groups may progress towards the goals they have selected? The complexity of the social order in so-called post-industrial societies is tremendous. Big business and technology generally occupy a predominant place. However, as John Kenneth Galbraith clearly showed, "technostructures," as he calls them, affect many aspects of the social order besides physical organization. Technology may be defined, along the lines suggested by Emmanuel G. Mesthène, as the organization of knowledge towards practical ends. Technology may thus represent the hard core of our society, but it also depends upon the contributions of a number of organizations that include universities, government, secondary organizations such as labour unions, and obviously business itself.

However, technostructure alone does not account for the whole field of social organization. Alongside it, other groups exist, notably primary groups such as the family, which continue to exercise a basic role in setting the shape of community networks as they exist in our complex urban societies. For example, these networks may crystallize around neighbourhood relations, covering groups of friends and neighbours, as well as relationships at work, thus encompassing the daily existence of individuals and nourishing their multiple inter-personal contacts.

The problem of social organization in modern societies is twofold: it first of all concerns the interaction of the technostructure itself with the overall social organization, and secondly, the ways in which individuals and groups become integrated with the various mechanisms of society.

The technostructure, consisting of those who are at society's helm, is today being attacked for many valid reasons. It has not succeeded in healing the various social ills affecting humanity. Some would wish to express their disapproval radically by trying to eliminate the technostructure altogether. But other, less rough-shod methods may work better. If one neither intends to abolish the technostructure, nor tries to adjust individuals to its constraints, what other alternatives are left? Is it for instance possible to devise a synthesis between the requirements of both economic and social ends? Is that not the real challenge of the present decade?

It seems quite feasible, indeed, to consider both industrial society and its future in two ways; either in the light of economic or technical requirements, related to factors such as yield, accountability, and efficiency; or else in the light of social requirements, based upon the human desire for self-determination, and related to the emergence of a humanistic consciousness whose new aspirations centre around the quality of life.

Is there an unsurmountable contradiction between the economic and the social viewpoints? Or else is it feasible to envisage a dialectic leading to new syntheses and new ways of life? I believe it is. To take an example: organization experts emphasize how important it is to ensure full membership participation if an organization is to function effectively. And Michel Crozier, in his study of the bureaucratic phenomenon, concludes that the great problems of modern organizations are not caused by machines, which can always be repaired, but by men, who are always able, through passive or active resistance, to paralyze any operation. In other words, the need for efficiency and the wish for self-determination are complementary.

The problem is, therefore, how best to reconcile economic and social criteria. The purposes of social organization must be re-examined in the light of both. And within every form of organization, the members must be given an opportunity to choose the solutions that will satisfy both orders of requirements. This implies reforming people's outlook, at the leadership and at the grass-roots level, as well as re-shaping organizational frameworks. That is a reformist, middle-way approach, suited to our Western societies. It seems to me that in Québec in particular, where we need to concentrate on building a solid social framework, it would be singularly ill-advised to tear everything down in the hope of rebuilding something better. It is preferable to draw the best possible advantages from the existing structure, subject of course to promoting the necessary changes in organization and in outlooks. If it proves impossible to reconcile economic ends with social goals, the whole of society may be heading toward paralysis.

2. Québec's special problem

The problem common to all liberal societies takes on some special features in Québec. Québec is a late-comer to modernity. We are all of us acquainted with a far less industrialized, far less urban, far more traditional

Québec than today's. Pre-industrial and post-industrial features still co-exist, occasionally producing a curious mix. The age of the workshop and the age of automation live side by side. Another special characteristic is the vigour with which the desire for self-determination expresses itself in Québec, bearing in mind its relatively low social density: the voices of citizens' committees, or of the *Opérations dignité* in the backwoods areas of the Lower St. Lawrence and of the Gaspé Peninsula, can no longer be ignored by the leadership, even though they may have difficulty in grasping the sense of the message.

A third special feature of Québec is the relative weakness of the social and political mechanisms, a weakness we face every day.

Yet another special feature is Québec's physical, geographical, and intellectual closeness to the United States and hence the need, perhaps greater here than elsewhere, to meet the American challenge. We can always decry the United States but we would find it difficult to survive in isolation from the rest of the continent. We are therefore confronted by the double need to accept the presence of the United States and, for those of us who are Francophone Quebeckers, to try to adapt to it *à la française*. That is a demanding challenge indeed.

3.   The mechanisms of modern societies

Modern societies are complex entities. It is useful to examine their foremost mechanisms, for they offer reliable pointers to the society's well-being.

Which are these major mechanisms? Business is one of the first, and everything impinging on the business world. Then the major interest groups, including labour unions and some of the institutions specific to our democracies, advisory committees, and the great mass media. There are also universities and research institutes and, last but not least, government.

A number of questions come to mind: How do these major mechanisms operate? What are their links with each other, universities with business, labour unions with government, and so on; and what role do members play within each?

It is patent that the conditions in which each mechanism operates are far from satisfactory. The relations between them are inadequate, and member participation, covering both individuals and groups, is also unsatisfactory and poorly provided for. Much space would be needed to develop each of these points, and failing it I shall merely provide some illustrations.

a) The operations of the various mechanisms   Let us first examine a very timely issue, that of economic planning and of socio-economic development. Much discussion is being devoted in Québec to the ultimate goals of economic planning and development, but more attention should be given to realistically evaluating the methods of implementation. Economic planning is only feasible if at least some established methods of consultation exist between a society's major mechanisms. Several such methods are possible: indicative, imperative, planning, and so on; but without synchronization or mutual adjustment between the major mechanisms it is impossible to have true planning.

Until recently in Québec, social and economic development has essentially been directed to the poorest outlying regions. That is how the Bureau de l'Aménagement pour L'Est du Québec (BAEQ) came into existence in 1963, a unique project whose story is particularly instructive.

That experience was valuable, but it must unfortunately be recognized that, in spite of the qualifications of our researchers, and of consciousness-raising among four to five-thousand people in the Lower St. Lawrence and Gaspé regions, five years after the filing of the BAEQ Plan, virtually nothing had yet been done in the area to follow up on the Plan's recommendations. What are the main economic poles of attraction in the area? Some say Rivière du Loup, others Rimouski, or even Matane. If, after so much discussion, no agreement is yet forthcoming on this point, might it not be because there are no real economic poles in this enormous stretch of land? Might not the real poles lie in Montreal, Toronto, Chicago, or New York? More and more, people are coming to realize this when discussing Québec's development.

We might as well admit it: there is only one major development pole in Québec, and it is Montréal, itself a relatively minor industrial, financial, and commercial centre when viewed on a continent-wide scale. Yet how can Montréal be claimed as a Québec pole, when it is almost exclusively under foreign or English-Canadian control? Francophone Quebeckers have little say in running things in Montréal, and this in turn has definite consequences for Québec's government, in that it is responsible for Québec's development. The government cannot give orders to Montréal's large corporations; all too often, it must close its eyes to avoid seeing flagrant inequalities in the participation of the Francophones and Anglophones in the economy and control of business; it must accept equivocation and procrastination, and not look too closely at the fact that Montréal does not contribute its fair share to Québec's development.

Without jeopardizing Montréal's competitive position on this continent, the city must become a development pole extending out to Trois-Rivières, Sherbrooke, Québec City, Rimouski, and Seven Islands, and therefore encompassing all the outlying areas; the Montréal business community must turn into a powerful lever for Québec's social and economic development.

b) Inter-relationships between universities and the other major socio-political mechanisms The extent of interplay between universities and society is a good example of the kind of interactions that exist between the various mechanisms of society.

Much criticism and a variety of accusations are today levelled at universities, and it is indeed quite proper to question their role and activities. A great many university curricula seem outdated in the light of contemporary societies' needs. One may also wonder whether universities provide the right career training for today. And is not serious research in Québec all too often conditioned by goals established in American research centres? Such criticism is not groundless. The worst form of colonialism is not political, but intellectual, and it is the form from which Québec most suffers. Colonialism arises out of the fact that Québec researchers have to import both the problems they work upon and the conceptual premises upon which they base as much their world-view as their attempts to organize society.

Since research is at the root of technology, and since technology is at the source of social and economic innovation, it seems ridiculous to speak of priorities for Québec if Quebeckers are not involved in setting their own society's basic guidelines, that is in formulating the very assumptions that determine the directions of research. It is obvious that in spite of the best intentions of the university leadership, of teachers and of students, the current situation is far from satisfactory in Québec.

But to evaluate this depressing picture correctly, account must be taken of the context in which Québec universities are operating. All too often we forget to bear in mind the antecedents which up to a certain point determine the present. It is easy in such circumstances to be unfair to the existing leadership. Québec has experienced, in its universities as well as elsewhere, two revolutions in less than twenty years. During the first, between 1950 and 1967, the paternalism of Québec's universities gave way to liberalism; but, barely were they becoming adjusted to liberal criteria than, under the spur of the student protest movement that began in 1968, the universities were again required to reexamine their role and to adopt yet another stance, that of the social university, at the service of society. In Québec as elsewhere, universities are being challenged, as indeed is the whole of society. Universities are accused of allegedly being at the service of an unfair and repressive society. One may agree or disagree, but it cannot be denied that, in spite of much effort, the problem of making education democratically open has not yet been resolved. Our universities overflow with students who should not be there, whereas a number of young people who should be in higher education, are not. This is a problem that cannot be solved by adjustments in the educational system alone. It necessarily involves the broader context of society, its culture, and its other institutions.

Particularly since 1965, we have seen a tremendous growth in the universities' administrative machinery: once having been paternalistic, university authorities have now become the servants of computers. Relations between universities and government, particularly relations with the Department of Education, give rise to a series of problems. Another difficulty concerns the definition of the universities' social functions: what are these social functions and how should the university fulfil them? By what criteria should the universities' social usefulness be judged? Are they the same as the criteria applicable to business? If not, what is their distinct nature?

An example: graduates' career possibilities. It is too late to be blaming the universities in 1971; already in 1961 a number of people were protesting against the misleading idea that increased education would make Quebeckers wealthier, that jobs would automatically follow as a result of a longer period of schooling. In the short run, things improved because the level of ignorance in Québec was very marked. (For instance, in the Lower St. Lawrence and in the Gaspé, six years' schooling was the average, clearly inadequate in a contempoary society.) But in the long run, it is unreasonable to think that graduates can create jobs. On the contrary, jobs have to be created for graduates. And the jobs do not exist. Is this the fault solely of the government? It is not, at any rate not exclusively. Much depends upon the choices people make, and also upon contemporary economic circumstances, which govern everyone's opportunities.

University reforms must be geared to the nature of the institution. It is all too often forgotten that in every society a place is needed for thought, a place whose sole concern is the education of human beings; and if that place is not the university, where else is it to be found? To dispense useful knowledge, the university must of course also seek support from other social organizations; it cannot alone settle every problem of professional qualification, research, employment, and so on. It must seek support not only from government but also from business. Yet today in Québec, relations between business and universities leave much to be desired.

The solution cannot be to reduce the research carried on in universities. It would be more to the point to increase the research carried on in the business world where it is clearly inadequate, and to establish better co-ordination between basic research for which universities must be primarily responsible, and applied research which business can pursue more consistently. Government also has a sizeable responsibility for research. According to the Science Council of Canada, opportunities for research in Québec are practically nonexistent. Even today, assistance from the Department of Education is insignificant in advancing scientific research. Furthermore, the difficulty of setting-up research programs relevant to current needs is increased by the fact that French-speaking universities lie outside the main North-American and European technological and industrial communications network.

This separation from the main North-American and European communications network has several consequences. Even with equal qualifications, the graduate of a French-speaking university finds it more difficult to make a career in business or even to find a job than does his English-speaking colleague. Neither the teachers nor the institutions themselves are well integrated in the communications network whereby students ready to work are discovered at the time the companies need to hire them. Few professors can directly call up a company president, few have easy social contacts in the business world, Francophone university teachers being on the sidelines in such informal communications. This really dramatic situation was strikingly brought to light in "Education and Economic Achievement," a study by Professor Donald Armstrong of McGill's School of Business Administration, prepared for the Royal Commission on Bilingualism and Biculturalism.

Before Québec genuinely becomes part of the main North-American network—and I believe this will take a number of years—we must find provisional solutions.

The first solution might be for Quebeckers to withdraw from North-America, so to speak, and to establish their own financial and industrial communications network; it would obviously be smaller but also more accessible and more controllable. Even though this would involve a certain amount of economic separatism, the smaller circuit obviously would have to maintain links with the principal one, because complete isolation would of course be unrealistic. Although this solution would not be altogether satisfactory, it must be considered with the other alternatives.

The second solution would be to use the government as an initial training ground before graduates move on into business. This would be to adopt a path different from that of the English-speaking graduates who get their initial experience in business before going on to government. French-speaking graduates, far more than their English-speaking colleagues, already tend to look to the civil service for their first jobs. One may thus envisage the broadening of the government production network by means of public corporations such as Hydro-Québec.

The third solution would be to establish better links with the existing business world and primarily with Montréal's big business. Such links already exist between McGill University and a number of large companies. They are not nearly so extensive in the University of Montréal or in Laval University. Lately, le Centre des Dirigeants de l'Entreprise (CDE) [an organization of company executives] and the University of Québec signed an agreement aimed at matching a number of university training programs and the needs of business firms. Hydro-Québec also has agreements with the University of Québec and with other universities. The federal and provincial governments subsidize sizeable research centres at Laval University. But these inter-relationships must be intensified, and must extend to all large-scale business.

The university as such cannot replace companies in the necessary area of on-the-job training. In-house training programs should therefore be elaborated, for they are inadequate or non-existent. Certain forms of research might also usefully be taken over by companies, subject to proper co-ordination and to the necessary institutional links with universities.

But this would require research centres with business and it would presuppose training programs meeting the needs of students. When the CDE plans agreements with universities on the subject of research, in-service training and so on, I am delighted to hear it, but cannot help noting that the CDE mainly represents small and medium-sized business and does not include the bigger companies save for a few exceptions. What practical effect are these agreements likely to have if the companies acting through the

CDE are unable to undertake large-scale research or to provide appropriate training for graduates?

Measures must be taken to intensify the links between universities and big business. I believe these measures should be initiated by universities without waiting for a first move from business. Largescale businesses should be encouraged to intensify their in-house programs of scientific research and also to make sound efforts to recruit university graduates.

4.   The government's responsibility

In every free society, the main responsibility for co-ordinating efforts to achieve administrative deconcentration, political decentralization, consultation, regional development, and community organization must in the end lie with government. In a society like Québec's, government may even have a greater share of responsibility than elsewhere since Quebeckers, as citizens, as members of secondary organizations, have more control over their government than over business. The question is whether Québec has sufficient power to play this role of stimulation and co-ordination. To meet its heavy responsibilities, the Québec government must also undergo reform.

Such reform must encompass several aspects of Québec's political life: it should leave out neither political parties, the National Assembly, the civil service, nor the government itself. A reform of the civil service is proceeding to ensure better co-ordination between departments and to meet the developmental needs of society. The procedures and the working methods of the National Assembly, the Cabinet, and the Prime Minister's Office will also have to be refurbished.

If the government were to take such steps, it would trigger a series of similar developments in all other areas of activity, in universities, business, and so on. It is then that a concerted effort towards reform, leading to the establishment of a society not only rational but also reasonable, would become possible.

B.   BUSINESS AND QUEBEC SOCIETY

The fact that we ponder how business can best fit into Québec society shows that a problem exists. Indeed, in most industrialized countries the problem does not arise—or at any rate is not raised—because it is taken for granted that business represents one of the main forces behind social, cultural, economic, and political integration. If by integration we mean first of all the conditions under which units join together to form new aggregates, and secondly, the conditions under which these new entities maintain their

The remaining section of this chapter contains the text of an unpublished lecture delivered at a study-session organized by the Conseil du patronat du Québec (Employers' Council of Québec), Montreal, 26 May 1972.

unity, it must be recognized that business has been both the main spur behind the great changes which marked the emergence and development of modern societies, and the main factor which consolidated and ensured the survival of these societies. In large countries such as the United States, France, Great Britain, or Germany, or in small countries such as in Belgium, Holland, or Sweden, business is routinely challenged, praised, or criticized, but no one would dream of claiming that it is not properly integrated in society—on the contrary those who criticize the capitalistic system, overwhelmingly business-oriented for the past 150 years, blame it for unduly dominating social values and the whole organization of society. How is it then that in Québec, business leaders themselves question the lack of integration of business in society—problems that are not redundant since the opponents of the current economic system, and even liberal economists and sociologists, denounce the situation prevailing here as "colonialist" and as "satellite-oriented"? The relevance and urgency of this questioning for Québec is supported by the fact that as much is said about integrating Québec's society in the business world, as about integrating business in Québec's society.

The question most frequently asked is: How is Québec society to be integrated in the business world? This way of formulating the problem clearly shows both the restrictive nature of the North-American economic network and the "colonized" attitudes for which our leaders and our spokesmen are often blamed. More recently, the question tends to be put in a new way which shows a very different state of mind: how is business to be integrated within the network of Québec institutions, implying that Quebeckers themselves want to take the responsibilities for shaping their society.

The aim of the following discussion is to show very briefly how far business has been and continues to be a weak factor of social integration in Québec, and to indicate the main lines of the reforms needed to correct the situation.

1.   The place of business in Québec

Big business should be studied by anyone interested in the processes of social integration in a community. Business has an undeniable influence upon a society's dominant values—both those which provide cultural backing for the country's different institutions, and those related to the dynamics of social change and to the persistence of the political system.

The liberal ideology is the spirit which most pervasively influenced minds and institutions in the United States, and to a somewhat lesser extent, in English Canada. This ideology, initially elaborated in Europe and more particularly in Great Britain, took root in the United States through the example and the influence of a small number of business entrepreneurs who practised and propagated the famous "gospel of wealth" at the end of the last century.

It is in the name of the liberal creed that the Supreme Court of the United

States, up until 1933, defended the great capitalists' interests against the assaults of underprivileged groups and of popularly-based state legislatures. It is also this creed that the National Association of Manufacturers and, particularly, the United States Chamber of Commerce still perpetuate and promote, largely unchanged. It has left a deep imprint upon the United States, even though today it is being questioned and challenged on many sides, and businessmen themselves have come to accept practical compromises, in the context of the welfare state and of the emergence of a technostructure that is forcing them to make a number of adjustments.

It would be tempting and easy—but it is unfortunately outside the scope of this chapter—to quote many statements by leaders of industry in the United States, by American politicians, and even by clergymen, in order to show how vastly outlooks and attitudes towards business differ between Americans and Quebeckers.[1] Of course the Québec Chamber of Commerce, the Conseil du Patronat, and in somewhat more subtle and modern ways the Centre des Dirigeants de l'Entreprise (CDE), as well as some solo figures like Gérard Filion, repeat the main tenets of the creed with minor adjustments aimed at adapting it to Québec's situation. But until quite recently their voices were drowned among a concert of denunciations of "materialism," tinged with a contempt for business which was perhaps one way of masking our incapacities. We never had our version of the American Episcopalian Bishop Lawrence, for whom anything verging on profit, savings, or competition was inherently holy and led to God. But we did have our Monsignor Paquet who, roughly at the same time, was proclaiming that "our mission is not so much to handle capital, as to bestir ideas." In his footsteps, many others here preached, acted, and spoke along the same lines. For the past decade or so, expressing such negative feelings about the business side of things has gone out of vogue. I mention these viewpoints not so much to describe bygone days, as to convey how much the anti-industrial ideology and the agricultural emphasis that prevailed here for so many years were related to our economic situation which they reflected and took for granted, and also to give an idea of the many obstacles standing in the way of social and economic development. Today, these are eagerly sought in Québec, despite outstanding reservations about the capitalistic forms of development. In this field as in others, Quebeckers, like all other people, are heirs to their past.

It can at the very least be stated that there has never been any great enthusiasm in Québec for business in its capitalistic forms. Business has not been perceived here as a stimulus to social change but rather as an Anglo-Saxon institution, alien to, if not inconsistent with, the French-Canadian outlook and attitudes to life rooted in Latin and Catholic traditions. Gilles Auclair's studies for the Commission on Bilingualism and Biculturalism have clearly brought out that, on the whole, the virtues and qualities that French Canadians most value are different from those enshrined in the American liberal creed; that French Canadians do not have the same spontaneously favourable feelings towards business as do Americans, and engage in a different style of management.[2] These propensities of French Canadians in fact coincide with their low position on the North-American economic totem pole.

Private enterprise is lauded for the material and cultural goods with which our society overflows. Well and good; but at least four different questions should be asked:

Do we owe all these goods solely to private enterprise or rather to a number of organizations including business, government, labour unions, and educational and research institutions?

Do these goods always satisfy real human needs? John Kenneth Galbraith has pointed out the flagrant inadequacy of public services (parks, recreational facilities, public libraries, and so on) among a super-abundance of private goods available to those who can afford them—an imbalance which even the growing hold of the welfare state does not quite manage to redress.

Who and what causes the unequal distribution of goods and services among the various layers of society and among different social groups?

As regards Québec more particularly, does the relative affluence of individuals here depend upon the energy of Québec's own business, or is it essentially a side-effect of North-American economic expansionism?

I shall only attempt to answer, and briefly at that, the last of these questions. If the attitudes of French Canadians towards business are indeed ambiguous, to say the least, it is because the factual picture is rather sombre.

Especially in the second volume of Book III of its Report, the Commission on Bilingualism and Biculturalism has shown in detail how much less Québec benefited from the decisions of industry than Ontario. According to Fernand Martin and André Raynault,[3] there are 632 American subsidiaries in Toronto as compared to only 137 in Montréal and, furthermore, a great majority of the Ontario subsidiaries are far more dynamic than Québec's. As compared to their competitors, Québec-based businesses show little desire to innovate: they conduct no research (R and D remaining with the American mother-companies); they have a slow growth rate (Montréal's competitive position is deteriorating and its industrial infrastructure is aging); they operate in the least profitable areas, few of them penetrating the spearhead industries based on the new technologies; and finally they have so far in no way supported the Québec government's efforts at planning, even though—it must be admitted—the government itself has not taken any strong stand, since it has so far not quite dared to involve the area of Metropolitan Montréal in its programs of economic development. Furthermore, in Québec as in all other provinces, out of all the ethnic groups save Italians, most of whom have only recently settled in this country, it is the French Canadians who least benefit from industrial and business activities both in terms of personal income and of entrepreneurial status. There are practically no French Canadians in top management in the bigger Québec companies, for the economic elite co-opts its new entrants, and the North-American industrial network, as Jean-Luc Migué has so clearly shown, is not in touch with French Canadians (the cost of communications being too high for both parties).[4]

It is therefore hardly surprising that a great many Francophone Quebeckers have a negative, rejecting attitude towards business in its capitalistic form, particularly towards multinational corporations, most of which, in Québec, are U.S. dominated. In fact, Québec entertains ambivalent attitudes toward the United States. The government is far more receptive to American investment than is the federal government (some even refer to a clash between nationalisms, the Canadian nationalism and the Québec nationalism) but, conversely, there is widespread and growing antipathy towards American subsidiaries which are blamed for being totally dependent upon the headquarters companies and therefore for serving the political and economic interests of the United States, not necessarily compatible with Québec's. (Everywhere else, as well, the subsidiaries of American companies are the targets of more criticism than those of other companies, doubtless because they are more visible and also because they more forcefully convey American imperialist and military interests).

On the other hand, we know that in spite of all the efforts of governments and the rather more half-hearted efforts of the companies themselves, disparities in the distribution of goods and services have remained as extensive as fifty years ago, and in some cases the gap has even grown. Despite surface appearances on occasion, the wealthy are becoming ever wealthier and the condition of the poor, although not generally deteriorating, remains stationary. The middle classes, for whom tax systems are especially harsh, and who are the preferred targets of criticism by the underprivileged, are rapidly moving towards an intolerable quandary. But neither governments nor business leaders are overly concerned with improving this situation, doubtless because they correctly gauge that the middle class is too closely tied and too loyal to the capitalistic system to revolt. While capitalism is everywhere unfair towards the lower layers of society, thus laying itself open to attack which, unless it produces major corrective measures, may one day overthrow the system, the situation is particularly serious in Québec since, in our case, social hierarchies correspond to ethnic divisions. Anglophones (Americans and Canadians) occupy the top posts and are in the highest income brackets, while a vast majority of Francophones remains on the sidelines in the lower brackets. Marcel Rioux concluded from this that in Québec there is equivalence between social classes and ethnic groups, Anglophones in general representing the bourgeoisie and Francophones constituting the proletariat. These are the reasons mentioned for accusing companies, in Québec, of being dominated both by American and Anglo-Canadian imperialism. The desire to turn Québec into an independent country also in some measure stems from this situation. According to this view, only a government under its own control would permit the Québec people to give Québec business a vitality of its own which, although not excluding necessary co-operation and economic partnership with the United States and with English Canada, would nevertheless allow Quebeckers to invest their own money in areas of activity chosen by themselves, would permit them to raise the level of their collective prosperity, to do business in their own way and to adopt a way of life as best suits them.

This is the back-drop—hardly conducive to optimism—against which the integration of business in Québec may be considered—integration as regards management, control, and influence upon the rest of society. The problem is twofold: what are the reforms that would permit business to adapt itself better to the collective goals defined or approved by the government? And will business leaders, particularly those from multinational corporations, accept the cost of such reforms? I can only put forward some elements of solution to the problems of reform. It will be up to the business leaders themselves to answer the second question.

It is obvious that Québec has entered a new period in its history, the post-Quiet-Revolution phase as I have already called it elsewhere. As compared with the Quiet Revolution, during which Quebeckers could for the first time fully taste the fruits of modernity without regard to their cost, and during which they also began to seek fuller mastery over their fate without worrying too much about the means thereto, the post-Quiet-Revolution phase is marked by basic changes in society: changes in values as well as in forms of social organization, which jeopardize the social order, worry the leaders, and breed far-out revolutionary projects. Every collectivity searches its heart: how are aspirations towards a fairer and more humane individual and collective life to be reconciled with the inevitable constraints of coherent development? Manifestoes, white papers, working papers, reports succeed each other at lightning speed; many proposals and submissions of course seem excessive or contradictory (at any rate if they are evaluated in the light of strictly economic or technical criteria). In spite of their erratic character, all these efforts denote the emergence of a new culture, a culture whose full flowering presupposes the creation of new relationships between economics and politics. When looking for a better integration of business within Québec society, these upheavals have to be borne in mind since they deeply affect the entire social order.

The new context of business in Québec requires the setting aside of the methods of economic advancement prevalent in societies where business is well integrated in the community, namely methods centred around the advancement of individuals. Much is made, and has always been made, of a number of fine individual successes among French Canadians, and today as yesterday, the names of those who have managed to reach the top echelons of business are given much prominence. But, today as yesterday, the number of individual successes is very small. Whatever may be said and done, it is impossible for Quebeckers to adhere collectively to the American creed of economic success through individual effort, because the number of the chosen is far too few to give any likelihood to such a belief. The co-opting of members of boards of directors, and the absence of Quebeckers from the North-American communications network, virtually prevent them from hoisting themselves in any significant numbers to the top of the economic hierarchy. The few exceptions, by the nature of things, are doomed to become Anglicized or Americanized—if this has not already happened by the time they have ''arrived''—so that they leave far behind them their native community, which draws no benefit from such isolated cases of success.

At the other extreme of the possible range of choices, we find those who favour dropping capitalism and replacing it by a socialist economy. Although this trend was long the province of scattered individuals or of small marginal groups, it has of late been considerably strengthened by the creation, in low-income urban areas, of avowedly marxist political action committees; and by the appearance, in and around the Corporation des Enseignants du Québec [The Québec Teachers' Union], the Québec Federation of Labour, and particularly the Confederation of National Trade Unions (CNTU) of a series of proclamations strongly influenced by marxism. Although the authorities of these federations have not yet decided whether or not to officially espouse a socialist economy, and although it would be unrealistic to assume that each of the hundreds of thousands of their members fully supports the concept,[5] these trends highlight the degree of disaffection which currently exists in Québec in relation to the dominant system, throughout organizations which, while striving to achieve their own goals, until recently did not question the bases of a regime of which they are part of the indispensable mechanism. Although the term ''socialist''—even when tempered by the qualification ''our own form of socialism'' (le socialisme d'ici, as it is called)—currently conveys a number of ambiguous positions which have little in common with marxism, or even with European social democracies, and has little that might alarm a ''capitalist,'' nevertheless the trends and movements that call themselves socialist, by their diversity and potential strength, reveal the rapid rise of political radicalism in Québec. Doubtless, it will prove no easier here than elsewhere to ''break the system.'' It should be remembered that in no industrialized country has it proved possible for socialist political parties who came to power by normal democratic means to carry out a socialist change-over in their countries. Both Léon Blum's Front Populaire, and Ramsay MacDonald's first Labour government, had to admit they had not been elected to overthrow the system but to restore prosperity and to alleviate poverty among the most miserable.[6] Short of revolutionary assaults, such as were seen only in feebly industrialized countries, it is unlikely that, in the short run at any rate, we shall experience a socialist regime in Québec, whether or not it becomes independent. While it is true that Quebeckers have little sympathy for capitalism, as much may be said of their feelings towards socialism. In a democratic regime, vast numbers of middle-class and working-class voters, not to mention farmers, will act as a brake upon political parties with the strongest socialist leanings. Nevertheless, the current disaffection and the wide-spread rise of exasperation with the present socio-political regime must be taken seriously by all those who wish to avoid rough clashes. It is of course easy enough to disparage or underrate the social movements which currently reflect and express these dissenting trends. And it is not difficult to demonstrate the unrealistic nature of a number of action manifestoes. But the real question is this: what alternative approaches and ideas are there to offer?

A number of people see a solution to the problem in improving the economic position of French Canadians through the development of a native capitalism, that is through reproducing American economic institutions on a Québec scale and through the efforts of Quebeckers themselves, in the hope of promoting the rise of a typically French-Canadian capitalist class. This approach is hardly promising, the examples of Ontario and of Québec having shown that locally-owned companies, once they have reached a certain size, are very vulnerable to offers of merger from larger and generally foreign corporations. Such mergers can of course be prevented by appropriate legislation. But how are the companies to be assisted when they cannot grow or even survive without a sizeable injection of fresh capital which they do not themselves produce? Could the state, or could a public investment corporation meet the huge requests for assistance that would be coming in? A more promising approach might lie in the spread of the co-operative formula, which seems particularly suited to French Canadians. Yet no one believes that co-operatives could become, in the current climate, a preponderant force in Québec's economy.

A broader formula, comprising both capitalistic enterprise, public or joint ventures, and co-operatives, would probably offer the best chances of economic advancement for French Canadians. To create a base for Québec's economy, at the time of the Quiet Revolution a number of Québec corporations were set up, such as the Caisse de dépots, the Société générale de financement, SOQUEM, SOQUIP, ROXFOR and SOGEFOR. The Parti Québécois, if we are to judge by its manifesto *Quand nous serons vraiment chez nous* [When we'll really be on our own], basically intends to continue along the same lines. Through the joint action of the State and of private enterprise (since the State, through its planning and development policies, happens to be far more enterprising here than private initiative) it is hoped that a Québec economic network may be set up, connected to the larger North-American network, but under the control of the Québec community, to give French Canadians the industrial base they require to set up their own economic hierarchies and to develop capital, skills, and management ability which they have so far lacked, opportunities having been inadequate to provide them with experience.

This effort to create a Québec economic network through collaboration of the State, business, and labour unions, is at this time favoured by leaders in most areas of activity and by the public. It is without doubt an approach which will continue to be followed and which, in spite of recent stumbling, seems promising. It may however prove that these ''investments in nationality,'' to quote Albert Breton, are extremely costly. It will doubtless be possible to create in Québec an independent economic network, but it will have grave problems to overcome: the competition of the large North-American networks; the absence of appropriate communications channels; and the sudden severance from American science, technology, and innovation. The situation might also further the marked preference of French Canadians for ''non-competitive'' public enterprise, which offers more security but encourages a certain *dolce far niente*. On the other hand, the lack of vigour which marks most Québec firms leads them to put excessive trust in the ''supportive'' role of the State, to which they tend to look for solutions to all their problems and for succour in an otherwise chronically wilting economy. From this state-centred mentality could emerge the rise of a kind of socialism—a non-ideological socialism, somewhat after the heart of small company executives—which would doubtless not turn out to be very profitable in economic terms.

In two ousanding studies, Jean-Luc Migué recently put forward a formula which, while keeping several elements of the above, corrects it. He favours Québec's industrialization through the organic integration of international business and technology in the institutions of Québec society.[7] Québec society, argues Migué, has never known how to make the best out of the multinational corporations established here. But how can there be proper integration of the ''Québec arm'' of international business ventures? Migué mentions two factors of integration which seem to him essential. First, the systematic and almost exclusive use at every level, but particularly at the upper echelons, of local manpower and executives, as is being done in most countries in Europe and elsewhere, including Mexico. In this way, of course, the thorny problem of French as a working language would be solved in practice. Secondly, measures to ensure the active participation of multi-national corporations in Québec life; the establishment of coherent research programs, in co-operation with universities; co-operation in drawing up vocational and professional training programs, provided by educational institutions; help to charitable institutions, the provision of fellowships and bursaries to students; executive training programs abroad, and so on. These measures would be all the easier to apply as top-management would be in the hands of Quebeckers, thoroughly familiar with local conditions.

This natural and organic process of integration in Québec society of multinational enterprise, once it has acquired a Québec management and a sufficient independence from headquarters in English Canada or abroad, would without any doubt be strengthened if the government were to implement the economic support and development policies I listed previously. However, in this new context, the broad goal of such economic policies would no longer be to develop a Québec economic network, but rather to promote the better integration—through appropriate controls and incentives—of multinational corporations and of Anglo-Canadian companies in the economic and social life of Québec. This solution may at first sight seem particularly difficult, but it is obviously far more promising than all those outlined earlier.[8]

It is a solution that would allow Quebeckers, first, to participate fully in the great scientific, technological, and industrial networks of the world, while helping them to preserve and even to re-discover their own identity, since they would then no longer be acting as isolated individuals, but as an identifiable collectivity. In thus becoming an integral part of a vast scientific and industrial communications network, they would have access, at the lowest possible cost, to a far more extensive range of jobs—Québec, North-American, European, African, and Asian—than could be offered by a purely Québec network. In the normal course of group life, and not through costly individual effort, they would acquire competence, skills, and a feeling for management which they lack today. They would have under their control a set of economic circuits of their own, circuits also organically linked with the vast international economic network. In brief, they would have available a complete economic base, giving the Québec community a possibility of acquiring its own reserves of capital, of benefiting from the vigour of large-scale international business, and of moving about comfortably in the business world, thereby giving those who might so wish an opportunity of working elsewhere in North America, Europe, or Africa, without having to sever their roots. That is undoubtedly the royal road to the integration of business in Québec society, a road which would at the same time ensure the collective economic advancement for which Quebeckers are increasingly and justifiably clamouring. Before concluding that this road would be too costly to follow, the business leadership, particularly in multinational and Anglo-Canadian companies, should ask themselves searching questions about the cost to them, today, of the flagrant under-utilization of Francophones in Québec's economy and about the discontent engendered by this under-utilization.

The business world in Québec has given itself a praiseworthy goal, namely co-operation between the main partners, labour unions and government, in matters of general public interest (and I have already suggested the inclusion of scientific research institutes and universities as well). But we have to recognize that our industrial societies are nowhere near this goal. There is as yet no society in which this integration has been fully achieved, and, particularly in our liberal societies, conflict takes up a major portion of the social spectrum. We are at present seeing in Québec a disquieting intensification of recourse to radical confrontation methods by labour unions, and we are up against a tough movement of dissent among young people, as well as a rise of parallel organizations among underprivileged groups. In other words, the traditional methods of discussion between business, labour unions, and government seem unable to contain and to absorb the new pluralisms produced by social change. It is urgent to find new areas of harmony, new ways of achieving consensus.[9]

From now on, the search for co-operation will have to concentrate upon the pursuit of common goals such as economic growth and social development. But we must remember that, as long as the main partners in this process remain unequal, things will remain at a stand-still. Business, on its side, must not fear to get rid of the traditional ideological and institutional supports which have for so long upheld its sway and given its leaders psychological security, but which today are, at best, noble traces of the past or, at worst, fanciful illusions. Business must have the courage to choose the path of radical internal reform, reform guided by a major concern: that of helping the integration of business into Québec society, which is itself engaged in a process of profound change.

CHAPTER 4

Political life: hopes and disappointments

Not unlike religion, politics evokes mixed feelings of reverence and defiance. In modern politics, does not the welfare state come close to assuming a divine status? And do not the priests of both politics and religion sometimes profess and propagate ''the good word'' in strange ways? Some of the faithful, having lost trust in religion, pour all of their hopes into politics, whereas others treat both politics and religion with the same rebellion, rejection, or indifference.

Politics deserves neither extremes of fervour nor of aversion. If it is an evil, it is a necessary one, while if it is a blessing, its nature can only be terrestrial. Especially in periods such as that facing Québec today, when political action has an essential impact on social and economic development, politics must be divested of the husk of false mystery with which societies are accustomed to surround it. It is ultimately far more useful to examine the effects of political decisions on the life of the people—decisions such as the one to build a dam at Manicouagan, or to control the James Bay rivers—especially in matters of economics, university education, or scientific research, than it is to peddle attractive political formulae that sometimes amount to little more than empty phrases. It is more important than ever today to strip politics bare, to examine its workings with a sharp eye, to gauge with accuracy the abilities and the work of public men, to weigh the nature of the interaction between the political and the social order—in brief to review carefully how the system works and the quality of the product it delivers.

It is by examining the ground roots of politics, rather than by elaborating theoretical hypotheses, that one may hope to determine its true worth, and, more particularly, find out the extent to which the Québec political scene fits the goals it is designed to serve.

A. THE LIBERAL PARTY AND THE CHOICE OF A LEADER FOR THE POST-QUIET-REVOLUTION ERA

Over and beyond the burning issue of the choice of a successor, the forth-coming leadership race in the provincial Liberal party raises the problem of the current political predicament. We are entering a new decade. The se-crets it still hides will, in less than four months, begin to reveal themselves, sometimes slowly, sometimes in a rush, as events unfold. No one can fore-tell what secrets the future may hold. Yet, we can be sure of two things: the great space adventure will continue; and we shall go on living with the ever present threat of nuclear war and annihilation. These expectations, from the thrilling to the apocalyptic, condition our outlooks today; and it is quite proper for us to search for present signs that may reveal the future's out-line. The many unknowns lurking behind the choice of the leader of a party that hopes for power, inevitably lead to such attempts at divination or dis-cernment.

It is likely that the seventies will differ far more from the sixties than these did from the fifties. Lester B. Pearson and Jean Lesage each in his way represented middle-class democracy, just as Louis St-Laurent was the last incarnation of the democracy of the great business bourgeoisie and of the establishment. Jean Lesage put great perseverance into acquiring a po-litical style which made him almost irresistible for a number of years. Like other men of his generation in every area of activity, for whom plain sail-ing began after the great thaw in 1959-1960, he suddenly became outdated. The mirage of the politics of greatness he had inaugurated blinded him to the symptoms of otherwise obvious unrest, some signs of which, like the sweeping electoral gains of the Créditistes, had already begun to surface during the early years of the decade.

Indeed, one has the feeling that among the men who most influenced the course of events between 1960 and 1966, a number had so long seen things social and political at a standstill, that they never quite managed to adapt to rapid change. The great rifts between past and present, the new tides, took them by surprise. The anticlerical *mouvement laïc,* aimed at secularizing Québec's institutions; the educational revolution; economic progress; the assertion of nationalism; and, more recently yet, the voluble emergence of young people—this multiplication of demands and new ideas (in some way initially triggered by Liberal slogans and by the party's political platform) in the end produced withdrawal if not rejection in a fair number of people. Subsequently, as befits good reformists, they turned their energies to tam-ing these demands.

1. Jean Lesage, a man of contradictions

Jean Lesage is himself a striking example of a man conservative by temper-

Section A of this chapter contains the text of an article that appeared in *Le Devoir* on 17, 18, and 19 September 1969.

ament, who became a herald of progressivism through the force of events.

A politician, who became leader of his party and premier, cannot be judged without some of the hindsight provided by time. Jean Lesage should certainly be credited with having very actively contributed to the re-shaping of a formerly inefficient and poorly-thought-of civil service. He surrounded himself with young, enthusiastic, competent ministers and col-laborators; he rightly attached importance to financial and fiscal problems; he promoted a policy of industrial investment; he continued to push for an improvement in federal-provincial relations, thus continuing a policy started under the late and regretted Paul Sauvé; and, above all perhaps, he emphasized the right and the duty of Quebeckers to acquire a sense of col-lective self-respect. Given the circumstances at the time, and the outlook of the main opinion-makers, that is no mean achievement. Well-served by a fine intelligence and by irresistible will-power, Jean Lesage adopted a style which combined distinction, grandeur, and efficacy, and which delighted Quebeckers. Over a period, he came as close as it is possible to be, to em-bodying Quebeckers' emerging aspirations.

But in other fields—alas too many—Jean Lesage exhibited an incon-stancy which betrayed the intense conflict in him between what he needed and sincerely wanted to be (that is, a reformist) and what he was by nature and education: a representative of the traditional elite. All too often, evi-dence of the new spirit (the spirit of *Cité libre*) in the fields of education, economics, and labour threw him into a spin. He knew that the situation re-quired him to be a reformist premier. But his conversion to the spirit of re-form was precarious. To convince himself as much as others, he constantly needed to proclaim his progressivisim. Hence the enormous importance at-tached to words during the Quiet Revolution. Was it correct to speak of "The State of Québec," of "special status," of "positive nationalism"? How many debates, then considered crucial, gave rise to a sea of slogans (Masters in our own house, The future is our guide, The keys of the king-dom, Education is wealth, The State is ourselves, etc.) and too little else in the way of projects and political decisions! Jean Lesage did not always at-tach the same meaning to words as did his main lieutenants: thus he soon stopped using the expression "the State of Québec"—which French jour-nalists had in their ignorance launched during his first official visit to Paris in 1961—when he saw what an explosive charge it conveyed in René Lévesque's mouth.

The fact that Jean Lesage kept control and often himself led the charge must largely be credited to the *équipe du tonnerre,* a dashing team which included men younger than himself and true reformists at heart. At their head, Paul Gérin-Lajoie must be remembered for his intelligence, tenacity, and for the efforts, unfortunately largely unsuccessful, devoted to getting the goals of his educational reform understood—his style, however, will survive; and René Lévesque, who knew how to turn Hydro Québec and the Manicouagan project into symbols of collective economic emancipation, this impetuous magician of formulae and slogans, sometimes disheartened, was a master of handling the game. These men understood the sense of the events they had themselves contributed to shaping, for it is they who thought of the projects which they then persuaded Jean Lesage to promote.

That is how Québec got its nationalization of the electric power companies, and its Ministry of Education. To claim that Jean Lesage was above all a catalyser is tantamount to saying that he accepted reforms, but not without having looked, in some fields at any rate, for ways of short-circuiting them. But he cared for greatness, and soon became aware of the fact that reform brought dividends; intellectuals praised him and journalists joined in the applause. Between 1964 and 1966, he turned a deaf ear to those among his advisers, conservative or openly reactionary like Bona Arsenault, who warned him about the unfortunate effect on the population of some well-intentioned but poorly implemented reforms. But in June 1966, the Lesage government was beaten at the polls, at the close of an electoral campaign conducted almost single-handedly by the premier himself— probably according to his wishes—a campaign throughout which he was at no time clearly shown in command of the full support of his main lieutenants.

Once plunged in the opposition back-waters, Jean Lesage never again came on strongly. In politics, it is not only the leader's image that matters, but also the team's spirit, and it is this which in the long run determines the fate of a government, of a political party, and of the leader himself. After June 1966, there was no longer any *équipe du tonnerre*; all that remained in the eyes of the public was Jean Lesage, leader of an opposition party, ill at ease in his new role, torn right and left by men who often unwillingly bent to his authority, forced to grant appreciable status to the president of Québec's Liberal federation, Eric Kierans, who on his own undertook a round of speeches throughout the province. Lesage was a leader disavowed or abandoned by many of his former and his new lieutenants (the disappointment of the new ones, left without status as a result of electoral defeat, was especially bitter, which explains some of their subsequent actions), lieutenants who one after the other, lost faith or gave up the game. In these circumstances, there is small wonder at Jean Lesage's decision to resign. The poor timing and the attendant conditions of this resignation glaringly confirmed the untenable position in which he was placed by the failure of the *politique de grandeur* to which his name had been tied.

One feels a certain nostalgia for the style, and for the team of men who still seem so present today through their achievements and in the projects they had started and which are being continued catch as catch can. I am convinced that these men did not deserve electoral defeat. Theirs was a mistake of timing or of priorities when, upon the adoption of Bill 60, they set up the Ministry of Education and the Conseil supérieur de l'education. The hurtling rate of reform doubtless needed to be slowed down. By forging ahead as they did, they unwittingly proved right the conservatives of every dispensation who were both more numerous and more clever than the Liberals had assumed. Thus, the ups and downs of a parliamentary system, tied to the electoral success of political parties, may deprive the people of worth-while leaders, even when these are difficult to replace, especially at short notice.

2. The requirements and impermanence of leadership styles

Jean Lesage's resignation brings out yet another aspect of the current political condition: leadership "styles" are both particularly demanding and particularly ephemeral. A leader may just start feeling at ease in his role of leader, after arduous training and careful grooming by public-relations experts, when he is already claimed to be out-moded. Ill-humoured public opinion looked askance at Daniel Johnson, who had barely managed to find himself when his premature death promptly surrounded him with a halo. Pierre Trudeau may just as easily lose favour at a moment's notice. Mao, Joseph Stalin, Konrad Adenauer, Winston Churchill, Charles de Gaulle, Gandhi, not to mention George Washington, Bismarck, and Napoleon, will survive the dust and clay idols which artists fashion for a day of glory. To make a political leader, as much as to make a man, no practical substitute has yet been found for the right raw material.

No man can play the role of political leader without allowing his weak and mortal person to be dramatized. Like the father and the priest in religiously inspired societies, the political leader is a symbol, and serves as a pivot for authority in a society. The only alternatives to the dramatizing of authority are rough-and-ready might, or anarchy. The crisis of authority we are experiencing today does not primarily stem from the persons exercising authority, nor from those submitted to it. The cause lies in the breakdown of the protective layers that used to shield authority roles. The signs and symbols surrounding the father, the priest, and the political figure in their respective roles have been drained of their spiritual significance: those who fill roles of authority no longer inspire the same respect, veneration, or confidence as in the past. They are no more than men, often aging and weak, whose image feeble propaganda attempts to enhance with "cosmetics."

Sometimes the image-makers are credited with successes which result, rather, from political circumstance. Public relations, like propaganda, only work effectively when they flow with the tide. But let them try to swim upstream, and they fail pitifully. An image can create an illusion for a time. Sooner or later it fails to disguise the reality behind the leader, his personality, the team, their actions.

Beyond the deeds and misdeeds of public relations, the question that comes to mind is: how permanent is the furious rate of turnover we have seen of late among political leaders? Will it remain a lasting feature of our system, or is it simply a passing phenomenon, resulting from a momentarily fluid socio-political situation? Since the Second World War, socio-economic development has followed a fairly constant upward curve; but until quite recently, the changes were mainly quantitative: more expansion, more democracy, more politics. Leaders in all areas got increasingly overworked, they have had to be more accommodating with their colleagues and subordinates, to bear in mind an ever-growing array of data—but nevertheless they have been managing to get through their work, whose quantity has grown, but whose nature did not substantially change. This is how, short of accidents, they have managed to remain in charge for fairly long periods at a time. But now, we are up against qualitative change: a new society, still nameless, it taking shape before our eyes. The leaders must learn to adapt. Diefenbaker, Pearson, Duplessis, Bennett, Douglas, Caouette, and others stayed on, and are some of them still at the helm, despite their being outmoded and their discomfitures: they gauge themselves by the old standards. But Jean Lesage and Pierre Trudeau are in an entirely different situation: their new style, of itself, forces them to embody the new era.

Of course it is less hazardous to observe the sun setting on a passing day than to prepare for the breaking of a new dawn. Many are the false prophets, many are the rash adventurers who heedlessly break their wings. Jean Lesage, so dazzlingly launched, so sturdily promising, did not manage to survive the early rays of the sun. His stature had undeniably grown between 1958 and 1964. But in spite of all his efforts, he could not keep pace with the dizzying rate of change. He was, in the long-run incapable of embodying uninterrupted change, which is of the very essence in our new times.

The world which is taking shape appears refractory, capricious, savage. It frightens, yet yearns to be tamed. *A priori,* there is no suitable precedent, helpful for understanding the current situation. But there is little likelihood of error in saying that the most urgent task is to find, in every area of activity and particularly in politics, leaders able to formulate collective aspirations and needs, to set the tone and to give society a new vitality. Such leaders must survive for a long time to re-orient and stabilize organizations, human relations, and social roles and functions.

It may be that Jean Lesage's successor will be a transitory figure. Perhaps conditions have not yet ripened to the point where Quebec's Liberal party can select a leader who will stay in charge for the next ten years. We must beware of cancelling out Jean Lesage's grave decision. And so we must be alert to the needs of our time, to be able to discern what traits his successor should have or should be able to acquire. As to selecting the person himself, this may be left to the skill of the delegates at the leadership convention—a convention which, it is somewhat prematurely assumed, will be ready to do serious business.

3.   Québec up against the problems of the next decade

a) The National Question   The coming decade will be critical for

Québec. Like the people of every community, Quebeckers are facing specific difficulties, in some sense congenital and apparently permanent, which they will have, just like their fellow citizens from other provinces, to continue to face and try to attenuate by means of solutions that remain to be discovered. Will the next decade bring an answer to the question posed so insistently, if unclearly, during the sixties: what does it mean to be a French Canadian? It may be imagined that the search for a collective identity will continue (although it may not necessarily reach its goal) along the two main lines which it has followed during the last decade: that of the status of the French language, and that of the political status of Québec society.

The next leader of Québec's Liberal party will inherit the heavy responsibility of continuing Jean Lesage's work, which first managed to revitalize Québec society and which, at one time, almost seemed to have found the right political approach to our problems. But the new leader will be working in particularly difficult circumstances. The impatience of some, the fatigue of others, multiple collective pressures, perhaps the threat of subversion, the spread of terrorism—all of these may cause sharp pressures which might drive leaders into "ignoring" the root problems, setting up a police state, taking hasty decisions, creating multiple social ebbs and tides without lasting effect.

On the national issue, the leader must have a clear, frank, unambiguous line of thought. But he cannot be expected to act alone. I preclude a referendum—which I take to be as precarious as public-opinion polls, but infinitely more dangerous: X percent for, Y percent against, so many undecided on a given day, at a given hour, in given circumstances—but in a totally unknown state of mind! What the leaders will have to launch instead, with the support of the population, is a series of specific programs so that, by 1980, we may at least have an incipient solution to the problem of our collective identity. In the past ten years our politicians have said more than enough about Québec's "problem." We have available—in the report of the Commission on Bilingualism and Biculturalism—the major elements of an answer, pointing to practical solutions. A political party, whose leaders might prove unwilling or unable to take the necessary steps that will set the mechanisms of change in motion, can only be a party disastrous for Québec and for Canada. It is no longer possible to put off action. Time, which has so far served us well, is running out.

b) Problems of Civilization   Like every other society in the coming decade, Québec will be facing problems in common with all of Western civilization if not the whole planet. This situation will seriously complicate the search for solutions to our own problems. The challenge for Québec, apart from the major world-wide concerns of our times, is to find theoretical and practical formulations that will fit the circumstances of the post-Quiet-Revolution era.

In Western civilization ever since the Second World War, the body has grown disproportionately to the head and particularly to the heart. There has been incredible technical development, based especially on advances in mathematics and quantitative methods. The human sciences, following the example of behaviourism, imagined they were adopting the right path when they undertook to parrot the quantitative methods of natural science. They met with failure and already, even outside what has been described as critical sociology, there is talk of post-behaviourism. Alas, political science has little to offer political men seeking practical formulae and methods of action. Yet I am convinced that it is from the human sciences, rather than from technology, that the first creative spark will come to transform civilization. Those who today attack the human sciences for upsetting well-established habits, are in fact acting counter-productively; they do a disservice to the goals of development they claim to be pursuing. They are men of the past, history will brush past them or else both will die together.

c) The main issues at stake in the post-industrial era   To examine some of the main challenges posed by the so-called post-industrial era, is to reinforce our belief in the primary role of the human sciences. Automation draws in its wake a series of radical changes affecting all of economics as well as, because of the need for planning, every area of human activity. We are imminently threatened by massive unemployment even among highly-skilled manpower. There is also the strange phenomenon of relative poverty among the well-to-do, who are caught up in a mad race to raise their income, ever-eroded by taxes, and to "keeping up with the Joneses." What will be done with the time set free by automation, early retirement, the enormous increase in the ratio of older citizens? What will happen when cities become unlivable, when women convince themselves that they can only be fulfilled by working outside the home, while there are no useful outside jobs to offer them? When efforts to curb crime fail because they do not touch the root of the evil, namely the long-eroded protective social structures which nothing yet adequately replaces? When we are forced to admit that the situation of the under-developed areas of the world worsens instead of improving? That taxes collected from the rich only temporarily relieve the poor and have no impact upon the causes of poverty? Even beyond all this, the problem of goals arises particularly acutely: why live, study, work, grow old?

These and other similar problems, upon whose solution we must concentrate over the next decade, all essentially fall into the framework of the human sciences. To achieve success, all of society's major forms of organization must be questioned and so re-arranged as to allay today's deep discontents.

4.   Since the crisis is political, the remedy is participation

We are into a general crisis, but it surfaces in political terms, requiring political remedies initially. We are witnessing such an intimate mingling of the social and political areas, that the very concept of politics must be reconsidered. Thus the reform of an institution such as a university, for instance, cannot take full effect without a concomitant reform of the political system. Modes of behaviour adopted within social organizations can only bear fruit if the political framework is favourable, or at least if it moves in the same direction.

Were we living in religious times, we would see the current crisis as a spiritual one. And we would then have a better chance of understanding the present situation. But we can no longer, even in Québec, expect much guidance from the clergy, which is itself experiencing the swirls and eddies of uncertain fortune. Because our era is secular down to its very bone marrow, we claim that our crisis is primarily economic, social, or preferably political.

Today, politics are total. In one way or another they encompass the whole of man. And what we ask of politics is that they be the catalyser of a renewed civilization, the engine of a rejuvenated socio-economic mechanism. The difficulty of the task thus laid upon politics is only equalled by the eager expectations of communities. Political leaders—and with them, social leaders—who procrastinate for another ten years, one year, even for one more day, run the risk of being tarred and feathered tomorrow.

It is not by chance that the remedy prescribed as a cure for the ills of social organizations is labelled participation. Politics has long been a fertile ground for experiment and for participation. Unfortunately (except for some scarcely-known cases that may not lend themselves to imitation, such as the People's Republic of China, the USSR, Israel, or Yugoslavia) only very rudimentary participation has taken root. Liberal systems have been practising incomplete democracy. Representatives are elected—and in this field there has been a great deal of success in eliciting participation—the same representatives being subsequently re-elected or replaced. The simple act of voting should not be deprecated, because it marks a stage of maturity reached by men after almost uninterrupted subjection throughout all of historical time. But the participatory democracy at which we must arrive must go beyond this. It must address itself to all citizens: "the government's task is your task." It must give them the necessary means of action to fulfill this responsibility. However, if the citizens lack the will to respond promptly, or if, because of ineffective methods or means of action, participation proves wasteful, then we must fear the rejection of participation as a formula, and it is unclear what other approach might adequately and soon enough take its place.

A rough-and-ready definition of participation might cover the contributions of every kind made by a person to the organization to which he belongs. The following questions may then be asked: Why such contributions? In what form and how? What are the changes in outlook and set-up required for an optimum degree of participation?

More than ever in the past, contemporary men need to take an active part in the activity of governing, because daily work no longer offers the full personal fulfillment it did in traditional societies, where work not only provided men with their livelihood but also with a framework for living. Political decisions are today intimately interwoven with men's everday lives, so that it would in some sense amount to slavery were men unable to make real choices in taking the decisions that determine the course of their own lives. Moreover, the active participation of citizens is also required so that today's governments may function democratically and efficiently: as in all big organizations, any resistance by the "human factor" may jeopardize operations as much if not more than can mechanical resistance or disfunction.

One may distinguish three forms of political participation; those based on integration, representations, and personal involvement. *Integrative participation* gives a person minimum political existence. He is part of a system, a subject. All that is required to ensure the legitimacy of the political system and of its leaders, is that the agents of political socialization should transmit the necessary standards and attitudes to the people.

With the introduction of *representative participation,* the whole body politic becomes sovereign. The person is promoted to the rank of citizen. The act of voting whereby he chooses, by methods specific to each country, those who will govern in his name, represents a basic mechanism which makes this method of participation possible. The assembly of elected representatives makes it possible for all the people to get together, without needing everyone's physical presence. Political parties are the churches where representative participation is celebrated.

As to the *participation of personal involvement,* it is still in the process of taking shape, and so had best be referred to in the future tense. Basically, it will maintain the advantages of representative participation, but will require some deepening and broadening of a number of undeveloped aspects. Needed, for example, will be the full development of the politics of consultation, today all too often used as no more than a sedative. Reality will have to catch up with fiction in the field of decision making. The sovereign people will no longer be content to play the useless role of a straw king. Co-management, self-management are still words that frighten, because those who now use them are often unfamiliar with the very rudiments of management. But the aspirations and the needs covered by these words are too powerful to be ignored by those who are in a position to help the new world come into being.

Just as the introduction of representative participation did not occur through a gradual progression of integrative participation, but in fact through successive waves of revolutionary assault upon a crumbling order which refused to die; so, too, the changeover to a participation of personal involvement will require a radical departure in people's outlooks and in forms of organization. Personal involvement implies a system of dialectical interaction between the base and the summit, as opposed to a system of consultation at the summit alone, which reflects the techno-structure as we know it today. I purposely avoid using the word "revolution," for these are problems best approached without passion. However, it is really a new world, let us say a world re-born, that will arise out of the new modes of personal involvement.

The changeover will require men to be different from today's common run. Today, not more than 2 percent of the public is very involved within its respective organizations; only 10 to 20 percent are more or less active; while 75 to 80 percent may be considered as inactive. Arriving at a point where people will generally feel personally involved in negotiations and decisions relating both to their personal interests and, beyond, to matters affecting the whole community, will require a fairly long period of intensive education. It will, moreover, require a profound reform of society; for, as long as half the people or more must sweat from morning till night to earn a basic decent living, it is useless to expect any irresistible mass movements toward participation.

Liberal political mechanisms and institutions must be replaced or renewed. Institutions such as political parties and parliaments, in their modern form, arose out of the introduction of the social tool of representative participation. Now that a different social tool is needed, the institutions need re-thinking and re-shaping. Can this be done thoroughly enough, and soon enough?

They must become attuned to a society devoted to planning, to intimate interaction between all its parts. Just as the Manicouagan dams did not get built with oxen, so must the civil service and the government learn to work with the tools of the electronic age. An end must be put to paper-shuffling activities and to the mentality that cloaks everything in the confidentiality of the Official Secrets Act. Better relations must become the rule between administrative departments and government on the one hand, and the public on the other.

Decision-making is, ultimately, the crux of the matter. This is where our efforts must lie. What are the mechanisms of consultation or coordination and of feedback that will ensure maximum efficiency and optimum involvement and support? How can the necessary unity of leadership be reconciled with the required diversity of operations in different contexts, geographical, physical, denominational? How are goals to be redefined? (For it must be remembered that a system may work quite well and yet be deficient if its smooth operation merely reflects inadequate goal setting).

5.   Portrait of the future leader

The seventies will see the real accession to power of the sovereign people. That is the true meaning of the expression "participatory democracy." Should it fail, grave upheavals may engulf all of organized society. The people's political leader will have to assert his authority and firmly see to the proper handling of public business. Available will be a vast array of machines to provide the necessary technical and human data. But it is above all the leader's talent for talking with people—advisers, assistants, representatives of community groups and associations, the public as a whole—which will be one of his outstanding characteristics. As happens in practically all big organizations, and also in politics: people will from now on want their leader to live among them and not in some distant oligarchical Olympus. The break-up of so many voluntary associations is a first sign of this trend: it is easier to break up a voluntary association than to overthrow a political system. But if pressure mounts sufficiently, the political system can also be toppled. The leader of a great political party in the seventies will manage to involve vast numbers of people in the decisions he must take. At the same time, over and beyond the necessary changes and the concomitant moves and falterings, he will base the legitimacy of the system and its stability on the consensus which must underlie the satisfactory progress of any nation.

B.   POLITICAL ACTION AND POLITICAL PARTIES

Governments pass, while political parties generally endure. This helps us distinguish between them. But, when we try to evaluate the actual or the possible contribution of political parties to political action, further clarification is needed. Indeed, this is probably the most shadowy area of political science. One may be tempted to say: "Let us ignore the parties, in the grip of their electoral funds, and let us rather discuss other ways of promoting political action." Such an approach would not be unwarranted, bearing in mind the history of certain parties. However, the actual relationship between political action and political parties is, I believe, far more complex than is generally assumed. Moreover, whether we wish it or not, parties change according to the circumstances in which they are operating. It is up to us to determine whether we wish to influence the factors affecting such change.

The expression "political action" covers three different orders of political reality: first, a series of actions (voting, belonging to organized groups, dissent, revolt) through which individuals and social groups express their wants and their political preferences, and seek to influence political decisions (namely, the input); next, the various projects, programs, decisions through which the head of the entire body politic, namely the government, authoritatively expresses itself vis à vis individuals and groups, (namely, the output); and, thirdly, the means used to forecast and to guide the public's reactions to political actions and decisions—including, when required, correctives to such actions and decisions (namely, the feedback).

Section B of this chapter contains the text of my opening address at the convention of the Québec Liberal party, held in Montréal, 11-13 September 1970. The text also appeared in *Le Devoir*, 12 and 14 September 1970.

Seen in this threefold light, political action must be examined in terms of the social goals it serves, it must be perceived as a network of interrelationships between the rulers and the governed, and finally it must be evaluated in terms of the communications or of the dialogue it promotes. Political parties, whether in power or in opposition, are clearly one of the mechanisms of political action seen in this way.

The art of ruling has never been an easy one. It has become exceedingly complicated. Today's rulers are as good as, and doubtless better than, yesterday's. But the tasks they must accomplish are more demanding. On top of this, economic circumstances are at this time particularly difficult in most countries. There is little point in asking the rulers to get us the moon. The fat governments of the sixties have been replaced, in leaner times, by governments equipped with pruning shears. But we may well ask them, nevertheless, to attend to mending the cracks that are appearing in the structure, and that they actively concern themselves with the future.

In response to an economic theory that postulated that all inequities were, in the long run, self-righting, Lord Keynes said: "Never forget that, in the long run, we'll all be dead." Very true; but at the same time, more than ever, through accelerating change and through expansion in the scope of the decisions taken today in many fields, the long run casts its shadow over the short. As the father of modern sociology, Auguste Comte, used to observe: "The present is pregnant with the future." Thus, whether we think of regions, of social groups, or of areas of socio-economic activity, the effects of long-term trends underlie the problems that require immediate attention. In limiting solutions solely to the means at hand, in refusing the help of experience seen as obsolete, or of forecasts seen as unrealistic, there is a risk that difficulties may be multiplied rather than reduced. What is ultimately most lacking in attempts to undertake enlightened political action is not so much theory—theories are a dime a dozen—but rather a good compass and a good, strong guard-rail. This is what I discuss in the following section.

After some brief comments on the methods of political action, I shall outline the actual and the potential contributions of political parties to such action.

1. The methods of political action

Politics is both the art of taking the decisions needed to satisfy human needs, and of making the process acceptable to citizens. What is most puzzling about the conflicts between rulers and ruled is the difficulty in reaching agreement in spite of many provisions for consultation and negotiation. One is very much under the impression that political logic moves in a blind circle. The government heads one way, the people push the other way; in spite of the many messages exchanged, they are apparently unable to understand each other. How are we to account for this curious paradox? And how are we to go about remedying it?

In my view, neither the substance nor the structure of political action is primarily to be blamed. Nor should the men involved be blamed. It is rather the form—or what we may call the style—of political action which seems deficient. This style, rooted in the ideas of eighteenth-century philosophers and shaped by nineteenth-century practices, no longer meets the requirements of our times. Two simple illustrations will show the extent of the gap, produced in less than three generations.

At the end of the last century, public expenditures in all countries represented a mere fraction (one to two percent) of the gross national product, itself ten times smaller than today's; whereas today public expenditures, even in so-called liberal systems, are of the order of 25 to 40 percent.

At the end of the last century, a few pieces of legislation a year were sufficient to meet the needs of society; today, in our welfare states, advances in social security and the protection of the social order require thousands of laws, regulations, and orders.

Whoever we may be, whatever our profession, whatever the area of the country we inhabit, politics has invaded our lives and it is virtually impossible to escape its hold. This political invasion of our daily lives is a new phenomenon in history. Whatever the problem: the status of nations, war, or threat of war, pollution, social, economic, or regional disparities, urban crime rates, balanced economic growth, or social unrest—it is always to politics that we turn for a remedy though the ills are not always caused by politics, and it is almost invariably politics that bears the onus when a solution is not immediately forthcoming. Basically, the traditional methods of communications and of political control are still in force: but they mainly cover parliamentary activities and to a lesser extent the government's work. As everyone knows, the true levers of political action, on the output side, are today in practice in the hands of top civil servants who are beyond the control of the people and who sometimes even dominate their own political heads, the ministers.

For example, what will a citizen gain by discussing his problems with his member of Parliament, when economic and technical constraints make the latter powerless? We may well deplore the weakening of parliaments since the 1940s. But the problem lies elsewhere. It lies in the growing difficulty that MPs experience in adequately carrying out their main task, that of adopting legislation. When whole segments of the people refuse to be identified with the actions of their elected representatives; when, moreover, practically all MPs adopt a given stand on a particular question whereas a majority of the citizens most directly affected adopt a contrary position (as we recently saw during the debate on Bill 63, supposedly designed to promote the use of the French language in Québec) the conclusion seems clear: there is a crisis of political authority. It is healthy to remember that legitimate rule can only be based upon the consent of the sovereign, namely of the people.

It is not through mere parliamentary reform, nor even through amending the relationship between civil servants and ministers, that the yawning gap between citizens and their elected representatives can be mended.

What most pressingly needs reform are the methods of political action. These have remained as they were when social needs and political issues were seen as distinct; and thus continue to be based upon the assumption of contrary or conflicting interests. For today's citizens, as for their fathers, the State is still a distant "they," alien and almost inimical, whereas in actual fact politics is inextricably tied to people's daily lives, affecting practically every moment. This is, generally, only dimly perceived, if at all. On the other hand, the rulers all too often see citizens as intractable children to be cajoled or punished according to circumstances or to the temper of the moment. Slowly our systems turn into a kind of techno-demagoguery, the apex of a period that adopted such complex tools for action that only a limited number of people know how to handle them—a period in which the tremendous yearning for a more instinctive life is rising to the surface in alternate waves of pleading and of anger, and in the search for a charismatic leadership of a kind previously unknown.

As against a system judged heavy and oppressive, community action is being promoted, as is in certain quarters a return to nature. Could the waves of dissent, which appear in the form of spontaneous movements, or fronts, or of pseudo-political parties, be an early sign of an upheaval which will affect the whole world, or, as with a number of such movements in the past, will they subside without leaving any apparent trace of their existence?

It bears remembering that there is nothing inherently ridiculous about the idea of self-government, an idea which inspired the popular movements that led to the great democratic revolution. What is ridiculous, is the claim that citizens can manage their own affairs alone, without the assistance of delegates and of civil servants. We thus come back to the perennial question—how can a people rule itself?—a question posed by numerous thinkers including Plato, Thomas Hobbes, John Locke, Jean-Jacques Rousseau, and John Stuart Mill. However, we must recognize that modes of representation and management methods then believed to be sophisticated, no longer meet today's changed circumstances. Co-operation and concertation will today require far closer relationships than in the past between rulers and ruled, as well as individuals' and social groups' more direct and more extensive participation in political action, at each of four levels: initiating action, planning it, decision making, and implementation. It is clearly no longer a matter of simple participation, consisting of contributions (wishes or advice) toward decision making by others. Rather, the people concerned will take on the responsibility for their own problems, in co-operation, of course, with those to whom they have for a time given the task of attending, on the people's behalf, to the administration of things and to the government of men.

The goal will not be to eliminate whatever tensions grow out of the need to organize human activities in one way or another and to distribute within society the proceeds of men's collective labour. The goal must be two-fold: to elicit new attitudes towards the sources of such tensions, and to introduce methods capable of preventing or of channeling such tensions.

Among these methods, the following come to mind: the establishment of advisory bodies and methods of consultation, intimately linked with decision-making centres, and administrative deconcentration as well as political decentralization, reaching out to individuals within their groups and within their own settings so as to promote their full participation in the activities that affect them. The implementation of such methods of government will require radical reform both of outlooks among people and authorities, and of the whole framework of political action itself. Let us try to examine the extent to which political parties can be involved in achieving such a vast changeover.

2. The contribution of political parties to political action

Modern liberal societies have two major mechanisms for converting social issues into political problems: interest groups and political parties. Voluntary associations give a considerable fraction of the population a means of making themselves heard—which the rulers do not always appreciate but which is nevertheless essential for the proper functioning of democracy. Political parties very appropriately have considerable weight in our democratic system. The parties' contribution to political action may be all the greater as they influence three important levels of activity: the formulation or presentation of claims or of demands upon the political system, decision making within that system, and finally the evaluation of the results of political decisions. Thus, if we wish to review or to reform the methods of political action to provide for better consultation and concertation, it is impossible to leave out the political parties.

Parties engage in what may be classified as three types of activities: electoral, governmental, and mediating. The electoral activity is the one best known, and it is also the one parties best fulfill, perhaps indeed the only one they adequately accomplish, as suggested by the ease with which they fade in the background as soon as an electoral campaign is over. People are less familiar with the parties' governmental and mediating activities, and, quite possibly, it is because these have never been carefully looked into, that they have failed to acquire their proper impact.

The governmental activity of parties is obvious. But to understand it clearly, a distinction must be drawn between two contexts in which a party functions, namely within and without the political system. In the first case, the party closely intermingles with the components of the political system, particularly the legislature and, if the party is in power, also with the government; but also, although less clearly and often improperly, with the administration and even the judiciary. In the second case, it acts as an independent organization with its own roles to play. In this way, the party as a framework for members of the legislature is not the same thing as the party that serves as an electoral machine or as a mediating body between the rulers and the ruled. But in practice these demarcation lines are often askew, as electoral considerations may twist parliamentary concerns; not to mention the fact that close relationships often develop between legislators and the top people in the party apparatus.

Thus, necessary and useful links exist between the party's two facets. However, a healthy society requires the functional distinction to be preserved. This is particularly important in the case of the party in power. In 1946, shortly after becoming Britain's Labour prime minister, Clement Attlee reminded philosopher Harold Laski, then chairman of the Labour Party's Executive Committee that, "as soon as a party leader becomes head of the government, his actions must solely be governed by his view of the general interest of the nation and not in any way by guidelines laid down by his party." Of course, since he is called upon, while making up his mind, to listen to the position of interest groups and even to that of other parties, he cannot be deprived of the right to lend a careful ear to the views of the members of his own party. In this way, therefore, the party acting "within the political system" should, in the general context of the political platform on whose strength its candidates were elected or brought to power, be careful to be governed for the good of society as a whole and should indeed, as a party, be subsidiary to the legislators, the head of the opposition, the prime minister. Correspondingly, "outside the political system," the party should strive to achieve its own specific goals, and should concern itself with its supporters, its electoral "machine." In brief, it should fully and quite properly attend to its various partisan activities.

At the same time there is no doubt that, to be able to fulfil all of its tasks adequately, a party must maintain a high degree of internal cohesion. Constant division on points of principle between a party's non-parliamentary leaders, or major conflicts of authority between the leaders of the party's two facets, would inevitably cause crises dangerously reducing the party's efficacy and perhaps even precipitating its breakup. "A party within the party" cannot be tolerated without seriously endangering its future, nor can grave internal rifts or divisions.

On the other hand, there is nothing wrong with the non-parliamentary leaders having differing viewpoints or giving different priorities to certain problems. Provided the unity of decision making is safeguarded (the principle of the ultimate authority of the parliamentary wing of the party being accepted on policy decisions), there should be debate between the party's two facets, provided this debate is a dialogue and not a sterile conflict. Such creative tensions prevent the party from getting bogged down in routine and from letting itself either be dazzled by short-lived success or paralyzed by set-backs. The tensions are a guarantee of perpetual vigour and constant renewal.

The interplay between the party's two facets will be all the richer and more profitable if it is accompanied by a division of labour. There are roles which party officials cannot legitimately play, notably legislative and government roles, and there are organizing tasks that belong to the party apparatus and in which the parliamentary wing cannot become involved without risking impropriety.

It is, for example, no secret that MPs and ministers, whose term of office is relatively short, are instinctively reluctant to devote their attention to matters only likely to become pressing in some years' time. By definition, they are men interested in the tasks at hand. In fact this is one of the main reasons why it is so difficult to legislate upon matters of major importance that have long been kept hanging fire before the necessary social solutions are elaborated. On the whole, a very long time elapses, between twenty-five and seventy-five years, before a social question becomes a political issue and comes up in the form of proposed legislation. Commonly, no advantage is taken of this long interval. In fact, for as long as possible, the subject tends to be ignored. When the government finally decides to undertake consultation or negotiation, it is under threat of a white paper, or of a pending bill, that the people are called upon to present their views. It is then practically impossible to proceed to a cool and clear-headed review of the points at issue; it becomes necessary to act in the heat of the moment, while passions run high, and the resulting urgency favours neither consensus for the common good, nor carefully pondered solutions.

Here it should be recalled that political parties are privileged in not being limited to specific issues that affect a limited segment of society, as is usually the case with interest groups. Rather, parties must turn their eyes towards the major problems affecting the whole of society. Indeed, they are led into doing this by the tasks which are theirs as a result of the fact that they are one of the mechanisms of government. Why is it then that the parties, which must survive the ups and downs of political life, are not concerned to examine the vital long-term problems which will sooner or later have to be faced and solved, such as the future of Canadian federalism, social, economic, and regional desparities, pollution, ethnic and linguistic problems, the status of universities, the distribution of electoral seats, and so on?

Any conclusions from such wide-ranging discussion would not be binding upon the parliamentary wing of the party, but would provide it with ample material for thought and with a basis for possible action. This would enhance the role of the ordinary back-benchers who are today more or less marginal within the legislative process, largely because they seldom know how to frame the relevant questions and are frequently short of adequate information to help crystallize their personal views on the subject-matter of up-coming legislation.

But it is through emphasizing their mediating activities, which happen to be complementary to those mentioned above, that political parties could best help to establish a broader degree of consultation within society. They are splendidly equipped to provide for exchanges of views with the people, and their electoral prowess shows that they can set off impressive movements. For this to happen, however, MPs would need to take as much interest in political action as they do in their own re-election, and the party would of course have to be considered as more than a simple vote-gathering machine, which it still all too often is.

It has become a habit to review this aspect of the activities of parties by distinguishing between mass parties and cadre parties. Mass parties, which have many supporters generally recruited from similar social backgrounds, are thought to be more ideological, more programatic, and more concerned over the political training of their members than cadre parties which rely mainly upon last-minute promises and upon patronage to get their candidates elected.

But this distinction, it would seem, has become too simplistic. For the past fifteen years, mass parties have seen the number of their members dwindling, their doctrines progressively watered down; and the after-taste of their former victories or defeats has prodded them even closer to the methods that have proved electorally successful in the hands of cadre parties. It would be a pity if, in the end, only the parties unlikely to succeed at the polls should remain concerned with providing ideologies and citizenship training.

We are currently seeing the emergence of parties (there are pointers in the wind in the Gaullist U.d.r. and in the Communist Party in France, as well as here in the Social Credit and the Parti Québécois) which are neither mass nor establishment parties and which, thanks to the coming-of-age of public relations, television, and the development of new propaganda methods, have both the skill of traditional mass parties to provide citizenship training, and the ability of cadre parties to reach the voters. At the same time, there are various signs among traditional parties, both mass and cadre, of early changes which may lead them to attach growing weight to their mediating activities. Thus they are less concerned over the size of their membership than over their influence upon the whole population. What they seek above all, is to be able to rely on a certain number of active supporters, well distributed geographically and in all areas of activity, people who are no longer seen simply as election organizers, but as community mobilizers.

This mediating activity, or the link that parties provide between the political system and the people, takes on a variety of forms. As instruments of socialization, they provide citizens with the means of understanding or evaluating the government's intentions and actions. Parties thus contribute to clarifying public opinion, whose vagaries and contradictions are sometimes so harsh or disconcerting to politicians. But at the same time, it would be undesirable for the rulers to use parties as advisory bodies or as channels for administrative deconcentration: there would be too much risk of favouritism or corruption. These major goals can better be served by using interest groups and civil servants acting at the regional level. On the other hand, governments should promote the legitimate forms of parties' mediating activities. Thus they might study the possibility of public funding for the costlier of these activities, subject of course to appropriate criteria and conditions.

But we should not delude ourselves. We are still far from the link-up parties (*partis-relais*) or the community-mobilization parties (*partis d'ani-*

mateurs) which Daniel Johnson championed here for a while and which, because of their twofold nature, I call electoral strategy and community— mobilization parties (*partis de stratèges-animateurs*). Old historical anchors will need to be cut, old habits set aside. But even more than the public interest, electoral considerations are bound to push parties in this direction.

What needs to be defined above all is a healthy dialectic between the party's role as a government mechanism and its role as a socializing organization. This clarification should be sought without delay.

In this way, if the decision-makers so wish, parties may, without giving up the electoral activities which are their primary goal, cease avoiding the true problems, as they all too often have done so far, and may thus become powerful tools for bringing together, whenever necessary, the rulers and the ruled. They could undertake tasks of information and of community mobilization, hold symposia, carry out inquiries, take the pulse of public opinion, and contribute to its enlightenment. Moreover, they could seek the views of individuals and of groups on various matters, provide a forum for public discussion, and become the agora freely and spontaneously chosen by people when they want to discuss their common concerns.

The many study groups, discussion clubs, and citizens'-action committees which are springing up everywhere show the people's great hunger for involvement in politics, and at the same time show the inability of organized interest groups and of political parties to play one of their major roles adequately: that of providing a continuing link between the rulers and the ruled.

As regards political parties at least, a serious and courageous effort is needed to correct the situation and to turn them at last into effective tools for political action. If parties manage, in line with their proper purpose, to create and maintain a continuing dialogue between the rulers and the people, they will do much to circumvent the threat of break-up that now hangs over our civilization.

C. POLITICS BETWEEN CULTURE AND ECONOMICS

Claims of every kind assail political men. It is quite likely that the claims upon the political system of cultural and of economic agents are among the most pressing. Cultural needs can be homogenous or heterogenous, and so indeed can economic ones. And these two may be in harmony or in conflict. Moreover, politics has its own ends and possibilities, sometimes

The remaining section of this chapter contains the text of my address to the Convention of the Québec Liberal party, held at Mount Orford, 25 August 1973. Portions of the address were published in *Le Devoir,* 27 August 1973, in *Le Soleil,* 28 August, and in the magazine *Maintenant,* no. 136, May 1974. For a more analytical view of the interaction between politics, culture, and economics see my paper: "La politique entre la culture et l'économie: Pistes de recherches," Académie des sciences morales et politiques, *Travaux et Communications,* vol. 2 (Montréal: Editions Bellarmin, 1974), 93-108.

more akin to cultural goals than to economic, sometimes the opposite, or again both structurally and functionally far removed from either, if not altogether antagonistic.

If we further bear in mind the specific circumstances of time and place, there is no doubt that a careful review of the interaction between culture, politics, and economics presupposes a complex analytical framework. It is not my purpose here to develop such a framework. One does not proceed to mark out a research trail before the land is properly cleared of brush. Canada and particularly Québec will provide me with a number of examples serving for such a preliminary brush-clearing operation.

These examples illustrate the kinds of interaction between culture, politics, and economics that are currently typical of Canada and Québec. Such a wholly empirical approach may sin by incompleteness and partiality. I take this risk, comforted by the thought that this is a context in which there are few impalpable truths.

Canada offers a splendid example of the constant use of state machinery to pursue industrial projects with carefully sought-out cultural spin-offs. Impressive public works sponsored by the government, such as the Great Lakes waterways, the Trans-Continental railway, and more recently, the Trans-Canada pipeline, the Trans-Canada highway, and the St. Lawrence Seaway were not merely aimed at compensating for the gaps left untended by private enterprise, but were in equal measure designed—sometimes against the natural grain of north-south rather than east-west industrial and cultural movements—to arouse and consolidate a feeling of national identity, promoting Canadian unity and counter-balancing the attraction the United States exercised in some areas of the country.

Moreover, the impact in Canadian territory of American legislation governing subsidiaries of American firms in this country, has on several occasions and again quite recently led the Canadian government to adopt measures aimed at protecting Canada's economic and political sovereignty and at promoting a "cultural" nationalism—called Canadianism—which, although never virulent, is quite explicit and has fairly strongly influenced parts of the public, notably intellectuals, politicians, and businessmen.

It is in the more or less consistent pursuit of these cultural goals that a number of Royal Commissions of Enquiry were set up, such as the Rowell-Sirois Commission on Federal-Provincial Relations, the Aird Commission on Broadcasting, the Massey Commission on Arts and Letters, and the Laurendeau-Dunton Commission on Bilingualism and Biculturalism. In line with these commissions' recommendations, important cultural institutions were set up: the Canadian Broadcasting Corporation; the National Film Board; the Canada Council; and national cultural programs were devised such as federal assistance to universities, the Official Languages Act, and the policies on bilingualism and multiculturalism. Of late, the gradual restructuring of most government activities in the fields of natural, life, and human sciences, as well as in the arts, within the Ministry of State for Science and Technology and the Department of the Secretary of State, suggest that the Canadian government wishes to give a very high priority to the promotion of culture.

What Margaret Atwood[1] so clearly showed with respect to Canada's English-language literature also applies to politics: English Canadians' main concern is survival. In this they are no different from French Canadians who so long seemed to consider survival their main raison d'être. But while survival for English Canadians means the maintenance of an identity separate from that of the United States, for French Canadians it implies a day-to-day struggle against the forces of assimilation at work in the whole surrounding North-American continent.

In the field of economic policies, Québec long observed the original liberal creed, that is a non-interventionism that could only benefit the most powerful business and industrial ventures. In the Québec context this could only mean submission to North-American imperialism.

We may ask: does this subservience of economic policies still persist today, or has the Québec government on the contrary recovered a certain autonomy, perceptible in its actual decisions and actions? This question can of course only properly be examined within the Canadian context. As we know, the history of Canada's economic policies may be seen as a long struggle to ensure the country's economic independence. That is why Québec's attempts to set its own economic policies must perforce start with a margin of operating freedom obtained with respect to the federal government.

Three major aspects must be borne in mind here. First, the province of Québec has a large stock of non-renewable natural resources, badly needed by the United States and by the rest of Canada. The Québec government may be expected to use this advantage to get its competitors to act in the interests of the province's economic development.

Secondly, a kind of industrial and trade balance already exists in Canada, notably between Ontario and Québec, which requires all parts of the country to bear in mind their common interest if they want to maintain an appropriate rate of economic development. It is true that Ontario leads Québec in the number and size of headquarters of companies established there, in industrial and financial ventures, in qualified manpower, and in population; and that this advance grows from year to year. But in spite of this increasing imbalance between the two provinces the interdependence remains intimate if we remember that thirty to forty percent of the goods manufactured in Ontario and not used by that province are absorbed by the Québec market.

Finally, and this perhaps is the most important aspect of Québec's economy: since 1960, the Québec government, more than that of any other province, has adopted economic policies coloured by a home-grown nationalism, a Québec nationalism not unlike the nationalism that the Canadian government has always practised visa-à-vis the United States.

On the other hand, in the field of cultural policies, the hard fact to be faced is that it is not the Québec government, but the federal government, which by-and-large has taken the main decisions and launched the principal projects that have brought Québec into step with modernity.

Québec then, even more than Canada, offers a rich source of material for empirical research into the relationships between culture, politics, and economics.

French Canadians, forced to the sidelines of the industrial development that took place in Québec from the end of the nineteenth century and especially since the 1920s, have long accepted and continue to accept, though more and more reluctantly, that their government should repeatedly exhibit marked servility towards industrial and financial concerns, whether continental or international, settled in Québec or interested in so doing: mining or lumbering rights yielded for a song, special tax exemptions, no restrictions on methods or scope of operations, not to mention the supply of cheap and accommodating labour . . . People went so far as to take pride in the fact that the province was "a paradise for foreign investors," and even today one may hear occasional expressions of official concern that Québec may be losing this "good" reputation.[2]

Such a subservience of Québec politics to powerful English-Canadian and American industrial and financial interests helps to make clear the Québec government's ambivilent attitude towards culture. On the one hand, its economic policies follow the original liberal creed, and this, in the Québec context, means submission to North-American economic imperialism. But on the other hand, Québec governments until recently strongly supported and propagated a humanistic, Catholic, and agriculturally-oriented culture. This was of course electorally astute, given the strength of the rural vote, disproportionately favoured by the electoral distribution of legislative seats. But it also put the most important social and cultural levers into the hands of elites, both lay and clergy, whose official attachment to traditional values guaranteed the survival of a paternalistic and reactionary political regime.

We must remember the co-existence, in the Québec of those days, of two very different official models or cultural patterns: the one, governing relations with big business, aligned with laissez-faire ideology and leading to a condition of economic colonialism, the other, devised for the natives , keyed to tradition, and reducing the people to the rank of subjects.

During Alexandre Taschereau's long reign (Taschereau was the perfect example of the colonized "gentleman"), and also under Maurice Duplessis, there were countless instances—sometimes wry, more often tragic for the community—of governmental capitulation to the great industrial and financial interests. The following event is typical of the chronic colonialism in which Québec then floundered. The scene happened in the mid 1950s, at the summit of the Duplessis era. Maurice Duplessis, and the local bishop, Monsignor Labrie, were inaugurating the new Betsiamites power station, surrounded by the usual religious and lay dignitaries, workers still on the project, and the local population. In his address, as usual, the premier praised the merits of the religious and rural traditions which Québec so faithfully maintained (so faithfully, indeed, that in the eyes of the rest of the surrounding English-speaking world, Québec had become "the quaint old province"). In turn, Monsignor Labrie then lauded the "Chef" who was so good at giving Quebeckers sound and healthy policies. Meanwhile among the group, the directors of the firm contracted to do a large part of the work, the McNamara Dredging Company of Toronto, were pondering the sizeable profits they were making on the jobs, here and elsewhere, given them by the Duplessis government. Observing the touching picture of natives, mutually congratulating each other for so well preserving the cultural models and the political methods that kept them in a state of economic colonialism, the English-speaking businessmen's thoughts turned to the future. "Too bad that man (Duplessis) has no son—one of them whispered to his neighbour—otherwise this kind of set-up could last another forty years." His neighbour whispered back: "If I were a resident of Québec, for sure I'd vote for the good cause." (Yet in fact, Québec's English-speaking businessmen and the English-speaking community never voted for Duplessis on any large scale. The vast majority voted Liberal as they had always done, merely contributing handsomely to the Union Nationale's electoral fund, which was the only contribution expected of them, since the overwhelming support of the rural ridings was more than enough to ensure victory for the party at the polls.)

Lest it should be thought that this subservience to big business vanished with Duplessis, here are two recent examples, out of a whole gamut of possible instances of the Québec Government's weak-kneed attitudes.

One is the painful episode of Bill 63, designed to "promote the use of the French language in Québec," adopted in the fall of 1969 over the indignant protests of countless people who really had the future of French at heart. The bill had doubtless been drafted under the direct and immediate threat of breaking off negotiations regarding several hundred-million dollars' worth of foreign investments which Québec badly needed, and it had most certainly been influenced by the fear of angering and alienating the industrial and financial establishments settled in Québec, as well as the whole of Québec's English-speaking community which plays so large a role in the Québec economy. Another instance is the stinging personal failure experienced by Premier Robert Bourassa when he vainly pleaded the cause of French at the General Motors plant in Ste. Thérèse in the summer of 1970.

Amazingly, one still hears voices urging the government to steer clear of courageous language policies which might antagonize investors and Anglophone Quebeckers! Is that not also the political caution advocated in the report of the Commission of Enquiry into the French Language in Québec, set up by a hesitant government and somewhat reluctantly kept going, on a promise that it would remain "reasonable"?

Finding it impossible to identify with a cultural model based upon the modernistic values that prevailed in the surrounding world, French Canadians adopted a cultural model which allowed them to build their society upon a solid foundation, even though the model supported and entrenched their economic dependence.

Had they, instead, leaned towards marxism, they would have defined their condition as one of colonialism and would have identified their ethnic group with the proletariat. Their elites, instead of offering the young the models of the stoïcs and of the holy martyrs of the Church, would have talked in terms of "tribal kinglets," "banana republics," and "white Negroes of America."

But Québec's clerical and lay establishment, with their strong rural roots, generally shared the religious and political beliefs of the people and stood to gain from economic colonialism and political paternalism. As trusted guides, they formulated and conveyed a protective ideology well attuned to the situation. Most of them, by now established in the cities but uncritically attached to Québec's ancient rural role, erected a symbolic and long-invincible barrier against the industrialization and urbanization fast gaining ground around them.

A singular aspect, which reveals the extent of the leadership's influence upon the culture of a people, may be observed in the fact that the French-speaking ideologists were ardently supported in their self-appointed role by English-speaking intellectuals. These went so far as to claim that French Canadians outdid them! They movingly observed that French Canadians, unlike themselves, were not tainted by the materialism of the business world, and had a special gift for appreciating and cultivating the things of the mind. Whether this was unconscious rationalization or a cynical attempt to forestall any thoughts of revolt among the natives, is now immaterial. It is a fact that such guilt-absolving confessions by English-speaking intellectuals friendly to French Canadians could only contribute to reinforcing the Francophones' beliefs about themselves.[3] With such ideological brainwashing, no wonder the French Canadians took to despising things economic and industrial, and to celebrating, in full North American mid-twentieth century, the sole relevance of classical humanistic culture. To this accompaniment, they enjoyed games of political patronage, whose strings some of them learned to pull skillfully and profitably, all this under the indulgent eye of the big Anglophone financial interests and of "big brother," the federal Liberal party, which—according to no less an authority than Pierre Elliott Trudeau, today Canada's prime minister under the wing of the same party—furnished one of the obstacles to the emergence of democracy in Québec, since it was itself benefiting electorally from the situation, and thus refrained from providing political education in the ways of representative and responsible democracy. Symbolic rewards cost a great deal less than having to abide by carefully worked out and rigorously controlled economic policies.[4]

The fact that this cultural model, based upon ruralism and upon Roman Catholic and classical humanistic values, could so long survive in the middle of an America strongly bent upon the pursuits of modernism, was of course linked to the survival of corresponding institutions. These were singularly resilient: notably, an integrated educational system ranging from grade school to university, with the famous classical colleges serving as its heart and brain (the fortunate minority who attended these colleges cannot help remembering them with nostalgia); the parish system, marvellously designed to perpetuate traditional community solidarities, but impermeable to modern industry and technological innovation; the paternalism of a clerical and lay establishment raised in a farming background; so exalted a view of educational activity, that people hardly felt it called for remuneration; the abandonment by the state of its prerogatives in the cultural field, more particularly in education, owing to the fact that governments could count on the unshakeable loyalty of both lay and religious ideologists and agents of socialization—in brief, all the necessary factors combined not only to maintain the cultural model but also to make it appear as the only worthwhile and "natural" one.

One might be tempted to say that the coming to power of Jean Lesage's Liberal government in 1960 provided a radically new departure in the interplay of culture, politics, and economics in Québec. But this would be too sweeping a claim. On the one hand, well before 1960, new elites, trained in the best schools of social science in the Western world, and supported by the new electronic media, were denting the defences of the established order. On the other hand, even the Liberal party's electoral platform in 1960 was largely inspired by rural and agricultural motifs. Still today, many vestiges of colonialism persist in economic policies, and tradition-bound cultural patterns survive, especially in people's view of political authority. It is nevertheless true that a strong desire for modernization has come to the fore in Québec since 1960. Initially known as the Quiet Revolution, this new spirit has been reflected in economic policies whose symbolic value betrays kinship with the Canadian government's economic policies towards the United States. Dashing slogans of course held the spotlight, slogans such as: "Masters in our own house," or "Québec has the know-how," to which even the Committee for an Independent Canada could find no appealing alternatives. But it is particularly the projects and achievements of the successive Québec governments since 1960 that call for a comparison of the two nationalisms, the Canadian and the Québec variety, in the field of economic policies.

The decision of the Québec government to manage its own trust fund (Caisse de dépôts) and to establish a number of public economic corporations was aimed at making up for the shortcomings of the private sectors and at stimulating not only the economy but also the cultural life of Québec. The huge Manicouagan hydroelectric development, in the early 1960s undertaken by the Québec government and carried out by Québec and other French-speaking engineers, was of course aimed at strengthening the province's economic infrastructure, but its promoters, particularly the then minister of natural resources, René Lévesque, founded great hopes for cultural renewal on this achievement. The effects were indeed soon felt: a great flowering of all the arts, and the appearance of modern aspirations and lifestyles. The 1962 decision to nationalize electric companies at a cost of several hundred-million dollars, turning Hydro-Québec into the sole provider of electricity in the province—Ontario had created its Hydro in 1917!—is easier to justify in terms of symbolic rather than economic arguments. Premier Robert Bourassa had similar goals in mind when he announced the James Bay hydroelectric development project in 1971, but this time Quebeckers were less inclined to rise to the bait. Hydro-Québec, the Manicouagan dams, the James Bay, all these are among the tangible symbols of Quebeckers' new technical skills. They show a current trend in favour of adopting new, modern values and of jettisoning a Catholic and classical humanistic culture, not devoid of greatness, but long used as a tool of political subservience that kept French Canadians in an economic position where they were, as the saying goes, perpetual "hewers of wood and drawers of water."

Meanwhile, the old protective dikes abruptly gave way, as we see in the profound religious crisis Québec is now experiencing, the enormous upheaval in the rural way of life, and in the sharp waning of the electoral influence of the rural vote. The Department of Education, created in March 1964, abolished the religious orders' control over educational institutions; CEGEPs (Collèges d'éducation générale et professionelle, i.e. community colleges) replaced the elitist classical colleges. New modes of community organization, more spontaneous and more permeable to change, began to appear as parishes lost their hold upon community life. Among different social and geographic groups, and in all areas of activity, new cultural models sprang up, sometimes at the initiative of a government long felt not to hold responsibility for educational and cultural activities, and sometimes out of the spontaneous desire of citizens who wanted to "take their fate into their own hands."

In this new set-up, not only are political decisions and actions often a source of far-reaching cultural changes, but they also reflect a wish to establish a new approach to economics, one that would more effectively counter-balance the moves of the great industrial and financial barons. Thus, an awareness of interdependence and an effort at exercising controls on business are gradually replacing the old, unashamedly colonialist attitudes.

The main question that Québec's political parties must currently ask themselves in the field of economic policy is: should Québec continue, especially with regard to Canada and the United States, to put its eggs into the basket of "nationality," as Albert Breton put it, or should it principally aim at utilitarian economic policies (full employment, optimum returns on investment, and so on)? And, should it choose economic policies of the latter type, how can it hope to escape economic domination by English Canada and particularly by the United States? How can it counter-balance the political, social, and cultural impact of American legislation governing American subsidiaries in Québec? Whereas, if it chooses to continue economic policies with symbolic or nationalistic overtones, such as establishing key industries, supporting small and medium business, prestige projects such as the hydro-electric development of the James Bay area, or financial support to community undertakings or projects, up to what point can the Québec government commit itself financially in the short and medium run without thereby having to let up on priority programs in the fields of health and welfare, education, recreation and so on? Unfortunately we are no longer left with reserves comparable to those that enabled the Quiet Revolution's nationalistic economic policies to be financed from 1960 to 1965. And so, who can afford to foot the bill, which is likely to go on growing even as the public treasury gets closer and closer to the bottom of the barrel?

The time has now come—or else it may never arrive—for a Québec political party to adopt a coherent platform on cultural matters, on the understanding that, should the party be brought to power, this part of the platform will exercise a particularly binding commitment on the government. Jean Lesage's team, it is well known, used to mock the Department of Cultural Affairs, considered as Georges-Emile Lapalme's brain-child. Have things really improved since then? When can we expect to have an independent Québec body like the Canada Council? When will we have a radical reform of the program of research grants, currently organized in totally outdated and arbitrary ways? When will we have coherent policies for the humanities and the social sciences? When will a daring and realistic language policy be adopted? When will we see a necessary counter-reform in the huge world of education, where administrators, teachers, and students are increasingly distraught, so arbitrary are the standards, so mindless the controls, and so inoperative the current methods of participation?

The efforts at rehabilitating politics started in the 1960s are continuing catch as catch can, with rather more misses than catches. It must be admitted that Québec's current government has been unlucky. It was barely beginning to hold its own, when the tragic events of October 1970 took place, so to speak clipping the government's wings. Subsequently, crisis has followed upon crisis, and it is only for a short while, since mid-1973, that a climate more favourable to coherent political action has existed in Québec.

Three kinds of problems deserve a closer look.

The first concerns political misdemeanour. Political parties must realize that vast networks of political corruption, patronage, partisan spying, and fraud of all kinds have recently begun to be unveiled at an apparently growing pace; they rivet the public's attention upon the parties' top leadership and upon members of the government, and are rapidly sapping whatever faith in politics the public may still have. Parties must therefore include in their programs measures aimed at preventing such violations of the basic rules of public and private ethics.

A second set of problems centres around the ever-tougher political confrontation between a utilitarian, technical approach (based upon factors of economic yield and administrative efficiency), and an approach which gives precedence to social and cultural factors, (aimed at justice, human dignity, and protection of the environment).

While this trend affects both governments and interest groups, it is neither the one nor the other which initiated it. It is the result of a new public awareness, a consciousness of newly-emerging values that reflect new requirements and arise out of circumstances to which the agents of culture, politics, and economics have contributed, most of the time unconsciously, through the exercise of their respective tasks. It is precisely this new set of circumstances that will galvanize into action a few of the people, more conscious than others of the needs of the times; and the cry as well as the pressure will then be taken up by as yet undetermined action groups.

This is the new context that has produced the Ralph Nader phenomenon, as well as an assortment of movements seeking to meet community needs by awakening the co-operative sense and the initiative of community members. This is what has been happening in many citizens' committees in Québec, in the poor neighbourhoods of St-Henri, St-Roch, Guyenne, in the *Operations-dignité* villages of the Lower Saint-Lawrence and of the Gaspé Peninsula, in Cabano, Manseau, and elsewhere. In these and other instances, such citizen groups also join together to defend common interests against daily assault by the promoters of private enterprise and sometimes even public enterprise, as recently illustrated by the citizen committee formed to fight, with success, Hydro Québec's hydro-electric development plan for the Jacques Cartier River.

Finally, a third order of concerns centres around an issue crucial to all Quebeckers, that of political independence.

Even Québec's independence movement, in its way, gives evidence of new modes of interaction between culture, politics, and economics. But, at the same time, many Canadians and Quebeckers, right or wrong, view independence as a political choice to be made as between economic and cultural values. This shows that, even in a modern context, one cannot assume that there is full and final integration between politics, economics, and culture. It may even be true that, today, opportunities for conflict and division are more numerous and more serious than ever.

It must be realized that the concept of interdependence is devoid of meaning unless it applies to a society which already has a certain degree of independence. In our era of forced technological and economic interdependence, people's desire for independence can only rest upon whatever degree of original synthesis or symbiosis they have achieved (or can achieve) between culture, politics, and economics. It is out of such a synthesis or symbiosis that nations arise, and through it that separate societies maintain their distinctiveness.

Now Québec today, as yesterday, constitutes a distinctive society within the North-American continent and within Canada.

Where opinions differ, however, is over the degree of political self-determination required by Québec to enable this distinctive society not just to survive but, primarily, to develop in line with its own characteristics.

I believe it is a mistake to use the argument of the interdependence of peoples to try to freeze Québec into its political status quo. People's inter-dependence will doubtless lead to the emergence of a world-wide collective consciousness, to which men will surely attempt to give some political form, foreshadowed by the former League of Nations and by today's United Nations. But it is likely that, side by side with these broad world-wide organizations, strong solidarities will also underlie narrower and smaller political alliances. Whether these subdivisions continue to coincide with today's nation states, as is doubtless likely in many cases, or whether they represent new local or regional political rearrangements, as is already evident in a number of areas including Québec, is largely immaterial.

Neither does it seem particularly useful to apply the concept of sovereignty piecemeal, as in the case of Québec's claim to cultural sovereignty. This claim was advanced several times in the past, and Premier Bourassa took it up in December 1972. Sovereignty can only be political, and it is indivisible, as it is founded upon a *sui generis* symbiosis of culture, politics, and economics. Apart from any short-lived advantages it may bring when used as an electoral slogan, I fail to see why any political party or government should get involved in the pursuit of purely cultural sovereignty: it can only be a mirage unless provision is also made for a strategy aimed at insuring an adequate dose of economic and political independence.

It is not the responsibility of Québec's Liberal party, at any rate for the present, to consider independence as a possible political solution for Québec. This is the platform of another party which is all to the good, as a choice is thereby offered to the people of Québec.

Québec's Liberal party must, rather, ask itself the following questions and embody the appropriate solutions in its electoral platform. Does the federal government apply economic and cultural policies promoting a sound synthesis of Québec's culture, politics, and economics? Do the governments of Canada's other provinces, in their own policies, promote an analogous development of Québec society? In the field of inter-governmental relations, should the Québec government develop new action strategies? Should it not first claim and obtain recognition of Québec's right to political self-determination? In effect, has not the time come for Québec's Liberal party to devise a new and final version of what the Canadian political system should be like, so that the fact of the two founding peoples or the two distinctive societies is at last recognized in theory as well as in actual practice?

If Québec's Liberal party is not ready to enter on such a daring new path, it should simply and frankly admit that all it can presently attempt is to achieve the most for Québec out of the current status quo. In this way, it will avoid falling between two stools, as other parties before it have done, much to their own discomfiture and to Québec's even greater loss.

A quick bird's eye view of the main trends in Canada, particularly in Québec, that govern the interaction of cultural, political, and economic activity, does not, unfortunately, give rise to much optimism. If the much sought-after modernity is accepted as a gauge, then the traditional values of the past may of course be judged harshly; but this cannot be done without distorting the real-life intentions of the people who shaped the past.

This is a question that historians have forever debated from every angle, without ever being able to resolve. The past may be evaluated in the light of its own context and of its own goals. But it is then difficult to draw lessons for the present or pointers for the future. Alternatively, by looking at the past in the light of today's issues, we may be divesting it of its own significance, even though the exercise may help to throw some light on what the future may hold.

In the light of developments during the past fifteen years, Québec is, I believe, proceeding to major readjustments in every field of thought and action. In some cases these may amount to revolutionary upheavals.

It is no longer feasible to keep putting off certain deadlines. Further delaying a cool settlement of the long-debated question of the political system that best suits Québec, and of the best ways of integrating the industrial and post-industrial economy in Québec society, is to accept seeing Québec rapidly reduced to the status of a mere tribe, or to invite the kind of terrorism that feeds upon a people's fear of extinction.

It is no longer possible to move into the future blindfolded. Basic choices have become burning issues. They are essentially political. But how can one fail to perceive that, over and beyond politics, the whole value order is at stake? What are the goals to be chosen? The priorities to be selected? What are the methods of action to be followed? All of these questions provide the material framework for tomorrow's culture.

Culture, politics, and economic activity in Québec will thus in the near future have to develop new organic interrelationships, in accordance with the wishes of a people who have reached maturity and whom a new collective pride moves to action. If this fails to occur, it is the process of final breakdown, already looming, that will come to pass.

CHAPTER

5

Politics and nationalism in Québec

This part of the book does not attempt to offer a final analysis of Québec's nationalism. Rather, it centres on the political dimensions of that nationalism, only secondarily touching upon its sociological and economic dimensions. In this work, I have mainly drawn upon secondary sources or upon my own earlier research. The extensive information arising from the inquiry into political cultures in Québec, which Micheline de Sève, Jacques Hamel, and I have been conducting for the last three years, has not been included here, since the main results of the study are not yet available. Moreover, the goals of our study were broader than the subject covered here. Here, I concentrate on the evolution of ideas without systematically looking for their interaction with the corresponding social movements, as we did in our inquiry. Finally, different methods were used in the two instances. While in the study of Québec's political cultures we moved from the particular to the general, here I proceed from general statements to an examination of the details. I use assumptions and examples, rather than an explicit analytical framework and carefully collated data as was done in the study.

In writing about nationalism, I hope to contribute to a better grasp of the nature of Quebeckers' historical consciousness. The approach is my own, but my concerns are close to those of Fernand Dumont, Guy Rocher, and Marcel Rioux: to give an account of the French Canadians' condition as a nation. Today, more than ever, we need such attempts at re-defining a people's past in terms of its present, to give us a glimpse of possible futures,

First published in French, but written with the Anglophone reader in mind. See *Nationalismes et politique au Québec* (Montréal: HMH, 1975).

however hazardous the undertaking. The apparent or real breakdowns in institutions and in modes of life since 1940, and particularly since 1960, make it very difficult for young people and even for adults to discover their ties with their forebears, and therefore to realize that they have a history of their own, one of great utility as a reference point, or benchmark, for defining themselves. This is the purpose of my writing: not so much to present new facts, nor even rigorously to marshal all the facts, but rather to give an overall view of a community of men who, because they have a past, may only—short of yielding to total empiricism and opportunism—fully perceive their current situation and their future possibilities by carefully bearing this past in mind. Historical awareness does not initially develop by producing new levels of consciousness, but rather through unceasing inquiry into a society's raison d'être, by the very members of that society. This presupposes a return to one's roots and a reconstruction of one's continuity with the past. Not only did our forefathers engender us, but they also conscientiously sought, with the aid of all the means available to them, to prepare the world we now call our own. And this is also what we have to do for our sons.

A further point: the old social constructs, even in societies which have gone through the radical break we call a revolution, invariably survive in the subsequent institutions and collective memories. The very words we use to describe today's circumstances in some way bind us to the past, since they were forged earlier on, to express the realities of a world now vanished and whose traces we are trying to find. What we must get to know, and this can only be done with empathy, by introspection and retrospection, are the specific ways in which the old formulae reappear today. The present of course is more than a repeat performance of the past. So, the real problem is to appreciate how the old constructs merge with new circumstances to produce today's realities and to pave the way for tomorrow's possibilities.

The past, whether that of an individual or of a collectivity, is never perceived as a single whole, but rather as a multitude of reference-points, set in patterns, each of which represents the product of experiences, good or bad, happy or unhappy. This then is why there is not one single French-Canadian nationalism, but several nationalisms, each related to a different notion of a French-Canadian "we." Consequently, there are several ways, not just one, of currently finding our roots in their collective past.

In this chapter I will therefore initially attempt to circumscribe the different approaches to the French-Canadian national consciousness; then, I shall try to give an account of the different ways in which Quebeckers today relate to their forebears, and shall outline the various justifications they use for their current choices, sometimes diametrically opposed although in good measure related to their different interpretations of the past. There is no more unanimity today among the sons than there was among the fathers in spite of their deep longing for a common solidarity.

To examine nationalism is to engage in the study of a particular ideology. According to a definition I advanced in *Société et politique: La vie des groupes,* "ideologies form a more or less coherent set of mental representations adopted under the influence of a group situation with reference to the total society or to one of its major components, with a view to providing the intellectual and affective elements necessary for identification with the group, to explain the group situation and to legitimize proposed courses of collective actions."

The ideology of nationalism, as I understand it, is twofold; in a variety of ways it unites two different ideologies, one national and the other social in character. To understand nationalism correctly, it must be placed not only in its cultural context but also in its economic and political contexts. A review of nationalism requires an examination of the total field encompassing both ideas and action, and thereby necessarily reveals the great historical praxes.

These ideas and actions do not occur at random; their interaction is not haphazard. Because they mingle within common social frameworks, because they use the same institutional channels, they constantly run into each other, are tallied in relation to each other, flow in harmony or get in each other's way, are consolidated or cancelled out in an unceasing round of attraction and repulsion. These compatibilities and incompatibilities give rise to specific socio-cultural constellations called national cultures, and to the specific uses of the "we" denoting various forms of "national consciousness."

However, retracing the path of Quebeckers' historical consciousness, beyond incidental discontinuities, is not my sole objective here. I shall also attempt to throw new light upon the current condition of social groups and of individuals. An instant snapshot cannot adequately reflect their successes and failures, their hopes and disappointments, their certainties and hesitations. It is equally important to evaluate the effect of past attitudes and behaviours which, like the silt of centuries, is what we build upon today. I shall be taking a careful, though brief, look at Quebeckers' past and present nationalisms; and this account will I hope help to avoid the shortsighted explanations all too often used today in examining present realities. Thus, the neo-conservatism which seems to be gaining ground in Québec's Liberal party, cannot simply be seen as the result of ordinary wear-and-tear in office, or of Robert Bourassa's personality. Similarly, to explain current tensions within the Parti Québécois, it is not enough to cite reasons such as the confrontation between the parliamentary caucus and the party organization, or the calling into question of René Lévesque's leadership. In these cases, as in so many others, one must be sure to understand the interaction of national and social ideologies in Québec, and above all, attempt to see the extent to which the specific network of these ideologies underlying each individual situation may have set the stage for it, sometimes without the knowledge of the actors involved.

A last concern guides me in this work. In examining Québec nationalism, there is all too often a tendency to restrict the analysis to Québec alone. But in the field of ideas as well as of human activities, Québec is open to the world with which it constantly interacts. These interdependences of course vary in time and space, and it is precisely their specific form at different points in Québec's history that it is interesting to note. Quebeckers did not themselves invent pre-industrial society any more than they did its industrial or post-industrial types. But within the narrow limits set by outside constraints, they have been in the past and are still today forced to devise models capable of responding to their own needs and their own goals as defined by Quebeckers' perceptions of their particular circumstances.

A.   THE POLITICAL DIMENSIONS OF QUEBEC'S NATIONALISMS

The concept of nationalism both as an ideology and as a social movement has been much written about. There are even a number of "theories" of nationalism. Among those most often mentioned, besides the marxist-leninist to which I shall be returning, considerable respect surrounds those of Ferdinand Tönnies which are based upon the distinction between community and society, of Karl W. Deutsch whose theories are geared to the concepts of communication and mobilization, of Louis Hartz whose suppositions are founded on the hypothesis that young nations represent but "fragments" of older colonizing peoples, and of Seymour Martin Lipset who emphasizes "formative events."[1] None of these, however, is comprehensive. I do not intend to delve deeper into the theoretical underpinnings of the concept of nationalism but rather to use it as an aid in understanding the developments that nationalistic ideas have undergone, and their relationship with political action in Québec. David Eaton's system model, as I have amended it in my *Société et politique: la vie des groupes,* will provide me with an explanatory framework.[2] However, before going into the heart of the matter, some definitions may be useful. In them, I shall try to abide as closely as possible by the generally accepted usage of words.

By nationalist ideology I mean a set of representations specific to a given community, called a people or a nation, characterized by an amalgam of features which include among others (none of them being of itself determining or even necessary) an origin, a history, a territory, a culture, institutions, and a language, common to the members of that community, providing a feeling of solidarity in its ties with the past and in its future prospects, often in the face of other communities seen as foreign or inimical; and also defined by its projects concerning the organization of the community's cultural, economic, and political life in ways that best suit it.

By nationalist movements I mean those forms of collective action undertaken under the influence of a perception of the national community's will to exist, often as a reaction to the undertakings of other communities perceived as foreign or inimical, aiming to mobilize the community's members so as to promote a sense of solidarity based on a shared past and a common destiny as well as projects relating to the organization of the cultural, economic, and political life considered proper for that community.

In studying nationalism, attention is often concentrated upon ideas alone—their origin, their content, and their interconnections—leaving aside the movements and ideas that underlie or interact with them in one way or another, impinge upon them, as allies or competitors, or as models or counter-models.

Such omissions inevitably lead to misreading the significance or the scope of nationalism. It is of course not enough to describe or to interpret nationalist ideas. It is just as important, if not more so, to examine their effects upon outlooks and institutions as well as the constraints that the latter impose on such ideas.

Nationalism, as a specific ideology, aims to gather together and meld various ideological patterns or approaches—those of social classes and of great secondary communities, such as employers' associations and labour unions, churches, ideological associations, partisan organizations, and so on—which act as carriers of the culture of a given society. It is also important to remember that, viewing things over a period of time, whenever a change occurs in the way secondary communities perceive the situation, an accompanying readjustment occurs in the content of the nationalist ideology.

Analysts are often content to see nationalism as a cultural category, and they only consider the other aspects of society, notably economics and politics, to the extent to which they can be viewed from the analyst's particular angle. Of course the various models of symbolic representations characteristic of the society (class models, community models of all kinds) must be taken very seriously because nationalist syncretisms are largely shaped upon them. But it is also important to relate nationalist representations with the data of geography, demography, technology, economics, social stratification, and politics. Such data impinge upon nationalist representations, influencing them to a greater or lesser extent, and being in turn influenced by them. In brief, nationalism arises out of the impulses, converging or divergent, of the total society and of all its component parts. But it represents active productions, whose feed-back has an impact on its subsequent development.

In a remarkable book, André-J. Bélanger points out the apolitical nature of Québec nationalism during what he considers the "great turning point" of 1934 to 1936.[3] Throughout his work and particularly in its introduction and conclusion, Bélanger converts this statement into a general hypothesis applicable to all eras of Québec history, the reformist trends between 1830 and 1840, as well as those of the two decades from 1950 to 1960 and from 1960 to 1970, which in the author's view only represented individualist assaults crushed against the brick wall of "the community spirit born of medievalism." Further still, Hartz's "fragment" dynamics, predominant in

André-J. Bélanger's analyses, would also apply to contemporary social-democratic and socialist nationalistic trends, whose political leanings are, at least apparently, far more marked. However, the author concludes (page 368): "From an archaic anarchism, idealized by the Groulx tradition, there is, after an interlude of liberalism, a passage over to an anarchism of the left, in its idealized or noble sense, where again the observer has to detect an apolitical approach sometimes dissimulated behind a feverish hyper-activity in the use of means."

André-J. Bélanger's contentions are at least useful in that they systematize current views. His carefully structured reasoning invites us to examine with great care the interaction between politics and the other aspects of society in the production of Québec nationalism. However, this would require a number of analytical tools which André-J. Bélanger, like most others who have so far dealt with the subject, have failed to elaborate.

It should be noted that, whether we take Canada or Québec as the framework of study, simultaneously or successively no matter, Québec's nationalism lies within the context of the nation state. As Karl W. Deutsch states: "The Nation State is still the most powerful instrument in the world for getting things done" and he considers that nationalism represents "one of the strongest political forces" of contemporary society.[4] And according to Anthony D. Smith: "In recent history, nationalism as a movement or ideology has become increasingly prevalent and perhaps dominant, even over communism."[5] The case of developing countries, most of which have just gone over from a colonial status to that of nation state, is very significant in this context, since nationalism plays the role of a pseudo-religion as was the case in Europe in the nineteenth century.

Today as yesterday, the secret of nationalism's attraction seems to depend far more on the symbolic satisfactions it gives than upon the needs it helps to fulfil. Thus, the success of a given pattern of nationalist representations is precarious, and likely to be ephemeral, as is again seen in a number of developing countries over recent years and in Québec during the 1960s. Undergoing many tensions whose nature and intensity fluctuate unforeseeably and often rapidly, depending on a variety of domestic and external factors, political systems are constantly forced to renew their supporting stock of ideologies, notably of nationalist ideologies.

Other ideologies, other versions of nationalism, are summoned up to fill the breach, and manage for a longer or shorter time to perform the system-supporting task expected of them. This unceasing absorption and rejection by the political system of the successive versions of nationalism shows that there is never any perfect and final integration between them. There are merely provisional accommodations as to goals and methods of action— accommodations which reveal the ebb and flow of social consensus. The dynamic nature of such interaction between nationalist ideologies as such and the use which the agents of the political system make of them must be emphasized. While on the one hand the latter can fully or partly absorb or reject a given nationalist ideology, or some of its aspects, on the other hand the ideology itself, elaborated as it is by autonomous social agents, may well refuse to serve the established political system and choose instead to support an alternative system. The period preceding the break-up of the Austro-Hungarian Empire gives us excellent examples of this.

Nationalism is all too often accused of necessarily conveying a rightist, conservative, and anti-democratic ideology. Yet there are many instances of progressive and democratic nationalisms of the left. Before the emergence of the various forms of corporatism and fascism, we have the examples of the French Revolution and of the early European nationalisms; subsequently there was also the Russian Revolution, and the later mergers of marxism-leninism with many nationalisms in Europe, Africa, Asia, the West Indies, and Latin America. It may well be that a review of Québec nationalisms, based upon a new approach, will reveal a whole gamut of political omissions and commissions concerning nationalism so far masked by the traditional viewpoints.

Nationalism fulfils four major tasks: as an ideology, it contributes to the legitimation of the political system which includes the possibility of affirming its illegitimacy; it creates a feeling of collective identity (that is, it gives rise to a specific sense of "we-ness"); it inspires specific political demands; and finally it masks or distorts certain aspects considered undesirable or destructive of the social reality. In line with those functions, nationalist spokesmen submit claims to the political system, and give it (or withdraw from it) a varying measure of support. In response, political agents provide them with indications on the will or the ability of the political system to meet their demands or to acknowledge their support. It is however possible that these requests and allegiances are only partly acknowledged or met, and since the political system itself plays an active role, they may even be taken up by the body politic but in ways different from the original intent of nationalist spokesmen.

Nationalism, as a particular means of making political demands, affects the system's capacity to mobilize the resources needed to achieve collective goals and to produce decisions binding on the whole of society. Nationalist support may be diffuse, extending broadly to the whole political system; or else it may be specific, aimed at one or more particular political goals, namely, according to David Easton's categories (which, broad as they are, will serve our needs here) the political community, the regime, and the authorities.

Nationalist support may also be forthcoming generally or, on occasion it may come to the surface only when specific issues are at stake. As earlier pointed out, support also covers non-support, which may go as far as active opposition, or it may be withdrawal.

Nationalism may buttress virtually all of a system's needs: the need for legitimacy, consensus, energy-mobilization—in fact, nationalism is one of the most powerful forces of political integration in a nation state. Of course, the spokesmen of a given pattern of nationalist representations may well refuse to give the established political system their approval, choosing instead to promote an alternative system or even to reject all political connection. In every such case, political agents or some of these will remain free to use nationalist patterns as they see fit; they may also arouse new patterns of nationalist representation. In fact, one of the most fascinating problems confronting the political analyst is to grasp the reasons why a given nationalism's support of the system flows or wanes, sometimes in line with circumstance: economic growth or social change, the emergence of new social elites or of new charismatic leaders; and to assess the leeway political agents have in their unceasing efforts to revive, to reorient, or to restrict an outdated, weakened, or even hostile nationalism, still necessary to the cohesion of a political community, to the maintenance of the regime, or to the legitimacy of authorities. Such efforts may include avoiding the pitfalls of a disintegrating nationalism, or of adjusting to a triumphant nationalism, and so on.

Finally, in order to understand the interaction between nationalism and politics, it is necessary to consider the two following points:

The first point concerns the elitest character of nationalism. Produced by the intelligentsia, nationalism cannot fully play its political role if it remains in the province of intellectuals alone. Communication networks must be established in ways that reduce the distance between elite and mass. And while the masses need not understand all the nuances of doctrine behind the national ideology, they should at least respond to the mobilization appeals addressed to them by nationalist leaders. Without at least latent mass support, nationalism cannot fulfil any major political function, unless political agents decide to use it for their own goals, which they can also do, especially if they operate outside the framework of liberal democracy.

The second point, one that is ignored though its importance should be obvious, concerns the inadequacy of nationalism, as an ideology, to sustain the political system. While an explicit official nationalist outlook generally underlies the nation state, the State can survive for a time even when its political agents fail to subscribe to any form of nationalism, as has probably been the case in Québec since 1970 under Robert Bourassa's government, although this government nevertheless feels it useful to proclaim from time to time the motto of "cultural sovereignty." It would in fact be difficult to show that a government managed to take and keep power solely thanks to the support of a nationalist ideology. Any nationalism is by itself powerless to provide political agents with the protective devices and rationalizations needed to overcome tensions within the political system and to get on with the business of government. Nationalism only reveals its whole strength, which can be overwhelming, when it is associated with another ideology be it liberalism, conservatism, corporatism, fascism, socialism, no less closely linked up with the political system, since it determines the nature of the regime. Whenever a given pattern of nationalist representations reaches its peak in political terms, this almost invariably coincides with its period of greatest identification with the ideology that defines the political regime. Things may get to a point, generally in periods of great stress, where the two are practically indistinguishable. It is then difficult to determine what degree of support the political system gets from one as compared to the other. But as soon as differences appear between the twin ideological supports, we generally see that it is the social ideology (that of the regime) rather than the national ideology (that of the political community) which most contributes to the persistence of the political system.

Nevertheless, the two-way relationship between the nationalist and the social ideology is so real that the one cannot be examined without taking the other into account. A good deal of effort will be spared if, when seeking to describe nationalism in a society's attempts for the different time periods, we relate the various forms of nationalism to the social ideologies either dominant at that time or considered relevant by the different nationalist spokesmen. Thus in Québec we might distinguish between conservative or traditionalist nationalism, liberal nationalism, social-democratic nationalism, and socialist nationalism. These are the nationalisms that left their mark upon particular periods: conservative nationalism was officially dominant from the beginning of the nineteenth century up until 1960; liberal nationalism has reigned since 1960, whereas the social-democratic and the socialist forms of nationalism have served as alternate ideologies even before 1960, but particularly since 1965.

I shall here be following this time pattern. It does not, however, imply that there was any linear development from one phase to the other. On the contrary, even though one particular type may have dominated all the others at any given point in time, they all co-existed. This was and still is the case in Québec. For instance, during the period when the conservative nationalist ideology was dominant, the liberal nationalist ideology surged forward appreciably between 1830 and 1845 and again between 1950 and 1960. Similarly, since 1960, the liberal nationalist ideology has predominated without having thereby pushed the conservative nationalist ideology altogether out of the picture. And it is all too often lightly claimed that the socialist versions of nationalism, emerging since the 1960s, have no roots in Québec's past.

1. Conservative Nationalism

Even when dealing primarily with Québec's recent and current nationalisms, it is important to look at those of the past since they, like all former social constructs, persist in the form of historical sediments or residues and thereby still exercise an influence on today's viewpoints. But the extent of this influence must be determined. Hartz's theory of ''fragments'' (which the majority of our historians, notably Michel Brunet's and Maurice Séguin's Montreal school implicitly accept, and upon which André-J. Bélanger's analysis rests) assumes that the patterns of symbolic representations brought by our early colonists have left a heavy imprint upon subsequent generations, forever forced to follow the ruts established in the mother country by the circumstances prevailing at the time when their fore-bears moved to the new land. On the other hand the "law" of historical residues or pseudomorphisms, to which Plato, Hegel, Marx, Weber, and others often referred, merely claims that the former constructs may reappear in unforeseen ways in subsequent social patterns, under the influence of the memory that survives among the descendants and of the traces that remain in institutions long after their disappearance as dominant social constructs. It must be noted here that these are by no means strait-jackets in the sense in which they are perceived by the "fragment" theorists, but simply predispositions whose nature and scope cannot be predicted and whose influence need not be compelling for it can largely if not altogether be side-stepped.

I shall in this section be referring solely to former conservative nationalisms, that is, those which predominated from the beginning of the nineteenth century until 1950 or even 1960 and which accept traditional society as reference frameworks. Even though elsewhere I shall often refer to this type of nationalism in the singular, I am here purposely using the plural at the outset. In actual fact, the two main nationalist leaders during the "conservative" era, Henri Bourassa and Lionel Groulx, even though they shared much the same views about the political regime which in their eyes would best suit French Canadians, happened to take very different even incompatible stands with regard to the political community of reference. Both were "conservative" in the sense that they expressed a preference for a certain kind of corporatism, while despising political parties and most institutions tinged with "Anglo-Saxon" liberalism. Although Bourassa and Groulx both favoured extensive "autonomy" for Québec, yet, whereas Bourassa always took Canada as his framework of political reference, Groulx, for his part, most of the time concentrated exclusively on Québec and on several occasions adopted a clearly separatist stance.

These viewpoints were conveyed, propagated, debated at length, and adapted to shifting circumstances by younger disciples (such as Esdras Minville, André Laurendeau, Richard Arès, François-Albert Angers, Guy Frégault, Michel Brunet), by newspapers and magazines (*Le Devoir, l'Action Française,* and later *l'Action nationale, l'Actualité économique, La Relève, Vivre, La Nation*), by movements such as la Société Saint Jean-Baptiste, l'Ordre de Jacques-Cartier, l'Ecole sociale populaire, les Jeunes-Canada, l'Alliance laurentienne; by interest groups such as the CNTU (the Confederation of National Trade Unions) until 1949 and the CFU (the Catholic Farmers Union); by political parties such as the Union Nationale and in a more amplified way, since they were latecomers on the scene, by the Créditistes.

I shall examine each of the following points in turn: the preconditions underlying conservative nationalism; its arguments; its political impact; and finally its political functions.

a. The pre-conditions underlying conservative nationalism   The roots of conservative nationalism reach far back into the past: the 1760 conquest was seen as the event which shaped the whole future of French colonists in America. The severance of ties with the mother country, France, produced the first consistent feature in the lives of French Canadians: their isolation. However, the great early nationalists, such as Henri Bourassa and Lionel Groulx, drew pride from the fact that French Canadians had founded homes throughout North America, in Ontario, in the prairies, in Louisiana, in New England. These great migrations were seen as "an integral part of the French mission in America." It is only their disciples who lost faith in the French Canadians' missionary calling. French Canadians were henceforth perceived as a lonely people, different from all others in America, and threatened by extinction in the huge "Anglo-Saxon sea" in which they formed small scattered islands. Only where they were gathered in larger numbers, on the shores of the St. Lawrence, cradle of their "race," could they hope for survival. But even there they needed to close ranks and to live according to their old ancestral traditions. Hence their marked ethnocentrism. Save among the first great leaders, conservative nationalism provided an image of a world turned in upon itself; yet, among all conservative nationalists, "we" and "the others" were clearly identified and differentiated from each other. Condemned to live as a permanent minority among strangers infinitely more numerous than they, French Canadians could only survive, it was emphasized, if they knew how to protect themselves against all sources of contamination by remaining within their own closed circle. Hence the individual and collective insecurity which conservative nationalism both reflected and attempted to exercise.

b. Conservative nationalist arguments   To offset its analysis of the situation, conservative or traditionalist nationalism firmly proclaimed the French Canadians' will to survive. This will to survive was nourished both by the claim to superiority of French Canadian culture and by the fact that this culture was the people's one and only true possession. However, French Canadians might only preserve their separate identity if they remained faithful to their past; it was thus incumbent on them to abide by their own traditions and to refuse or reject any change likely to jeopardize these. Language and faith were the most sacred of such traditions. And neither stood alone, as attested to by the often quoted saying "our language is the guardian of our faith." Conversely, should Christian and Catholic faith be lost, the language too would be threatened with disappearance, or at the very least would be made to serve goals alien if not contrary to the spiritual mission of the *race élue,* the "chosen people." French Canadians were perceived as having a spiritual role to play in North America, which they might only fulfil by resisting any seepage into their culture of "Anglo-Saxon materialism" and of pervasive Protestantism. As François-Xavier Garneau concluded in his *Histoire du Canada*: "May *les Canadiens* be faithful to themselves; may they be wise and persevering; may they resist the blandishments and the glitter of social and political novelty! They are not strong enough to give themselves free rein on this score. It is for pow-erful peoples to put new theories to the test . . . as for us, a part of our strength comes from our traditions; let us not stray away from them and let us change them only very gradually."

It therefore followed that French Canadians needed the protective frame-works of family, rural parish, and Church. It is only by faithfully following the guidance of their clergy, by supporting the local elites, by avoiding fra-tricidal struggle, that they could hope to remain true to their roots and to their calling. The good path involved abiding by the beacons of ancestral loyalties, buttressed by the well-meaning paternalism of the clerical and lay elites.

Thus, promises of happiness in after-life made up for whatever miseries this world had to offer; thus, too, the "revanche des berceaux," the re-venge of the cradle, provided an inexpensive dike against the unceasing as-saults of an ever-increasing "Anglo-Saxon" incursion; farming and crafts-manship also represented a sheltered way of life, free of the industrialization and urbanization that invaded and corroded the French-Canadian temperament, indelibly stamped as such innovations were with "the Anglo-Saxon spirit." It is chiefly against industry and cities that the conservative nationalists preached. The economy, as they saw it, had to be at the service of culture, not the other way around. Unavoidably, industry and the cities were to French Canadians places of "perdition," that is of assimilation into the Anglo-Saxon world. Too weak to invent ways of life that would suit them within the social framework already monopolized by the "Anglo-Saxons" and which would in any event always remain under their control, French Canadians could only get lost and lose their unique identity, should they attempt to penetrate these alien reaches. So convinced were the conservative nationalists of the suicidal nature of any organized attempt by French Canadians to reach out for modernity, that they wanted society to stay within its traditional framework of farming and craftsman-ship. The solutions to the serious problems confronting French Canadians included "a return to the land": the promotion of farm settlements in new areas, often ignoring their hopelessly unsuitable soil, by "opening-up" parishes and offering land grants; and campaigns to buy "local goods." As late as the second quarter of the twentieth century, even though most of these nationalists were by then living in Montreal—one of North America's cities with the fastest industrial growth rate and with, moreover, one-third of Québec's French Canadians!—the nationalists continued to advance the same goals and to defend the same solutions, just as if nothing had ever changed.

The mottoes and the anathemas of conservative nationalism became more and more schizophrenic as the movement towards modernity became more and more inescapable in Québec. Thus, left to its own devices, the mass of the people acceded to industrial and urban life through the back door, as "hewers of wood and drawers of water." When they morally and intellectually awakened from the numbness in which traditional teachings had kept them, it was to get rid of the taboos that had so long governed their lives. But deprived of hope in a glorious future for the race and no longer able to remain faithful to "our master the past," all that was left to them was a vast emptiness.

c. Conservative nationalism and politics   It is a mistake to view conservative nationalism as apolitical. There is a very definite view of politics underlying this nationalism, a view which shaped the political education of several generations of students in our classical colleges, those outstanding educational establishments of Québec's traditional elites. The seemingly apolitical nature of conservative nationalism is the result of an optical illusion, for although it neither fits into industrial society nor easily adapts to the ideas and institutions of liberal democracy, it manages comfortably within a pre-industrial context, such as France's *ancien régime* or various corporatist regimes.

It might be claimed that the social "we" propounded by the nationalists is so vague in nature that it offers no basis for political action. That would be an inappropriate description of conservative nationalism. When the "propounded social 'we' " is matched with the well-known features of pre-industrial society, instead of being left in a social vacuum, it becomes very clear indeed. And if it may at first sight seem that this "we" offers no basis for political action, that is because the political prospects of conservative nationalism were doomed to be short-lived at inception. Indeed, the reference political system of the spokesmen of this form of nationalism was a highly decentralized federalism lined with paternalistic corporatism; whereas French Canadians were in fact up against an ever-more centralized federalism on the one hand, and on the other, a liberal democratic regime well in control, at least on the face of things. Despite this irresolvable contradiction, it is nevertheless a fact that conservative nationalism paid much attention to politics, and that there were generally close ties between conservative nationalism and politics during this long period from 1840 on, and more particularly from 1890 to 1960.

The support that conservative nationalism contributed to the established political system was of an integrative kind. Thus, for instance, it usually perceived the political community as consisting of Canada's population as a whole. For Henri Bourassa, and even for Groulx (although the latter remained less specific and definitely less keen on this aspect), Québec represented a sub-system of the Canadian political system. On this point, there is practically complete agreement between the spokesmen of conservative nationalism and their English-speaking compatriots. Both approved the federal form of government and lauded its merits. Conservative nationalists, as much if not more than their English-speaking counterparts, sought to consolidate Canada's independence, first vis-à-vis British imperialism, then towards the all-pervasive American influence that sometimes verged on annexationism. However, unlike the English-speaking and some of the French-speaking intellectuals and politicians, the spokesmen of conservative nationalism remained cool towards any attempt to stimulate various kinds of pan-Canadian nationalism or "Canadianism"—mostly doomed to failure in any event. They saw Canada as an "artificial" entity, its continued existence resting on a "marriage of reason." Their *patrie*, the country of their hearts, was still French Canada whose boundaries, though fluid, tended to become synonymous with Québec's. Hence the ambigous way in which conservative nationalists used the word "national." It applied to things Canadian as well as French Canadian, but more specifically to Québec, within its social and political frameworks. However, subtle conceptual and particularly emotional overtones separated each of these usages, only fully understood by the initiated.

The conservative nationalists were not alone in favouring a decentralized federalism. A number of English-speaking Canadians and non-nationalist Francophones adopted a similar stand. The conservative nationalists were, however, alone in turning this tenet into a specific ideology, which in fact became central to conservative nationalism. This ideology has become known as "autonomism." It embodies the firm belief that the culture and the specific interests of French Canadians will only really be protected if the government they control, namely the Québec government, has broad political powers vis-à-vis the central government, and possesses the firm determination in every instance to adopt positions upholding Québec's exercise of a wide range of political jurisdictions. "Québec first," the theory of a "pact between the two founding peoples," the "two nations theory," the doctrine of "associate states," "recovery of the powers yielded to the federal governments," and so on—all these claims and theories go to show the vital if not the markedly influential nature of autonomism as a specific component of conservative thought.

There is no dearth of pro-separatist statements in l'Abbé Groulx's work.[6] Indeed, in his early writings as well as in what he wrote much later toward the end of his life, he passionately espoused "un état Français," clearly intended to be Québec, and at that a Québec virtually independent from the rest of Canada. Yet the issue of separatism remained a point of discord among conservative nationalists. Henri Bourassa and his followers were fiercely opposed to the separatist solution. And even when Groulx expressed a preference for separatism, we feel it was a purely emotional response on his part. One gets the impression that, when he looked at matters dispassionately, he never thought the separatists' dream achievable. Moreover, he was always wary of those in power in Québec. In particular, Groulx accused Maurice Duplessis of having betrayed the hopes that had brought him to power in 1935, and of following in the footsteps of Honoré Mercier and of Alexandre Taschereau in jeopardizing Québec's natural resources to the advantage of foreigners.

Conservative nationalists were firmly opposed to the established political regime. Of course, the supporters of this ideology were unconsciously influenced by the old-style laissez-faire liberalism, then dominant on the Québec political scene. This may at least be assumed from their preference for a harmonious, consensual society, and from their *anti-étatisme,* whose full extent has been pointed out by Michel Brunet[7] and Ramsay Cook.[8] But in all things political, they also showed a deep antagonism to the liberal philosophy whose individualism and materialism were seen as corrosive of French-Canadian values. The low regard they had for the liberal and democratic regime may further be seen in the conservative nationalists' deprecation of political parties, their opposition to majority rule, to American-style employers' associations, and to labour unions acting as interest groups; going so far, for Groulx and a number of his followers, as a distaste for British-style parliamentary institutions.

As an alternative to the distrusted liberal and democratic regime, a form of corporatism was advanced, which second-wave conservative nationalists even attempted to build into a system. After an independent conception, this corporatism later came under strong influence from the European fascism of the twenties and thirties. In Québec it sought to build the whole of the polity on various occupational groupings frequently called "intermediary bodies," an expression from the *ancien régime,* which often cropped up in the statements surrounding the birth of "the Estates General of French Canada."[9]

While the promoters of conservative nationalism did not pursue their logic to its very end and neglected to take the practical steps leading to a replacement of the decried liberal and democratic regime by a corporatist regime, this was doubtless in part due to their feelings of incompetence and powerlessness, but it was also a result of the tremendous respect they had for any kind of established order. "Authority stems from God"; when Father Lévesque, in 1950, was to declare that "freedom, too, stems from God," nationalist circles viewed him as a dangerous revolutionary, which of course went down well with the authorities, not least with Premier Maurice Duplessis who quite correctly saw Father Lévesque as an intractable adversary. The political implications of conservative nationalism cannot be fully grasped unless one is aware, at the heart of this ideology, of the "leadership mystique" which gave rise to innumerable and ultimately rather sterile efforts to honour the heroes and founders of New France. L'Abbé Groux picked Dollard des Ormeaux, a nearly forgotten *colon* settler, whose brief and brave stand against the Indians at the Long Sault in 1660 won him death and—at Groulx's instigation—subsequent fame among successive generations of college students who had to show, in countless essays and patriotic speeches, how Dollard from one day to the next turned out to be the "saviour of New France."

Thus it was that conservative nationalism contributed its support, sometimes diffuse and sometimes specific, to the established political system. Whenever conservative nationalists felt tempted to upset the apple cart, a strong sense of incompetence and powerlessness ("we were born to be poor and humble") and especially an absolute respect for authority soon reminded them that, although they were patriots, their conservative allegiance was perhaps still stronger.

That is why, when the noble but impossible vision of a spiritual rather than a mundane mission for French Canadians faded away with the decline of l'Abbé Groulx's influence—Groulx having been a cleric first and foremost, and only then a nationalist—conservative nationalism's inherent optimism also disappeared. Forced to acknowledge that the State, and no longer the Church, had become the French Canadians' only protective shield, and that religious faith could no longer make up for economic weakness, Groulx's disciples—such as the Michel Brunet we knew at the end of the 1950s—gave way to pessimism and resignation. ("Things being what they are, the English cannot swallow us up, but there is no way we can grow.")[10]

d. The political functions of conservative nationalism   As Pierre Elliot Trudeau has argued, conservative nationalism certainly served as a screen to hide from French Canadians a view of their real situation.[11] (But, in actual fact, is that not true of any ideology?) Yet, as Trudeau claimed, while conservative nationalism upheld the dominance of anachronistic symbolic representations and institutions, it also lay as a leading obstacle in the path of democracy in Québec. This, indeed, is the title of one of his articles, originally published in English, and especially well known in English circles.[12] What actual evidence is there for this claim?

So great is the influence of the large, established ideological patterns, that it is possible, despite recent developments in the fields of thought and action, for conservative nationalism, though officially put on the shelf, to continue to exercise a certain hold on the minds of people—even of those who feel themselves above such changeability. And so one question arises: will French Canadians remain forever bound to conditions in their society that derive from a pre-industrial culture? A further problem: ought French Canadians to become aware of this fact, take on the full responsibility of such a problem, and use it as a point of departure in their present search for a culture better adapted to their desired life-style? It is in this direction that Edouard Cloutier's argument appears to be leading.[13] There are striking similarities between his approach and Hartz's "theory of fragments"; and there is a certain attraction about studying Québec's political culture in this manner. But the theory convinces me no more than does that of Louis Hartz. I am unable to believe in historical and cultural determinism so strong that they can permanently mould the intellectual and emotional temperament of a people. Was it not claimed in the seventeenth century that the English were, by nature, trouble-makers and revolutionaries, and that the French were submissive and conservative?

I am not challenging the conclusions of Gilles Auclair's work for the Royal Commission on Bilingualism and Biculturalism, on which Edouard Cloutier bases his thesis. Nor do I question other studies leading to similar conclusions. The attitudes and economic behaviour of French Canadians may betray a pre-industrial outlook. In this they would differ from English-speaking Canadians who bear all the characteristics peculiar to an industrial society. These differences once again would reveal the hold of the past as well as the grip of conservative nationalism on present-day French Canadians. It would, however, be rash to conclude as do the determinist interpretations, that contemporary attitudes are the necessary and permanent consequences of a kind of natural, immutable order of things.

Must we then conclude that the early model of cultural development which French Canadians should have adopted, or which is suitable for them today, is the liberal and democratic English or American style model, as is explicitly assumed by Pierre Elliot Trudeau and by most analysts, especially among the English-speaking? That assumption involves a quantum leap which currently available data do not warrant, at any rate not before a thorough study is undertaken of the most significant manifestations of Québec's political cultures.

It is here that I dissociate myself from Trudeau in his interpretation of conservative nationalism. While his arguments seem to me valid in demonstrating how conservative nationalism drew French Canadians away from the principles and the practice of liberal democracy, it is in my view inappropriate to condemn this form of nationalism outright without asking oneself whether it did not for a long time fulfil some useful social functions (such as bringing collective security); and it is just as rash to conclude, as if this were the only possible logical conclusion, that the ''rehabilitation'' of French Canadians after so many years of ''darkness'' must necessarily proceed along the pathways of liberal democracy, long laid down by the English and the Americans and to a lesser extent by some of the other Western nations (paths which the very same peoples seem to some extent to be abandoning today).

An altogether different alternative may be put forward: conservative nationalism flourished in three different cultural contexts.

First of all, it held sway within the political culture of the higher elites (upper clergy, federal ministers and MPs, the heads of big business, men of learning), where support for the essential tenets of conservative nationalism (Catholicism, Messianism, anti-liberalism, agriculturalism, political autonomism, etc.) in practice mingled with Anglophone cultural patterns in the various fields of activity in which its members were actively involved (religion, politics, business, academic pursuits, science).

Secondly, conservative nationalism had a strong foothold in the political culture of the lower elites or of the men prominent locally or regionally (parish priests, doctors, notaries, school-teachers, college professors, small-town businessmen). In all good faith, they accepted the creed—lock, stock, and barrel. They adapted it to the practical circumstances of their lives, and used well-tried methods of socializing that fraction of the young who had the ''chance'' of being educated in the classical colleges, prime means of training the next generation's elite. Finally, this is the group who saw to it that the *foi du charbonnier*, the strong, unquestioning faith of the simple, should survive among the population as a whole.

Third, conservative nationalism pervaded the political culture of the "masses"—an expression the elite never used (the faithful, the people, *les habitants* were the words in current usage). These people were given the basic training essential for their simple lives as farmers, unskilled labourers, craftsmen, or factory workers, and were armed with the beliefs that made them accept their lot unquestioningly, docilely. Theirs were not necessarily lives of hardship, but they were tied to low socio-economic status and to political subservience.

We are not in a position to prove or to disprove this hypothesis. It is a plausible one, since the same pattern may be found among other peoples, within traditional models of society in a colonized setting, where a three-tier hierarchical order prevails. Two studies have provided evidence that (except for Créditiste MPs, whose social roots are in the lower elite if not in the "mass" and whose attitudes and behaviour closely parallel it) French-speaking MPs in Québec and in Ottawa abide by the same values and political standards as the country's English-speaking legislators.[14] While Ward and Hoffman did detect certain differences, for instance as regards the MP's role in representing his riding and distributing patronage, Kornberg on the other hand concluded that, despite the different pressures exercised upon French-speaking and English-speaking legislators and allowing for party allegiances, both groups held to essentially the same standards and values. In the light of his results, Kornberg claims inability to bear out or disprove the "culturalist" theory. It may however be true, he says, that owing to the contrary pull of pressures upon French-speaking legislators—pressures on the one hand from their own ethnic community and on the other hand from their "English" working framework—they are subject to certain psychological conflicts in exercising their role as members of Parliament. Conditions would lend themselves better to analysis if a comparison were made, instead, between the attitudes and behaviour of members of the Québec National Assembly and the Ontario Legislature. It would also be useful to study French-speaking businessmen operating in English settings as compared to French ones.

All we can be sure of in regard to the upper elite, is that the arguments it used to legitimize its rule were virtually all drawn from conservative nationalism. Were their beliefs sincere, or rather is there evidence of a certain cynicism in accepting the compromises necessary to coexist with "les Anglais," whether in religion, politics, learning, or business? Is that the secret of the survival of French Canadians, that this survival in some way involved a "betrayal" by the upper elite?

The foremost political function of conservative nationalism may thus have been—based on a view of the situation that required the most stringent economy of means—firmly to uphold the status quo. This would help to throw light on the reasons that led so many Anglophones to sing the merits of this nationalism. It was a cheap way of maintaining the upper hand. It was easy for anyone to turn to his advantage the unsophisticated ideology of conservative nationalism. It is precisely what so many Americans, English Canadians, and, in their own way, the Québec upper crust did, with or without malice aforethought.

It must not be forgotten that it is among the best-educated Anglophones that were found some of the most ardent defenders of the damaging myth whereby it was claimed that French Canadians had no business flair but were gifted for the "higher enjoyment" of arts and letters. (Recent studies have on the contrary shown that Anglophones and particularly Jews have a far greater appreciation of art than do French Canadians, and that this is probably a result of their higher income and education.) Nor must it be forgotten that Anglophones at least tacitly if not actively encouraged the French-Canadian upper elite in its efforts to turn liberal democracy into a simple-minded travesty for popular consumption by merging religion and politics in a fashion exemplified by this typical Sunday sermon: "Remember, Brethren, that heaven is Blue and hell is Red"—The Blues and The Reds being the widespread popular names for Conservatives and Liberals. (Could it be testimony to French Canadians' independence of mind that a majority, nevertheless, in spite of such solemn priestly warnings, forthwith rushed off to vote Liberal, as was, for example, the case in the federal election of 1896, despite a severe warning from Monsignor Lafleche, according to whom a Catholic could not "unless under pain of mortal sin" vote for the Liberal, Wilfrid Laurier!)

Ironically enough, one of the foremost critics of such travesties of liberal democracy, Pierre Elliot Trudeau, is today contributing to their perpetuation. Having become prime minister of Canada under the banner of the federal Liberal Party which primarily benefited from such political folklore, he, too, now avidly welcomes French-Canadian votes though, today as much as yesterday, they are "ethnic" votes. He, too, follows the laws of electoral strategy: it is so much simpler to cultivate the "ethnic" feelings and prejudices of French Canadians than to encourage them towards democracy (which might possibly lead them to vote against the Liberals).

The dominant elites' use of conservative nationalism was also a feature of the provincial scene. Alexandre Taschereau and Maurice Duplessis, during the thirty-five years of their reign, knew how to wring every possible advantage from the major themes of this ideology (religion, laissez-faire, agriculturalism, autonomism, etc), thus keeping the people tied to the most rudimentary forms of political culture.

For a long time, French Canadians were kept by their elites in a state where they could not acquire a political culture that would have given them an image of the State as the instrument of all the people, or any notion of a pluralist society. Victims of the conscious or unintended connivance of their leaders with the English-speaking establishment, the political demands that the people managed to formulate—until very recently—were few and elementary, often symbolic, as in the instance of bilingual cheques. It was therefore easy for political agents to satisfy them. For a long time, French Canadians remained content with the crumbs off the tables of whoever was materially or intellectually wealthier: the English-speaking establishment and the French-Canadian higher elite. The Québécois were given every opportunity to "benefit" from patronage. It is evidence of their subjection that they took this in good stead.

Surprising as it may seem, very little is known about the precise nature of the relationship between the lower-tier elite, the local or regional "notables," and the mass of the people. While it is certain that these local elites believed in conservative nationalism and that this faith was both more spontaneous and less self-serving than that of the upper elite, their approach does not seem to have been doctrinaire. The local leaders were all the more easily obeyed as, apart from a few points of religious observance, they were not very demanding. The people could thus give the impression of following the directives from on high while generally carrying on as best suited them: no one was too concerned over the real feelings behind the proper religious and political practices.

But in fact, what were these feelings? Kenneth McRoberts shows that until the eve of the Quiet Revolution, Québec's population as a whole remained largely unmoved by the theme of political autonomy, even though it served as a leading electoral slogan from the end of the nineteenth century up to this very day.[15] In spite of all their strivings for more independence, French Canadians tended to be vague about the practical limits of provincial and federal jurisdiction, and unashamedly turned to federal authorities whenever the province was disinclined to meet the peoples' wants.

In the religious field, a major component of culture, as it is, the people apparently stood united behind their priests (and this was true even of agnostics who, if we judge by recent developments, must have been quite numerous; yet they had to feign religious belief and never failed to attend Sunday Mass). Nevertheless, many examples go to show that, in the case of major political decisions, the people did refuse to follow their religious and lay leaders despite the best arguments drummed up out of conservative nationalism's most strongly held beliefs. This happened in 1812, during the American invasion; in the 1837 uprising; in the two conscription crises during the First and Second World Wars in 1917 and 1942, and so on. In each such instance, supported by their local clerical and lay elites, the mass of the people dared to defy the wishes of the top leaders, openly though not with impunity.

McRoberts says he cannot explain why "the masses" were so unresponsive to the autonomists' directives. Might it not be because the latter's cultural values were different from those of the dominant culture? One may ask whether such "elitist" cultural patterns were ever sufficiently explicit to achieve the definite idelolgical status. Only a careful review of the precise role of the local and regional "notables" might help to elucidate this question. Were they simply a channel of communication between the higher elite and the masses? Or were they more or less involuntary accomplices of the masses? Or else were they trying to reconcile pragmatically the doctrine of the leaders with the practice of the common people?

Fernand Dumont has put forward an interesting hypothesis on this point, which fits in well with my own analysis.[16] Even though educated in classical colleges and universities, the local elites remained rooted in the common people, shared their every-day concerns and simple pleasures, and eventually returned to them to carry out their lifetime calling. Their prestige was derived from the special resources they possessed, such as their expertise (theology, medicine, law) or from their control over political or religious "patronage." Hence the respect given them by the people whenever they exhibited their special gifts in religious ceremonies, in the event of disease, or of legal proceedings. Whenever danger threatened, in the form of an epidemic, a drought, or even of unpopular government measures, the issues were dealt with on the basis of a kindly paternalism interwoven with a relationship of day-to-day equality in common pursuits. The ties of solidarity created by such simple and spontaneous relationships produced a kind of democracy which, direct and organic as it was, was no worse and in some ways better than English-Canadian and American liberal and representative democracy at the same period.

Was that the form of political organization that would best have suited French Canadians? We will never know, because the model was never applied throughout the whole of society. The top leadership, to avoid a possibly tragic confrontation, or through conviction, preferred to adjust to the dominant English economic and political institutions, thus limiting their own historical contribution to any full test of conservative nationalism.

But history is an unpredictable mistress, and it may happen that these former solidarities may again come to the fore and that Quebeckers may draw upon them, in tomorrow's new circumstances, to create their own framework of social patterns.

2. Liberal Nationalism

By common western standards, Québec is an exception to the rule. Whereas in Québec, nationalism's main ties were with the conservatives (this amalgam being so powerful that Marcel Rioux could still write in *Cité libre* in 1955: "The tragedy is not that there is a 'right', but that it takes up the whole place"), in Europe and in the United States the early nationalisms were generally associated with the then-triumphant liberalism. As Jean-Paul Bernard has shown, the decade from 1840 to 1850 was decisive in this respect.[17] While the repression that followed the 1837 unsuccessful rebellion strengthened the conservatism imposed upon Québec, the same decade elsewhere marked the first successful steps towards the great liberal revolution. Of course, during the latter half of the nineteenth century, and even more so after the First World War, conservatism remained fairly strong in Europe, where it appeared under various guises. It "turned modern" and even became the dominant political approach in countries where liberalism had never managed to take deep root, as it Italy, Germany, Austria, Spain, and Portugal. Québec's conservative nationalism drew inspiration from these European sources, notably from France, Italy, and later from Franco's Spain.

Jean-René Suratteau has convincingly shown that the earliest manifestations of nationalism were tied to the liberalism that carried the day in the industrially advanced countries between 1815 and 1848, at the time when the great nineteenth-century socialists thought it would not be possible for socialism to take root in the framework of the nation-state.[18] Thus, Anthony D. Smith writes:

But, taking the core doctrine as a whole and without reference to its real or alleged consequences, we can say that nationalism appears as a not unreasonable application of Enlightenment principles to the complexities of modern policies and societies. The core doctrine is schematic and tentative; yet it constitutes the necessary condition for the search for realistic conditions of liberty and equality, not to mention democracy, in an already divided world.[19]

Briefly, I shall follow here the same pattern of discussion as in the previous section: I shall examine the pre-conditions of liberal nationalism, its arguments, its political impact, and finally its political functions.

a. The pre-conditions for liberal nationalism Conservative nationalism was dominant in Québec politics from 1840 to 1960. This is not to say that during that long era this ideology flourished unchallenged. On the contrary, especially between 1840 and 1880 and from 1950 on, there were a number of individuals, periodicals, and movements who stood up in the name of a liberal creed. Chief among them were those who gravitated around the Institut canadien which after many harsh battles incurred the anathema of the conservative nationalists and foremost among them Monsignor Bourget, and was finally disbanded. Furthermore, during that period, liberalism was often associated with anticlericalism. Many of its spokesmen were non-nationalists and some of them anti-nationalists. How then to explain the fact that Wilfrid Laurier, who was prime minister of Canada from 1896 to 1917 under the liberal banner, got the widespread support of the French Canadian electorate? The answer lies in two facts: first, by that time the Liberal party had lost most of its former radicalism in Québec; and second, it was easy for that party to overcome the ideological handicap which might have survived by exploiting the "ethnic" feeling among the French Canadians and thereby get their vote. (It was Laurier who once said of the French Canadians that in politics they were swayed not by reason but by feelings. "Ils n'ont que des sentiments.") Both Louis Saint-Laurent who was prime minister from 1948 to 1957 and Pierre Elliot Trudeau, since 1968, have followed the path opened up by the federal-Liberals under Laurier.

The hold of conservative nationalism was indeed so strong in Quebec as a dominant ideology that it was not until 1950, with the creation of the periodical *Cité libre,* that the beginning of a process which would bring a reversal of the situation and lead to the assertion of a liberal nationalism as an official and dominant ideology in Québec came about.

Every conceivable claim has been made for the periodical *Cité libre;* all it now requires is a little serious study. Thus, for example, it was said and repeated that the periodical paved the way for the Quiet Revolution. It might be added that it pretty well took it over. It would be very interesting to examine how, starting with the Christian Personalism of the French periodical *Esprit,* and then under the inspiration of John Locke, John Stuart Mill, and Jean-Jacques Rousseau, the editors of *Cité libre* came to criticize conservative nationalism and its cultural, social, economic, and political instruments, and to put forward the idea of an alternative political regime. It is claimed today that *Cité libre* was anti-nationalist. That is not at all how I see its editors, in the early days at any rate. Its two main spokesmen, Pierre Elliot Trudeau and Gérard Pelletier, always opposed doctrinaire nationalism. In the name of the liberal democracy they supported, they fiercely fought against the authoritarianism and the clericalism that were part and parcel of conservative nationalism. However, they continued to draw inspiration from Christian and Catholic tradition, and in politics they remained faithful to the ideas of autonomism to the extent of firmly supporting Maurice Duplessis in most of his struggles against the federal government, notably in the notorious issue of federal grants to the universities, in which debate Pierre Elliot Trudeau took a very active part. (This issue was only settled in 1959, thanks to the wisdom of Paul Sauvé, and without the contribution of any of the intellectuals who are claimed to have fathered the Quiet Revolution).

The direct influence of *Cité libre* upon minds and events is overrated. Its authors were essentially individualists. The periodical was never wealthy and it lacked the means, perhaps also the conviction, to launch any significant social movement. The Rassemblement des forces démocratiques and, a little later, the Union des forces démocratiques were its stillborn children. Even the Institut canadien des affaires publiques, many of whose leaders were closely associated with *Cité libre,* and which greatly contributed to consolidating the position of intellectuals and to clarifying ideas at the time, did not need *Cité libre* to make its presence felt. In spite of sporadic contributors from the Québec City area, it proved impossible to set up a Québec chapter of *Cité libre;* it remained a Montréal periodical, hence its lack of historical depth and of social roots, which were in fact its main weaknesses. Another piece of evidence for *Cité libre*'s limited direct influence lies in the fact that, although it is often claimed to have given birth to the Québec Liberal party's 1960 platform, the claim is excessive. Georges-Emile Lapalme's *Mémoires,* a reliable source on this point, mentions that the platform was fully drafted by Lapalme himself at the express request of Jean Lesage who was no assiduous reader of *Cité libre.*[20] Lapalme says that it is not *Cité libre* that provided him with a source of inspiration, but rather the electoral platforms of the Liberal party in 1952 and 1956 from which sizeable quotes were taken. Indeed, in a number of ways the 1960 Liberal platform betrayed conservative leanings, for example in the importance attached to the rural as compared to the industrial economy.

Cité libre's interpretation of the current situation was often mistaken. Thus for instance it remained bound to conservative nationalism's illusion that Québec had a consensual and unanimous society, following sheep-like behind its leaders, lay and clerical. *Cité libre* contributed to building the myth of Québec's monolithic society. It still proclaimed this myth in 1958. No doubt, since conservative nationalism was still the official ideology, conservatism pervaded all social structures and especially politics. But, appearances notwithstanding, a look beneath the surface would have detected a very definite pluralism and a whole flowering of democratic aspirations among Québec groups.

A 1957 study of several citizen groups by the Institut Canadien d'éducation des adultes in fact revealed both the existence of vigorous democratic tendencies among a good many, notably in the co-operative movement and in labour unions, and an acute awareness of the corrosive effects of the constant road-blocks conservatism was setting in political life.[21] Indeed, it seems to me that it is especially by studying the efforts of action groups to achieve independence vis-à-vis the ideology of official leaders, by uncovering their hidden, underground ways of living out their beliefs, that one may really understand the circumstances that allowed liberal nationalism to take root in Québec.

Before becoming the ideology of the political authorities, this nationalism already existed as a sociological reality and as a hope. It underlay most of the many opposition movements outside of the legislature, including phenomena such as the Asbestos and the Louiseville strikes, the impact of Laval University's Faculty of Social Science under its Dean, Father Georges-Henri Lévesque, and even the Liberal victory of 22 June 1960. When the Confédération des travailleurs catholiques du Canada (CTCC)— the Confederation of Catholic Workers of Canada—adopted a new name in 1960, becoming the Confederation of National Trade Unions (CNTU) this was not regarded as a new departure but rather as a reflection of trends followed since the 1950s.

Cité libre also seems to me to have incorrectly assessed the importance for Québec and international events in the period that followed the Second World War. The periodical argued that Québec had to catch up to modern times. But the model it kept putting forward, despite socialist positions borrowed from European social democracies, was that of the European and United States liberal democracies. It failed to perceive the interest Quebeckers would find in the awakening of the peoples of the Third World, in the trend to decolonization, and in the accession to independence of nearly forty countries under the stimulus of a nationalism inspired at times by liberalism, at times by socialism, but in fact essentially new. That is why the onrush of a first wave of separatism in Québec in 1959, and the creation of the RIN (Rassemblement pour l'indépendance nationale) in September 1960, took the editors by surprise. They remained unable to understand the basis and the scope of the independentist movement. Even more, the tolerance they had so far practised, and had contributed to spreading, at this point began to wear thin.

Further still, *Cité libre*'s main editors showed relatively little awareness of the importance of current scientific and technological advances. They were the products of the nineteenth century's last liberal generation, rather than the spokesmen of our own scientific and cybernetic century. If they seemed modern to their readers, it was because the society they criticized seemed to them to have remained frozen within the confines of the seventeenth century. The features of the newly emerging political culture escaped their notice, and they completely misunderstood the meaning of the young people's revolt in the mid-1960s—a revolt for which they had, in some sense, helped to pave the way, but of which they became a target. The liberalism they were formulating came out with an old-fashioned accent. The pity is that they still live by it, and that their prominent positions on the political scene now enable them to turn their views into reality. They were not the initiators of liberal endeavours, and while these seem to be coming to term virtually without their contribution, theirs are the tenacious convictions that will now give them the midwifery role. The faith that moved them, thus, imperceptibly turned into a form of obstinacy, reminiscent of the conservative nationalists at whom they originally threw their barbs. Success will have proved costly: theirs is the new intolerance.

The editors of *Cité libre* never claimed the credit of having worn down the *ancien régime* and heralded the New. They were quite modest about the effects of their action. It is the early analysts of *Cité libre,* in the 1960s, who, without having properly studied the periodical, made claims for its influence. For its readers at the time, *Cité libre* represented the awakening of a new spirit, the liberal spirit expressed through open discussion in its columns, and through its open-armed welcome to the new pluralism that was appearing on the Québec social scene, much to the dismay and powerless disapproval of conservative nationalism. This is where *Cité libre* played its revolutionary role: it was a source of inspiration for all the groups which, since 1940 at least, were awakening to new hopes—hopes new for Québec, for they were already old elsewhere.

The principal merit of *Cité libre* is to have served as witness to an era. The periodical reflected the efforts of a generation of intellectuals, trained in social science during the war and the post-war years, to understand their society by means of a conceptual framework new to Québec. Over and beyond *Cité libre,* a new mood was evident in various areas, such as the co-operative movement, the labour movement, and the universities. There was also *Le Devoir*'s active opposition to obsolete social policies and to the Duplessis government's corruption. Another factor was the introduction of television, whose effect upon the period has never been properly assessed. There was, perhaps above all, as usually happens in such circumstances, the inner crumbling within the old regime, within the Church, among the aging elites, and most clearly of all, within that prime bastion of conservative nationalism, long believed unassailable, the Union Nationale party, in power in Québec since 1936, except for the five years of World War Two. The end finally came when *Le Devoir* broke the natural gas scandal and when Maurice Duplessis died in 1959—an end which many had despaired of ever seeing, even among those who today pass for the makers or prophets of liberal nationalism.

b. The arguments of liberal nationalism   Marcel Rioux considered the 1960 provincial election to have been "a global social phenomenon." He wrote: "the election was more than a transfer of power from one team to another . . . it affected all of society: it penetrated every corner, cast doubt on age-old truths and on solidly ensconced authorities, marked a breaking point with a period of Québec's history and the beginning of an era which many Quebeckers see as leading this land to greater political autonomy if not to total independence."[22] In retrospect, this was claiming too much. The 1960 election can only be considered as "a global social phenomenon" in the light of the great dreams it made possible. In actual fact, liberal nationalism, even at its inception, was far less "revolutionary" than it seemed to many.

The Liberal victory simply allowed everyone to say what many people had been thinking for a long time. It opened up hopes of finally achieving what had so far been unattainable. The replacement of conservative nationalism by a liberal form of nationalism had long been under way in Québec. That this was not evident in the 1950s is due to the mirage that occurs whenever a political system, generally the source of the dominant ideological imagery, is deeply cut off from important segments of society.

"High time for a change!" was one of the popular slogans of the 1960 Liberal campaign. The most frequently mentioned changes were of course practical: in the economy, education, social security, and so on. The government's follow-up was so swift that even the most impatient were taken aback. A good indication of this pace may be found in the fact that Québec, with the lightest per capita public debt in 1960, became the province with the highest per capita debt within five years. To support this new activity, it was essential to renew the ideological stock-in-trade. New themes were put forward, around Québec's will to break off its age-old isolationism, to step forward resolutely on the path to modernity and development. The expression which doubtless best reflects all these efforts at renewal was *rattrapage,* catching up. This expression became a symbol and an ideological argument for the most diverse groups in putting pressure on the Québec government which, in turn, also used it extensively in putting pressure upon the federal government.

In analysing the arguments of liberal nationalism, a careful distinction must be drawn between those related to the political community and those dealing with the regime and the authorities. The arguments related to the political community are highly developed. They go back to the overall themes of conservative nationalism, but with more conviction and with a radical change of emphasis. The regime is also different: liberal instead of conservative. But there is little ideological substantiation available for the liberal doctrine. Indeed, the main spokesman of liberalism during the 1960s was a politician, in fact a minister, René Lévesque. It is perhaps in the area of legitimizing political authority that tensions between the old order and the new proved strongest, but here again no clear exposition of principles and arguments was forthcoming.

Liberal nationalism under Jean Lesage from 1960 to 1966, as under Daniel Johnson and Jean-Jacques Bertrand from 1966 to 1970, and under Robert Bourassa since April 1970, has accepted the Canadian political community. This is an unconditional acceptance, in spite of occasional shades of revolt by Jean Lesage and Daniel Johnson, which mainly seem to have been a disguised form of pressure upon the federal government.

Québec's traditional autonomism never disappeared; it was in fact more marked than ever. But it ceased being mainly negative as it had been under Taschereau and Duplessis, when its aim was to check the federal government and prevent it from acting, even at the cost of Québec's development, if necessary. Now, under liberal nationalism, Québec's autonomism became positive. It sought to provide for Québec's rapid and favourable development. But the necessary programs had to go through the Québec government. So, instead of being defensive as it had been before 1960, Québec's autonomism became aggressive. Federal-provincial relations became intense, Québec's government throwing challenge after challenge to the federal government, notably the fiscal "ultimatum" cast by Jean Lesage in the spring of 1963 at the very opening of a federal election campaign. To help implement its policies, in 1961 the Québec government established a Department of Federal-Provincial Affairs, which was subsequently to become, in line with the Québec government's desire to play an independent role in the international field, the Department of Inter-Governmental Affairs. The expression which perhaps best symbolized these new autonomist tendencies was the phrase "State of Québec" which came into vogue after Lesage's visit to France during the fall of 1961. Another sign of the new spirit: Québec's French Canadians now firmly began to identify themselves as *Québécois,* Quebeckers.

Liberal nationalism also eagerly sought to clairify the nature of Canadian federalism and to define Québec's position within Confederation. "Québec's special status," "the two-nations theory," "associate States," all of these were approaches, for a time considered promising by a number of people, towards far-reaching constitutional reform. To help Quebeckers state their viewpoint, but especially to mobilize them, French Canada's Estates General were in 1964 set up with the financial and moral assistance of the Québec government. The Estates General faded away by 1969, leaving behind them a trail of broken friendships, disappointed hopes, and reams of paper covered with a flood of words.

The Québec government even played with the idea of separatism, especially in 1962-1963, under Lesage, and in 1966-1968 under Johnson. President de Gaulle's visit and his rallying cry from the Montréal City Hall's balcony on a July evening in 1967: "Vive le Québec libre!" served as a climax to the separatist temptation. A return to "realism," already begun by Lesage in 1965, came back in full swing when, after Daniel Johnson's premature death in 1968, his succession fell to Jean-Jacques Bertrand, an old-style French-Canadian nationalist. Robert Bourassa's slogan "cultural sovereignty within a profitable federalism" seems to be realism at its peak, even though (to be cynical) it is difficult, to assume that even this cannot be capped.

For a time, the federal government and English-speaking Canada were alarmed by the mounting demands for Québec autonomism. Of course, they came nowhere close to supporting Québec's federalist proposals. Edwin R. Black shows that, save for the old "compact theory," which found some favour in the 1950s both in English-speaking Canada and in Québec, none of the ideas on Canadian federalism advanced by Québec during the 1960s was favourably received in English Canada or seriously considered in federal government circles, even though the New Democrats and even the Conservative party for a time flirted with the "two-nations theory" despite inner dissension and dire electoral consequences.[23]

While being unenthusiastic about the climate of opinion in Québec, English Canada and the federal government attempted to forestall any possible head-on collision. Thus in July 1963, the Royal Commission on Bilingualism and Biculturalism was set up under the co-chairmanship of André Laurendeau, who had been one of the first to press for such a commission, and of Davidson Dunton, the English Canadian most open to Québec among the men of his generation. In spite of a clear-sighted Preliminary Report (1965) warning that Canada was experiencing the gravest crisis of its history, in spite of the famous "blue pages" of the Introduction to the Final Report drafted by Laurendeau, in which the Commission explored the extent of self-determination proper for Québec, the Royal Commission dragged on until 1971. The conclusion of its work was marred by a dramatic failure: the members of the Commission, worn out by stress and age, proved unable to agree on any political solution to the Canadian problem. As of the writing of this book, the latest constitutional developments have been the inconclusive work of the House of Commons and the Senate's Joint Constitutional Committee, and the smarting failure of the Victoria Federal-Provincial Conference in 1971.

Much the same climate of concern explains the entry on the political federal scene in 1965 of the three Wise Men: Pierre Elliot Trudeau, Gérard Pelletier, and Jean Marchand, who had refused the same bait in 1963. Like Louis Saint-Laurent, who in 1942, on the death of Ernest Lapointe, had allowed Cardinal Villeneuve to persuade him to enter the federal political scene in spite of his lack of interest for active politics, it was a feeling of "mission" that pushed these three men, who during the fifties, had been fierce defenders of Québec's autonomy and adversaries of the federal Liberal party (their sympathies leaning towards the NDP) to engage in such a spectacular turn-about. Wishing to counter-balance the "excesses" of Québec nationalism, they wanted to demonstrate the possibility for French Canadians to do as much for Quebeckers, if not more, in Ottawa as in Québec City. Fate seems to have been kind to them, for they have been holding the foremost leadership positions in Ottawa since 1968. At any rate it is impossible to understand the meaning of their actions and positions since then, if one fails to remember that, like so many of the French Canadians active on the federal scene since Confederation, they are, as they say themselves, primarily "missionaries." Furthermore, Trudeau in his political outlook is unfailingly and stubbornly a pan-Canadian nationalist in orientation, which of course corresponds to that of the Canadian business community since Confederation. Above all, he has so far succeeded in keeping Québec "in its place," which in the words of the late Prime Minister St. Laurent is that of being a province just like the others. For all those reasons Trudeau appears to be a prime minister of good stature: he is the right man at the right time.

While Québec has in the past century had a plethora of leftist conservative ideologists, historians, and philosophers, after the unequal struggle which the leftist liberals waged and lost between 1840 and 1880, it has had a dearth of articulate liberal thinkers. To find French-Canadian viewpoints associated with liberalism in the twentieth century, we have to go back to Errol Bouchette at the beginning of the century, and the somewhat later Esdras Minville. But as Jean-Charles Falardeau has clearly shown, their arguments in favour of industry and urban life were neither heard in their time nor well received subsequently. Liberalism verged on heresy.[24] The editors of Cité libre, speakers at the Institute des Affaires publiques, and a smattering of academic economists or sociologists—that is all the Québec intellectuals' contribution to liberal thinking amounts to since 1950. With today's economic and political liberalism in full swing, there are still only a few isolated liberal intellectuals to be seen, barely able to hold their own in the face of socialist thought (highly popular as it is among the younger intellectuals), and even in the face of the conservative constructs of the still highly vocal spokesmen of the traditional elites. Furthermore, this liberal thinking does not have its roots in Québec but borrows from foreign philosophers or ideologues, American or at best European.

There is no cause to be surprised that Québec's liberal nationalism has no elaborate tenets. As we remember, the 1960 electoral platform, inspired by Georges-Emile Lapalme, contained a good many conservative elements interwoven with old-style liberalism. Only the parts of the platform dealing with the culture and the role of the State, areas closest to Lapalme's own heart and experience, had a somewhat new ring. Only in the 1966 platform did the provincial Liberal party really voice its democratic convictions and its view of men as citizens. In 1970, and more especially in 1973, economic issues were highlighted over social and cultural ones, and the regime's liberalism was merely taken for granted. The Union Nationale party gave liberalism even shorter shrift: though it was perforce necessary to adapt to the circumstances that currently favoured liberalism, the old conservative clichés remained very much in force and popular with the party's supporters, essentially rural and traditionalistic. Both for the Liberals and the Union Nationale, "thinkers' " symposia were one thing, elections and practical politics quite another.

It is not among intellectuals but among action groups and politicians that the most far-seeing spokesmen of liberalism must be sought. From the middle of the nineteenth century, while conservative nationalism held sway over intellectuals' minds, treating industrial activity with consummate contempt, the business world carried on regardless, unashamedly assimilating the old Anglo-American liberalism in its laissez-faire form. In support of their arguments, the laissez-faire liberals had no compunction about drawing upon religion, here as in the United States. And the business world held firm sway over politicians, including Québec's premiers. These *rois-nègres*, tribal kinglets, as André Laurendeau once described them, in turn had no qualms about becoming the ardent propagandists of laissez-faire, especially in the fields of industrial expansion and of natural resources.

The Association professionnelle des industriels, Québec's main employers' association from 1943—when it was founded—until 1960, was the principal spokesman of this "pure" economic liberalism, characteristic of the business world. As Jean Louis Roy so well showed, Alexandre Taschereau and Maurice Duplessis were to take up the main themes of the old economic liberalism, blend it into their conservative doctrine, and thereby give it tremendous authority.[25] They lauded personal initiative and free enterprise and branded the immorality of embattled trade unionism. At the 1949 annual convention of the employers' association, Duplessis affirmed: ". . . nothing is new under the sun, and eternal verities are always true because they are eternal. A system wherein all belongs to the State is a harmful system . . . goodness lies only in a system of freedom for private enterprise, appropriate in the past, necessary in the present, and indispensable in the future. It is a system that obviates the dangers and disasters multiplying under State monopoly. It brings out the merits of talent, work, initiative, competence, and human dignity." What these resounding professions of faith led to, was the mounting wealth of big business, while the people remained as poor as ever.

A new turn of mind marked the liberalism of the Quiet Revolution, save in the field of investment where the old bent-of-mind persisted. The new leaders loudly proclaimed their faith in the welfare state, by then in existence in practically all the Western industrialized countries. Many of these men believed in the new liberalism as a result of their federal experience. Others, like Paul Gérin-Lajoie, Pierre Laporte, René Lévesque, and Eric Kierans, who were of the *Cité libre* generation, shared its social ideas. That is doubtless why pragmatism has been the rule in Québec's new brand of liberal nationalism. Its liturgy was rapidly making a clean breast of the vestiges of the old order, carried over until 1960. But nothing ever completely dies away. Thus the adoption of the merit system in the provincial civil service and of objective criteria in the awarding of public contracts did not lead to the jettisoning of patronage, but to the invention of a new expression: "good" patronage, to describe an ancient reality that refuses to vanish.

The principal theme of liberal nationalism became the motto *maîtres chez nous,* masters in our own house. It did not have too much impact on investment, where the traditional laissez-faire practices had produced far-reaching dependence upon the United States—a dependence as ingrained as a law of nature against which men were powerless. But it did have appreciable repercussions in a number of other fields: the introduction of a Québec pension scheme after hard-nosed negotiations with the federal government, the creation of a number of public financial or industrial corporations, and particularly the nationalization of electric power companies in 1962 and the building of the Manicouagan dam (a costly decision, whose symbolic value was nevertheless incalculable). These were some of the achievements which for a time drew upon Québec the eyes of foreign universities and of the international press. The State no longer rested content with its famous "complementary" role, which had so long lined the pockets of Québec's business potentates. It turned to investment and entrepreneurship, and was very soon engaging in these on a large scale. René Lévesque was the driving force behind this new economic impulse. He used to say that the State "is one in ourselves, the best of ourselves" and in him nationalism merged with the new liberal spirit.

Yet another of its trademarks was the "educational charter" of 1961 and, at last in 1964, the establishment of a Department of Education under Paul Gérin-Lajoie. I have elsewhere examined the arguments put forward in support of this crucial political decision.[26] Every reform in this field bore the liberal trademark: the State's new role in education, free schooling, open access to education, partial deconfessionalization, decentralization through the establishment of regional schools, the introduction of post-secondary education through the introduction of comprehensive two-or three-year CEGEPs, which put an end to the elitist classical colleges, the updating of curricula, and the setting of higher standards for teacher qualification.

Jean Lesage, whose reason leaned towards the new while his instincts held him back to the old, had said in 1961: "As long as I am premier, we shall have no Department of Education in Québec." He came to regret this statement bitterly, as he did a number of others made between 1960 and 1962. But he made amends by masterfully and very democratically leading the battle for Bill 60 in 1963, designed to establish the new Department of Education.

The Lesage Government's slogan *s'instruire, c'est s'enrichir* (education is a person's wealth) may not bear the mark of genius, but it certainly bore the liberal stamp. It marked a new way of dealing with education in Québec. Teaching had traditionally been seen as so exalted a task that no material or financial considerations should be allowed to sully it. Duplessis, who had scandalously ignored the universities in the old days, in 1956 attempted to justify himself by comparing the educational system to a house: "Who in his right mind would think of building the upper floors before having made sure that the foundations were solid?" he asked. He further referred to the universities: "You don't build a cathedral on a dunghill." Of education in general, he said: "Education is like alcohol; some people can't take it!"

More significant, though less spectacularly than in the two previous instances, openness to free discussion and to a great variety of opposition bear witness to the liberal nature of Québec's new regime. The new state of mind was perhaps best illustrated by the debate surrounding Bill 60. The traditionalist elites launched a great offensive which showed the extent to which conservatism, though no longer politically dominant, still exercised a firm grip. Alarmed at this resurgence of conservative opinion which, moreover, was out to mint political coinage out of the many inconveniences produced by reform, in 1965 Jean Lesage called a halt to all reform, claiming that the people, "out of breath," were no longer capable of keeping pace with the government.

Even the notion of political authority became imbued with the liberal spirit. This was perhaps the most difficult accomplishment for both government and people. Jean Lesage, who in many ways was an eminently traditionalist leader, several times drew back in exasperation at the swift democratization that went so far as to affect his own status or the role he was exercising. "The Queen does not bargain with her subjects" was his initial response to the civil servants' campaign for union accreditation. But political authority had to cease relying on meta-social criteria, as it had done in the era of conservative nationalism. It had to fall back upon competence. No longer a personal attribute, competence depended on how one performed one's duties. Further still: no longer boundless as of old (even though in practice tempered by a kindly paternalism, as in many traditional societies) authority was now more closely and effectively regulated, for the benefit of both rulers and ruled. Hence an end to arbitrariness in politics, and elsewhere. Another innovation was the spread of the community development and mobilization, inaugurated in 1963 by the BAEQ (Bureau d'aménagement de l'est du Québec), Eastern Québec's Regional Development Office, following a federal-provincial agreement under the Agricultural and Rural Development Act. More and more people were demanding participation in management and in decision-making, and were seeking self-determination. This "liberation" went well beyond the bounds of pure politics. The pendulum swung so far that leaders in every field, from bishops to parents, were caught off guard. Québec was up against the first authority crisis in its history.

c. Liberal nationalism and politics   Those who were not actively involved during the first four years of the 1960s cannot understand the impact of the times upon contemporary minds. One has to have been associated with the dreams and disillusions of that period, which came to be known as the Quiet Revolution, to be able to evaluate it correctly.

As we have seen, the transition from a period dominated by conservative or traditionalist nationalism to one characterized by liberal nationalism was no spontaneous development. It was, rather, the effect of slow mutations, originating as far back as the 1940s, in various sectors of society: labour unions, co-operatives, universities, the Church, the mass media, and even the family. How is one to account for the fact that these mutations, whose extent is clear today, were barely perceived at the time, and that well into the 1950s much was made of Québec's *immobilism*? How is it that the Union Nationale's defeat in the 1960 provincial elections came like a bolt from the blue, and that the supporting framework of conservative nationalism seemed to shatter unaccountably, despite the fact that it was rotten through and through and ready to crumble away on its own? I have elsewhere explained that this phenomenon resulted from the gap between the rates of change in the social and the political systems, as well as from the optical illusion caused by political ideologies which alternately play up conservatism and progressivism in a society.[27] It is obvious that between 1950 and 1960 Québec society was less conservative than it seemed on the surface, and that after 1960 it was less progressive than was then generally believed.

Somewhat startlingly, of the various elements of society, it was perhaps politics which at first offered the strongest resistance to the shift from old to new. Had things been left solely in Premier Jean Lesage's hands, especially during this first year in office, there is even reason to think that he would happily have let himself be propelled into the familiar rut of conservative nationalism. In a phrase reminiscent of Duplessis' countless colourful aphorisms, one of Lesage's speeches referred to the people of Québec as being "in calm possession of the truth." But times had changed; Lesage's catch-phrase caused a ground-swell of irony, and the premier, feeling ridiculed, swore he would never again be caught making a speech without first having read it.

Nevertheless, politics then triggered accelerating change and gave it its main momentum right up to 1965. Politics, more than any other institutional gauge, revealed the bare bones of problems. Boldly, the ministers responsible for the main portfolios, Paul Gérin-Lajoie, René Lévesque, Pierre Laporte, later Eric Kierans, and Jean Lesage himself, unveiled the major aspects of collective weaknesses: in education, in the field of natural resources, and of public goods and services, inadequacies in the civil service and in public finance, in social security, housing, city planning, and so on. Québec was lagging behind the times and had to adopt the necessary measures, however painful, to make up for the discrepancy. Bridges had to be established with the rest of the world, organizational frameworks rebuilt, outlooks modified. Politics became crucial. The state was turning into an essential lever of change: from one day to the next, the laissez-faire approach gave way to that of the welfare state.

The government's capacity to act and to decide mounted sharply. A plethora of young and talented civil servants, many of them repatriated from Ottawa where they had often discontentedly vegetated in low-grade jobs, others recently graduated from Laval University which had long readied itself for this role, came to support and sometimes to guide the efforts of the ministers working to modernize Québec speedily.

Stronger and more numerous political pressures came from all sectors: agricultural, industrial, cultural, social. For a few years, the government seemed to cope with these with the greatest of ease. In fact, most governmental activity in this regard was initiated by the government itself, amounting, as David Easton puts it, to ''withinputs.'' Political support also broadened and became more diversified. The traditional supports: parishes, the Church, the top clergy, and so on, moved aside to make room for the labour unions, particularly the CNTU, the co-operative movement, the professional associations and the universities. The time seemed remote when—as late as 1950!—Cardinal Léger could still write to the premier just before a meeting: ''At this crossroads of spiritual and temporal powers, we must between us settle common problems.'' (The Episcopate's last trumps were to be played—and partially lost—during the 1963 debate on Bill 60, concerned with the creation of a Department of Education.) Politics, like all of society, would become de-clericalized. The sudden diversification of political support would point up the extent to which Québec society was already a pluralistic one. The spurious unanimity that had reigned under the Old Order gave way to a variety of positions, some convergent, others sharply opposed. For a time, the government was receptive to all these trends and tolerant towards a broad range of opposition. So liberal was the regime that it considered as legitimate forces aimed at the destruction of the political system, for instance the separatist movement at the time when the RIN (Ralliement pour l'indépendance nationale) turned into a political party. However, there was less tolerance towards socialist movements which challenged the very bases of the liberal regime. This presaged a much sterner approach towards radical forms of opposition from 1965 on. Like any political system, after a short period of euphoria when the sky was the limit, the Québec political system came down to earth and made survival its prime guideline.

A number of people have blamed and continue to blame Jean Lesage's Liberal government for what they consider to be the missed opportunities of the Quiet Revolution. Of course, these missed opportunities are there for all to see. However, the problem is whether, in the actual circumstances of the time, these near-misses could have been avoided by the Lesage government or indeed by any other government wanting to liberalize Québec.

The many changes in behaviour and in values that occurred after 1960 only appeared revolutionary because they had been so long delayed. Thus the fact that Québec today has the lowest birth rate in North America (barely 13 per 100) happens to be striking because, as late as 1960, it had the highest rate (33 per 1000) after Newfoundland and New Brunswick. The sociological effects of this demographic change today appear as the most significant: the linguistic balance in Canada and in Québec no longer hangs on the "revenge of the cradles." In the field of education, too, such a big jump in size and rate of change occurred between 1961 and 1965 in good measure because of accumulated delays.

At first dazzled by the scope of planned reform and by the spectacular character of the Quiet Revolution's early achievements, Québec's population soon became disenchanted. Dissatisfaction grew and became evident in a number of fields. By 1965 the great hopes of 1960 and the early enthusiasm had faded. Why this fall from grace? There is a twofold explanation. First, the growing disparity of views between social and political agents regarding both the nature of the political community and the character of the political regime that would best suit Québec. Secondly, the rapidly growing impression of failure, notably in the field of education, where the monstrous size and the impersonality of many CEGEPs and the apparent lowering of the quality of young people's education led a number of people to deprecate reform and to regret the former classical colleges. Discontent also became rife in the cultural field, where the much awaited assistance to artists and writers never materialized; furthermore, the Québec government long delayed recognizing the language issue as a very sore spot, in spite of the fact that a growing number of groups, increasingly self-assured, were pressing for French unilingualism in Québec. The incidents surrounding the school dispute in the Montréal suburb of Saint-Léonard (where the local school board dominated by citizens of Italian origin, decided to opt for English as the language of instruction, which caused indignation among the French Canadian parents) gave a sign of the times. The political system at last woke up to the language problem in 1969, though it had been acute since 1961. However, it was the impression of failure in the economic field which most contributed to discrediting the Lesage goverment as well as that of the Union Nationale, which followed. In the end, a great deal of money and energy were invested without managing to reduce Québec's dependence on English-speaking Canada and on the United States: the control of Québec's economy today remains as much in the hands of "foreigners" as it was in 1960 and without any improvement in French Canadians' relative earning power as compared with that of the members of other ethnic groups. No longer the "hewers of wood and drawers of water" of yester-year, better educated than of old, Québec's Francophones still remain far removed from the command of most key posts. In Gérard Filion's words, they are now "beggars on horseback."

The ever more pragmatic approach of Québec governments since 1965, save for a brief interlude from 1966 to 1968 under Daniel Johnson, showed an absence of spirit, of imagination, and of common purpose. The vast dreams accompanying the beginnings of positive autonomism and the great Manicouagan achievements rapidly gave way to harsh disillusionment. After an initial period of tolerance, the Québec government clamped down on separatism. The federal government firmly re-established its upper hand when Trudeau came to power in 1968. Despite the slogan ''cultural sovereignty within a profitable federalism,'' and a few sporadic ministerial leanings towards autonomism, as in the case of Claude Castonguay in social security and Jean-Paul L'Allier in communications, the Québec government has been acting to all intents and purposes like a large municipal administration, as Claude Morin has pointed out.[28] The regime's liberalism has suffered a number of grave blows. After the War Measures crisis in October 1970, the government has shown growing intolerance towards any form of opposition, and growing inclination towards repressive measures. Recent evidence of this has been forthcoming in its treatment of the opponents of the Official Languages Bill, presented and adopted during the summer of 1974, and its arbitrary reaction to the Commission of Inquiry into Construction Union Freedoms (la commission d'enquète sur l'exercise des libertés syndicalisme dans le domaine de la construction)—the Cliche Report.

It has correctly been claimed that the middle classes primarily benefited from the Quiet Revolution. Since then, it has become increasingly evident that the Québec political system, in the era of liberal nationalism, is neither able to satisfy the needs nor to understand the aspirations of the people in underprivileged sectors and in outlying areas. Québec, like the societies around it but in its own special way, has entered a period of sharp polarizations.

d. The political functions of liberal nationalism   Liberal nationalísm has thrown light on the Québec government's possible range of action as a political sub-system of the Canadian political system. But the activities undertaken and the solutions chosen may be evaluated in very different ways, depending upon the socio-political viewpoint with which one approaches the assessment.

Liberal nationalism clearly aims at positive self-reliance, it safeguards the rights to every form of legitimate active opposition within the framework of democratic rules and procedures, it seeks the cultural and social advancement of both individuals and groups within the welfare society, and it favours modernism in all spheres of activity. More particularly, liberal nationalism seeks to promote a diversification and strengthening of secondary social organizations and the development of social and cultural pluralism. The pursuit of these goals has had a number of effects, intentional or fortuitious, foreseen or unforeseeable.

Now that the early euphoria is over, one is better able to evaluate how much leeway the Québec government has within the Canadian political system. Even in the eyes of the political agents, and particularly those of the social agents most involved in modernizing Québec, this leeway seems dismally narrow. The degree of political sovereignty required by Québec since 1962 cannot be provided without a deep constitutional reform of the Canadian political system. Such a reform seems far less likely in 1975 than in 1963, and this once again contributes to putting the Québec government on the defensive in its relations with the federal government, and to strengthening the hand of the separatist movement. On the other hand, Québec's economic dependence upon the United States and upon English-speaking Canada has not dwindled, despite much effort; indeed it has grown. Here again, liberal nationalism produced hopes it was unable to meet. This failure has moved a number of people to think that what needs changing is not so much the hopes, as the Canadian political community and the liberal regime itself. Finally, liberal nationalism has promoted a certain mobility among Québec elites. Prestige and influence have gradually been shifting from "privilege" (official social status) to "merit" (personal knowledge and competence). But here, too, the swing never went all the way. However, the hierarchical structure of social classes and the accompanying dominant-dependent relationships remains unchanged. There has been no social promotion for the masses. Thus, a number of people harbour the feeling that real equality of opportunity cannot be achieved within the present system. Only a socialist system would, they feel, insure fairness for everyone.

This then may be seen as liberal nationalism's main political function: it cleared the ground, freed the bottleneck. It thus paved the way for another political regime, which will either consist of a return to conservatism in some new form, or of a transition to some kind of socialism. The way the stage is set, as long as liberal nationalism persists, uncertainty about the regime and the political community that best suits Québec will doubtless continue to mount. Québec will find itself in full transition. Contradictions in the current situation go so deep, and the choices ahead are so perilous, that it is impossible to foresee the end-result of present-day processes.

3. Social Democratic and Socialist Nationalisms

Socialism, or even Scandinavian or British-type democratic socialism, has never managed to take root in profoundly conservative Québec. There have of course been marxists, or non-marxist socialists, in Québec well before the 1960s. However, it is only since the end of the 1950s that they have managed to surface and to form social movements with some following. Can socialism therefore be seen as one of the forces to be taken into account in Québec? Four kinds of consideration are relevant here.

First of all, unlike Québec Anglophones, French-speaking Quebeckers have so far always shied away from pan-Canadian social democracy, both in its old CCF form and in its newer New Democratic Party version. Yet never did the New Democratic Party, from its founding in 1960, spare any effort to attract French Canadians. Instances come to mind such as the election to the national presidency of the party of Michael Oliver, a thoroughly bilingual Anglophone, well known and highly regarded among Francophone intellectuals; the granting of a fair measure of independence to the party's Québec section and the appointment of Francophone presidents of the Québec wing, successively Robert Cliche, G. Raymond Laliberté, and F. Gautrin; the inclusion in the party's electoral platform of policies meeting the views of Francophone Quebeckers, even at the risk of losing some Anglophone support in Québec, and particularly of alienating voters elsewhere in the country, as happened in the 1968 federal election, after the party had given qualified approval to the "two-nations theory." In the July 1974 federal election, the New Democratic Party did worse than ever in Québec. What is it that keeps Francophone voters away: the "socialist" nature of the party? Wouldn't it rather be the failure, in spite of considerable effort, to dispel the "English" image the party has always had among the French-speaking public? The latter explanation seems to me the more likely. Social democracy's poor electoral showing in Québec, so far, seems due to the fact that it has never yet managed to develop any viable integration with a truly Québec national ideology.

Secondly, the rise of native Québec socialism coincided with the "liberation" movement, triggered by the 1956 provincial elections. The Union Nationale was returned to power, apparently stronger than ever but rapidly disintegrating from within. Yet it is the 1960 Liberal victory that finally gave the socialist movement a certain impetus with the result—apparently paradoxical but basically quite logical—that these late-comers on the scene promptly launched an attack against the regime, the liberal regime as it happens, that had at last given socialism a chance.

Thirdly, the appearance of socialism as a social movement coincided with changes in Québec nationalism during the 1960s, and more particularly with a strong separatist upswing. One might wonder whether the two factors are interrelated, and whether they enhance each other or stand in each other's way.

Finally, it should be remembered that there is more than a simple difference of degree between social-democratic nationalism, and social nationalism particularly in its marxist-leninist form. In fact these are two basically different forms of nationalism. There is more of an ideological gulf between social-democratic nationalism, as exemplified by the Parti Québécois, and the marxist-leninist brand of socialism advocated in Québec during the 1960s by intellectuals, particularly those of the *Parti pris* group and perhaps even more by labour activists such as Madeleine Parent, than there is between social-democratic and liberal nationalisms—particularly as, time aiding, electoral motives are inducing the Parti Québécois to moderate its social ideology.

It is very much in their social ideologies that distinctions exist between socialist nationalism and social-democratic nationalism. The former is doctrinaire and tries to arrive at a precise Marxist-Leninist definition of the theoretical bases of its action strategies. The latter is pragmatic and, when necessary, does not hesitate to adjust its ideological premises to the requirements of effectiveness, as has often been shown by the turn ideological debates have taken since 1969 within the Parti Québécois. Socialist nationalism assumes that socio-economic contradictions in Québec are far-reaching and must necessarily lead to a class struggle; moreover, socialist nationalism systematically pursues its radical critique of imperialistic capitalism and of the bourgeoisie, championing the working class and virtually limiting its activities to a gradual penetration of the urban proletariat—while social-democratic nationalism, on the other hand, promotes a consensus view of society and tries to gain the electoral support of the middle as well as of the lower classes.

These conclusions might militate against dealing in the same section with both the social-democratic and the socialist brands of nationalism. In fact I shall be dealing mainly with social-democratic nationalism, and shall only touch upon socialist nationalism to the extent to which it seems, as in the case of *Parti pris,* to have contributed to the appearance of conditions that allowed the Parti Québécois to be born and subsequently helped to crystallize certain ideological tensions within the party. Moreover, whatever may separate them, social-democratic nationalism and socialist nationalism are often obliged to take a stand vis-à-vis each other, if not to exercise complementary sociological functions, since both aim at doing away with the Canadian political community, both attack the existing political régime, and both condemn in varying degrees and for very different reasons the established political authorities. It must of course be recognized that there is no common measure between socialist nationalism's radical denunciation of liberal capitalism and the rather mild reforms advanced by social-democratic nationalism, especially in the Parti Québécois' essentially liberal version. Above all, the practical conditions of the political struggle in Québec since 1970 are such that socialist nationalists and social-democratic nationalists are in constant touch and are often forced to wage the same battles. The rise of the Parti Québécois, the only partisan organization that is both independentist and leftist, even leads a good many socialist nationalists to support it for practical reasons on given occasions, such as during electoral campaigns.

a. The pre-conditions for social-democratic and for socialist nationalism   It is impossible in one chapter to give due account of the simultaneous emergence on the Québec political scene of two different ideological forces: one national, separatism, the other social, namely social democracy and several varieties of socialism. It would be harder still to outline the background of many attempts at merger between these two ideologies.

Ever since Jean-Paul Tardivel, a forerunner of Henri Bourassa and of Lionel Groulx, separatism has always represented a temptation, a barely repressed dream in Québec. Separatism was long considered as a young man's notion, no longer befitting the adult. As recently as 20 February 1961, André Laurendeau, who had himself been a separatist in his youth, wrote: "It is proper, indeed quite acceptable, to be a separatist at the age of

25. This is no longer quite so at 35.'' It is only on the eve of the new order, in 1960, that separatism took root as a viable social movement.

Much the same is true of socialism: until the middle of the twentieth century, committed socialists were scarce in Québec, and most of those who come to mind had in other periods of their lives flirted with liberalism, corporatism, or fascism, or even with all of these ideologies in succession.

Also, until the very end of the 1950s, it was most unusual to see a thinker or a group of thinkers attempt to link separatism with socialism or even with social democracy. However, since then, a great many intellectuals have engaged in this exercise, as have a number of social movements including a recognized political party, the Parti Québécois.

Failing a substantiated explanation of such startling changes, a few pointers may prove useful.

First, let us mention the international situation during the immediate post-Second World War years. Throughout the world, especially in the former African and Asian colonies achieving independence, nationalism was awakening side by side with the emergence of varying forms of socialism, especially marxism-leninism, generally under the influence of the Soviet Union or of China. The merger of the two ideological forces almost unfailingly proved explosive. This was so because it placed side by side a newly acquired collective pride with an acute awareness of marked dependence accompanied by a raw fear of hunger. Karl Deutsch eloquently described the possible consequences of these tragic conditions: ''In some of the poorer countries governments will come to power that will prefer to go out with a bang than to see their people starve with a whimper . . . we can no longer drive any substantial minority, or any major ethnic or social group, to desperation.''[29]

Québec of course is no African colony. But this cannot prevent a number of Quebeckers from subjectively comparing their lot with that of African peoples or of American Blacks. The wide sales in Québec of Frantz Fanon's book, *Les Damnés de la Terre (The Wretched of the Earth),* and particularly the influence it exercised on the socialists and on a number of Québec separatists, is further evidence of the fact that the convergence of separatism and socialism here is part of a wider movement whose roots lie outside, as much as in, Québec. If most national liberations are propelled by socialist nationalism, why should Québec be an exception?

The favourable international climate is reinforced by internal factors. The separatist current grew up in the shade of a liberal nationalism strongly tinged with autonomism in the Lesage government's early years (1961 to 1964) and under Daniel Johnson (1966 to 1968); separatism took on weight and consolidated itself, as official nationalism became eroded during the Lesage government's last two years in office and when it was subsequently virtually abandoned under Jean-Jacques Bertrand and, again, under Robert Bourassa. This nationalist falling-by-the-wayside was accompanied by growing reservations in English Canada towards Québec's varying forms of political autonomism, and by English Canada's refusal to consider seriously the various approaches to constitutional reform or to the rejuvenation of Canadian federalism advanced by Québec's political leaders.

On the other hand, the great hopes of political, economic, and cultural rebirth in Québec, aroused by the Lesage government's adoption of the welfare-state philosophy, did not long survive. The government proved increasingly unable to meet the justified expectations of various sectors of the population, in labour unions, underpriviledged urban districts, impoverished rural areas, whose demands became increasingly insistent. Young people, who are acquiring an education in growing numbers here as elsewhere, were turning against the established system; and intellectuals, whom the lick-and-promise of the Quiet Revolution had not long satisfied, furnished most of the initial support for the Québec independentist and socialist movements.

Already at the end of the 1950s, the *Revue socialiste* edited by Raoul Roy was competing with *Cité libre*. On 8 September 1960, just two days before the founding of the RIN, the Action socialiste pour l'indépendance du Québec was set up. This movement, aimed at channeling the energies of the people who gravitated around the *Revue socialiste,* was the first to proclaim "the indissolubility of the national and of the social questions."

This is the background against which the RIN was born, fated to be torn by ambiguity. As André d'Allemagne relates, the dissensions within the RIN, first in the right wing under Marcel Chaput, who founded the Parti Républicain Populaire in December 1972, then in the left wing among the supporters of Andrée Ferretti in March 1968, give proof of the difficulty of combining Québec's national and social issues.[30] The Parti Québécois which, under René Lévesque's presidency, combined the Mouvement Souveraineté Association founded by René Lévesque himself, with the Ralliement National led by Dr. Jutras and Gilles Grégoire, inherited the same tensions, and it has not yet in 1975 managed to resolve them fully. (Shortly after the Parti Québécois' founding, the RIN disbanded, and its members were individually invited to join the Parti Québécois.) Currently, periodicals like *Liberté, Parti pris*—which challenged *Cité libre* head-on and took over its place—the *Revue socialiste* and, as of the time of writing, *En lutte, Mobilisation, Défi,* and even *Maintenant,* and *Relations,* have laboriously been trying to find a formula which would satisfactorily achieve the difficult fusion of separatism and socialism in Québec's own context. Echoes of these efforts have spread in concentric circles amid labour unions, political action committees, even among the Montréal chapter of the Société Saint-Jean-Baptiste and particularly the Mouvement National des Québécois (the newly adopted name for the Federation of St-Jean Baptiste Societies) which, as Jacques Hamel has shown, is closely following in the footsteps of the Parti Québécois in the socio-economic field.[31]

b. The arguments of social-democratic and of socialist nationalism Unlike *Cité libre,* the *Parti pris* group practically never considered itself to have played a major part in Québec's recent social and political development. The periodical was founded in October 1963 as a result of unsurmountable ideological divergences within the *Cité libre* team. The last issue of *Parti pris,* number 39, was published in the fall of 1968, following unsuccessful attempts by the editors to find a common attitude towards the recently-established Souveraineté-Association, which was soon to become the Parti Québécois.

The reason why so little influence is attributed to *Parti pris* as compared to *Cité libre,* whose impact has been considerably inflated, essentially arises out of three facts. The ideas promoted by *Parti pris,* unlike those advanced by *Cité libre,* were never endorsed by any major political party and did not become part of the dominant political ideology. None of the editors of *Parti pris* has so far come to hold any important office; and those who for a time held the limelight, like Charles Gagnon and Pierre Vallières, were by the nature of their actions shunted aside from the rest of Québec society. Finally, the highly doctrinaire approach of the periodical gave it the tone of a student publication or of an in-group review, thus keeping any intellectuals who were more concerned with discussing Québec realities than with debating marxism-leninism or trying to find the right ways of applying the marxist-leninist analysis to Québec events.

But, in spite of these shortcomings, *Parti pris* does not deserve the oblivion into which it has fallen. For nearly five years it was one of the main breeding grounds of intellectuals of the post-*Cité libre* generation who favoured both separatism and marxism-leninism. Paul Chamberland, Pierre Maheu, Jean-Marc Piotte, Andrée Ferretti, Charles Gagnon, Luc Racine, Gaétan Tremblay, and Pierre Vallières, who wrote and edited *Parti pris,* are highly intelligent people. André Potvin's thesis on the *Parti pris* nationalist ideology clearly shows the periodical to have been at the heart of the 1960s' debate in nationalist and socialist circles:[32] a debate on the proper ways of associating separatism with socialism; on the role of violence in achieving an independent and socialist Québec; on the kind of socialism best suited to Québec; on the appropriate ways of "decolonizing" Québec; on the conditions of the class struggle in Québec; and so on.

In actual fact, there is at least as much good writing in *Parti pris* as in *Cité libre.* Yet a study of *Parti pris* is inadequate to understand the nature of socialist nationalism, and particularly of the social-democratic nationalism it denounced, mainly because the periodical ceased publication in 1968, that is at the very time when a major cultural revolution occurred in Québec, played out mainly by students but penetrating the whole of society. Note must also be taken of the radically new departures occurring within the labour movement over the past five years; Louis-Marie Tremblay was the first to undertake a study of these.[33] Finally, mention must be made of the development and of the achievements of the Parti Québécois over the last six years. It would be impossible to do these movements justice here by providing a full account of their activities. The complexity of the subject also prevents me from attempting a preliminary synthesis, such as the one Micheline de Sève and I elaborated elsewhere, though from a different angle.[34] Dealing very briefly with the subject may fail to bring out clearly enough some of the radical divergences of view between the supporters of social-democratic nationalism and socialist nationalism; yet I shall nevertheless attempt to outline some of the salient points in their approach towards the political community, the regime, and the authorities.

In most instances, socialist nationalism and the Parti Québécois' social-democratic nationalism reject the Canadian political system. In this, they are very close to right-wing separatists such as those of the Alliance Laurentienne founded by Raymond Barbeau; but a basic division on the kind of political regime that would suit Québec, precludes any viable alliance between them, were it only tactical. However, the arguments in favour of rejecting the Canadian political system and promoting an alternative one within the Québec framework are very similar among all Québec separatists, whatever their social ideology.

A first series of arguments aims to show that the Canadian Confederation, the political system born out of the British North America Act, does not serve the best interests of Quebeckers; and that there is no good reason to think it can be reformed to any significant extent. The government, the House of Commons, the federal administration, and the Supreme Court all feature a permanent Anglophone majority, and it is therefore only natural that they should first of all serve the interests of the English-speaking majority of the country. Moreover, past attempts, including the most recent, to correct the situation and to introduce "equality between the partners" have always led to resounding failures, such as the fiasco of the Commission on Bilingualism and Biculturalism and the ineffectiveness of the Official Languages Act. In launching an offensive to promote multiculturalism throughout Canada, as the federal government has done since 1972, it has once again shown its inability to comprehend Québec issues. Further still: the relative position of French Canadians throughout the country is rapidly weakening, as shown by the 1971 federal census. French-speaking minorities, except in New Brunswick, are dwindling away and it is now impossible to change the demographic, social, and economic factors responsible. In a few years (except for the Acadians who will in New Brunswick still continue for some time to cling to their own myth of survival) there will be practically no French Canadians left outside of Québec. The ratio of French Canadians to the rest of the country's population can only maintain its downward trend, and already Statistics Canada forecasts it to be 20 percent in a few decades as compared to the present 28 percent. Even in Québec, given the current socio-political context, the ratio of French Canadians is falling off alarmingly, particularly in the greater-Montréal area. Bill 22, which declares French to be the official language in Québec, in the view of many people, is bound to have effects no less harmful than the infamous Bill 63 it replaced; which goes to show that even the French language cannot adequately be protected in Québec itself within the current political framework.

Hoping to redress the tragic situation of French Canadians within a renewed Confederation, as some federalists might wish, is ludicrous according to the spokesmen of socialist nationalism and of social-democratic nationalism. They feel that English Canada and the federal government have given ample proof of the unacceptability of such adjustments. Moreover, the socialists claim, Anglophones are right to oppose political decentralization or the granting of a special status to Québec, since such measures would weaken Canada, whereas the social, economic, and cultural circumstances, as well as international conditions, point up the need for strong government. The Canadian government would be quite misguided if it were to weaken itself in doubtlessly futile attempts to win over Québec. In brief it would be best, without bitterness or hate, to conclude that the Canadian government and English Canada can do nothing for Québec, and that therefore the only logical solution is to divide the Canadian political system so as to provide for two strong independent governments, subject to later arrangements between them to meet common economic, defence, and other requirements.

A second series of arguments draws upon the arsenal of justifications used since 1945 by African and Asian peoples to win their independence. The theory of political self-determination, that is the right of peoples to determine their own fate, advanced in 1917 by President Woodrow Wilson in defence of Central and Eastern-European peoples wishing to accede to statehood, was revived with renewed vigour after the Second World War. This formula's contagious success is no doubt due to the fact that it is held to be self-evident and akin to natural law, as expressed in the United Nations' Declaration of Human Rights. Both social-democratic and socialist nationalisms use the theory of self-determination as a corner-stone of their political thinking.

The other positive argument, also drawn from post-war international experience, relates to the right of colonized peoples to liberate themselves from their overseers, the colonizers. The various Québec independentist movements are not equally vocal in denouncing the colonialism from which Québec suffers in their view. But they all use the anti-colonialist arguments to some extent, socialist nationalism very aggressively, social-democratic nationalism, as expressed by the Parti Québécois, somewhat more warily. Anti-colonialism is directed primarily against the Canadian political system, a direct descendant of the 1760 conquest which put New France's French population under an English yoke. But it is also directed against the United States, respecting which Canada itself is largely defenceless. The socialist and the social-democratic nationalists feel that a reform of the political regime, given the fact of Québec's very specific cultural traits, would make it easier to ensure economic and cultural independence for Quebeckers in an independent Québec rather than within a political system whose English-speaking majority seems to them to have no identity of its own, or at any rate seems not to be very interested in preserving the original features that set it apart from "the Americans." Kari Levitt's devastating conclusions[35] on the extent of American power in

Canada, notably through the complex influence of multi-national corporations, has greatly contributed to strengthening the relevant convictions of the spokesmen of socialist and social-democratic nationalism; it is the Parti Québécois' economic expert, Jacques Parizeau, who wrote the preface to the French edition of her book.

While old-style European nationalisms were predominantly liberal, those that appeared after the Second World War—in Yugoslavia, Czechoslovakia, China, Korea, Vietnam, Africa, Cuba, South America—tend toward socialism. Most recent national liberations have drawn upon more or less home-grown versions of marxism-leninism. Ideologically, Québec is different from these, mainly because our post-war indepentist movements have had much difficulty in combining their doctrine with marxism-leninism in a way credible and attractive to a wide cross-section of the public. There are of course marxist-leninist trends in Québec. However, so far, socialist nationalism has only gained some measure of support where the marxist-leninist vocabulary has been played down at the very least, as for instance in the labour unions and even more strikingly in the Parti Québécois. In fact, even the social-democratic elements of the party's platform have been so far watered down that it practically aligns itself with the newer forms of liberalism, especially as its struggle for power sharpens. Thus, today, the revolutionary stance in Québec is not essentially anti-liberal—liberalism, as we have seen, does not have very deep roots among the people—it is the stance of socialism as opposed to conservatism.

The value system of socialist nationalism is its unifying thread. This value system plays up justice, equality, and human dignity. These of course are also part of the stock-in-trade of liberalism, as Pierre Elliott Trudeau's slogan in the 1968 General Election, "the just society," goes to show. The main difference between liberalism and socialist nationalism is one of targets. When socialists speak of human dignity, they do not mean the same thing as do the liberals—a difference clearly perceptible in, say, Montréal's protest movements. Socialists dwell mainly on down-to-earth living conditions, whereas liberals principally refer to the ethical aspects of existence. Moreover, the former consider human dignity to be closely tied to the group or class condition, while liberals see people above all in terms of their individual circumstances. The socialists speak of "community enhancement," the latter of "improved opportunities" for the individual to educate himself, to work, to do better in the tough struggle everyone faces, pitted against everyone else upon the road to success.

Socialists and liberals also have a differing view of goals and objectives. Liberals mainly perceive these in economic terms, as demonstrated by the Liberal party, both federal and provincial, whereas socialists attach far greater importance to social goals, caring even more about the quality of life than about economic growth.

The emphasis upon justice and equality also in fact, if not in theory, mark a distinction between socialism and liberalism. While liberals' professions of faith in justice and equality, however sincere, often reflect mere pious hope, for socialists the will to achieve a just and egalitarian order is a driving force which looks for ways of making this happen. Hence opposition to capitalism as a system of industrial production, and to the "bourgeoisie" as a dominant class, drawing unfair advantage from the inequalities produced by capitalism.

Yet another theme, popular during the 1960s in some socialist nationalistic circles, was that of anti-clericalism. This came through very strongly in the early issues of *Parti pris*. It is barely in evidence today, either because it is considered pointless, the Church no longer having the power it used to have; or else because people do not care to give needless offence to other people's intimately held beliefs; or because it may be that some religious feeling still survives among the social trend-setters.

Socialist nationalism carries still further the erosion of traditional authority triggered by liberal nationalism. In fact, it goes so far as to deny to the established authorities any legitimacy or any right to govern at all. In this, socialist nationalism is in tune with very deep, very widespread feeling in many social groups.

Yet socialist nationalism is not an anarchist movement; in other words, it does not attack authority as such. But how does it envision the re-instatement of authority? This would result neither from a reform in ways of life, nor from an educational campaign to change people's outlooks, but rather from the dissolution of the Canadian political community and especially from a radical change in the economic and political regimes. Replacement of the currently dominant capitalistic liberalism by socialism would promote class mobility and cause a replacement of the ruling elite. The bourgeoisie would no longer hold the key posts in every area of activity. It would be replaced by the people, or at any rate by their most enlightened spokesmen.

On most of these points, social-democratic nationalism as professed in the Parti Québécois stands midway between socialism and liberalism, being even a shade closer to the latter. Thus, economic goals are given a high order of priority in the Parti Québécois. It was learned early and painfully that short-term economic considerations have an appreciable effect upon voting patterns, and consequently the party adjusted its policy proposals in every field. (This is the kind of thinking that prompted the unfortunate document, at the beginning of the 1973 provincial electoral campaign, outlining Québec's budget after Year I of independence!) Also as regards justice and equality, the Parti Québécois advances a number of measures aimed at a more equitable social and economic order, while at the same time in practice coming to terms with the current dominant institutions and often unwittingly and indirectly contributing to their consolidation. On the whole, the Parti Québécois would willingly go back to the glowing days of the Quiet Revolution. Through a well-thought-out program of nationalisation and through strict controls over the economy, the party would seek the advancement of the whole Québec community, but it is likely that, as happened even when the Quiet Revolution was at its best, the middle class would be the prime beneficiary.

In its position towards political authorities, social-democratic nationalism as practised in the Parti Québécois is far less radically negative than is socialist nationalism. It feels it has a capable shadow-cabinet, but one cannot escape the impression that the change-over would just substitute one set of leaders for another, without replacing a whole ruling class by another, as socialist nationalism would wish. The Parti Québécois lags far behind the labour unions' position on this point. These in fact denounce the collusion between leaders—for instance, a CNTU document is entitled *La Grande trickerie (The Big Hoax)*—and fight to obtain "power for the workers," without however specifying very clearly which social strata the phrase covers or excludes.

In a thorough analysis of his own Harris polls, Louis Harris shows that in the United States over the past ten years, mistrust of all authority, religious, business, labour, political, and so on, has greatly increased and that such mistrust is general, rather than confined to particular groups, such as young people. The situation in Québec is analogous. At times, rejection of authority even borders on civil disobedience, as when court injunctions are disregarded: for instance in the case of the medical specialists' strike in 1970, and of the Common Labour Front strike in 1972, which led to one-year prison sentences for the three labour leaders, Marcel Pepin, Louis Laberge, and Yvon Charbonneau. And the fact that this form of social-democratic nationalism strongly attacks established authorities for their selfishness and incompetence, seems to me to be one of the main reasons why it appeals to the people.

The Parti Québécois takes a far milder stand. It theoretically opposes every form of acquired class privilege. But, should it come to power, its inherent technocratic leanings would make it rely heavily on the various "experts" best capable of exercising authority in the light of the economic goals and criteria the party deems essential.

This analysis raises two general questions: the first is related to the ways in which socialist or social-democratic nationalisms might come to power and highlights the crucial issue of the use of violence; the second deals with the links between independentism and socialism, raising the problem of which comes first in time as well as in importance.

Replacing the current social and political order by a new one must be a primary objective for all those who believe that it can be superseded by a far better system. But should the change-over prove difficult or impossible to achieve within the liberal democratic framework, must the goal be set aside, temporarily or for good, or else must it be pursued at all costs, whatever methods are necessary, even including the use of terrorism?

The use of violence may be approached in tactical or in ethical terms. Social-democratic nationalists tend to see it as a moral issue, its tactical implications taking second place; most socialist nationalists see it the other way around.

The FLQ (Front de Libération du Québec) brought to light Québec's revoluntionary potential. From Montréal's first bombs in the spring of 1963, up to the kidnapping of diplomat James Cross and the kidnapping and assassination of Minister Pierre Laporte in October 1970—i.e. over a period of more than seven years—terrorism became a part of Quebeckers' daily lives; and whatever may happen in the future, it will no longer be possible to erase it from the people's collective memory. Malcolm Reid,[36] Marc Laurendeau,[37] and others have revealed the roots of political violence in Québec and have studied the FLQ's notorious career.

Much attention was devoted in *Parti pris* to the doctrine of violence and to the possible conditions of its application in Québec. The periodical gave birth to the Mouvement de libération populaire, immediate forerunner of the FLQ. The MLP proved too short-lived to put into effect the violence in favour of which it argued. But *Parti pris* also exercised an undeniable influence in elaborating the new view of history which, in the 1960s gave Chénier, a leader in the 1837 rebellion, the place of national hero formerly occupied by the seventeenth-century pioneer soldier Dollard des Ormeaux—a new historiography that markedly gained ground when Montréal's Saint-Jean Baptiste Society came to adopt it. However, in *Parti pris,* the debate tended to turn theoretically around the marxist-leninist views of violence and on the conditions warranting violence in Québec as a tactical weapon at the service of the working people.

The October 1970 crisis and the severe repression that followed it (the War Measures Act, the arrest and imprisonment of several hundred people, Québec's "occupation" by the Canadian army, the permanent curbs on civil liberties) brought this debate to an end, at least temporarily.[38] In a series of articles in *Le Devoir* in 1971, ex-FLQ thinker Pierre Vallières made a sharp turn-about, stating that circumstances in Québec were not revolutionary ones, and consequently that the use of violence would only harm the cause of socialist nationalism, bringing to bear upon it the concerted anger of established authorities, whose strength would only be consolidated by terrorism. Vallières concluded that legal methods were the only ones likely to succeed in current circumstances, and he urged independentists and socialists to join the Parti Québécois, whatever its present shortcomings. Vallières' analysis did not carry the day entirely; Charles Gagnon, a former comrade-at-arms, totally rejected it. In fact, most socialists appear to have refrained from joining the Parti Québécois. As to violence, most socialist nationalists' views seem to be that, even though Québec's political situation has, from a revolutionary viewpoint, gone from bad to worse since 1970, terrorism would today arouse even less sympathy among Quebeckers that it did in 1970.

On its part, the Parti Québécois has always believed that Quebeckers are not a violent people and that social-democratic nationalism's only path to success lies through integrative or legal methods of action rather than through divisive or subversive ones. It has tried to build up its electoral strength and to reinforce its electoral strategy on the complex checkerboard of constituency politics; it has concentrated on fighting resounding battles in the National Assembly, on using the whole range of legal public demonstrations, on mobilizing a wide cross-section of the people, on supporting other ideologically kindred social movements' struggle against the party in power, on attracting intellectuals, and so on. Having always believed that any electoral success would be jeopardized if it in any way seemed to side with terrorism, the Parti Québécois even preferred to alienate some sympathizers, whose allegiance was not felt to be worth the risk. But, despite all such efforts at respectability, opponents have always stood ready—at any opportune moment, such as the October 1970 crisis—to denounce the Parti Québécois as an ally or as a front to terrorist movements.

An analysis of socialist and of social-democratic nationalisms' case raises another general question, that of the relationship between independentism and socialism.

Nationalism has always posed a dilemma for theoretical socialism. While nationalism holds a "unanimist" view of society, all individuals and groups being held as part of the nation, socialism is class-oriented, and holds the view that while some classes (e.g. the proletariat) are "good" and should hold sway over others, the bourgeoisie are "bad" and should be excluded from the nation. While the interpreters of marxism-leninism have continued to split hairs over their masters' positions regarding the national issue, after the Second World War one people after another managed to meld doctrine and practice in their own way, and to win a long succession of revolutions in the name of both nationalism and socialism. It is the very absence of such a victory that causes lack of agreement in Québec on the proper linking-up of nationalism and socialism.

While all the spokesmen of socialist factions wish to see, on the one hand an independent, and on the other, a socialist or social-democratic Québec, they do not all attach the same meaning to these two goals nor do they work towards them both with the same degree of zeal.

May independence be achieved in one fell swoop or can it be arrived at by stages? Must it be entire, or can it be relative, possibly even resulting from an agreement with English Canada to give Québec a special status within a new Canadian Confederation?

And again, must the only socialism worth a struggle be "pure" marxism-leninism, or would a simple Scandinavian-type of social democracy be acceptable?

Similarly, if one of the two main goals must be given lower priority to ensure the success of the other, should the less favoured one be independence, or socialism?

These questions have aroused inside debate, often bitter, ever since the resurgence of separatism and socialism at the end of the 1950s. Quarrels, breakaways, short-lived or still-born tactical agreements have proliferated, often seeming to involve total enemies rather than warring brothers.

The tension inherent in any attempt to merge nationalism with socialism, in defining the nature of a national community, shows up strongly in

Québec. Nationalism aims at integrating the whole national community, whatever divergences may exist in the viewpoints and socio-economic positions of the "nationals"; on the other hand, socialism gives priority to socio-economic factors, and may even see certain classes, notably the French-Canadian capitalist bourgeoisie, as "anti-national" and thus unworthy of becoming included in the new nation, short of giving up all class privileges and agreeing to put every talent at the service of the people's revolution—as was in fact done willy nilly in Russia, China, and Cuba. How, in today's Québec, is the tension to be resolved between nationalism's all-inclusive tendencies, and some of the socialist factions' attempts to rekindle the class struggle?

The Parti Québécois wishes to provide a meeting ground for left-wing viewpoints, but there seems to be no possible common ground, at least ideologically, between its own brand of social democracy and marxist-leninist socialism. Thus the Parti Québécois is itself nowhere near achieving the difficult merger between nationalism and socialism. It tries to arrive at some form of tactical unanimity at least, but has difficulty in polarizing the various groups, some of which emphasize political, others cultural, and still others economic factors. In its attempt to find a common denominator, the Parti Québécois is failing to gain the support of an as-yet undetermined number of people and of groups, because it is perceived either as an insufficiently independentist, or else as an ineffectually socialist party.

Guy Rocher wonders whether "the necessary socialism will prove possible." He aptly writes: "Hoping for political independence polarizes a lot of energies: should Québec soon become independent, the absence of left-wing political thought and of a socialist movement will be sorely felt. . . . The second goal, that of achieving a Québec brand of socialism, is more difficult to present and defend because it is less popular, it comes up against stronger resistance among the people, save in rather limited circles—and doubtless because it amounts to a fairly radical break with Québec's ancient and recent past."[39] But nowhere in his essay does Guy Rocher specify the kind of socialism he would wish to see in Québec. Does he favour a "home-grown" socialism as advocated by Fernand Dumont, a socialism which would reshuffle the ancient loyalties of French-Canadian traditional society in accordance with today's circumstances, or does he envisage trotskyism, marxism-leninism, or social democracy? The range of choices, alone, already indicates some of the problem's complexity.

Ramsay Cook clearly understands this:[40] the inherent tensions can only be released through an existing state or at least through a party capable of taking power. Such a state does not yet exist, but the party has been around for the past six years, for the Parti Québécois clearly fills the bill. Its ways of achieving success, the compromises it must accept on the way, the kind of merger that will ultimately ensue between nationalism and socialism in Québec for the moment remain unknown; but we can already hazard the guess that it will take shape in some form of social democracy with a strong liberal tinge.

c. Social-democratic nationalism, socialist nationalism, and politics   The political dimensions of the various forms of social-democratic nationalism and socialist nationalism stand out even more clearly than they do in the case of conservative nationalism and liberal nationalism. This is especially obvious when we look at what is expected of the political system and what support is given to it. Here again, it is important to distinguish between socialist and social-democratic nationalisms.

Socialist nationalism places no demands upon the established political system, save one: that it should do away with itself as a political community (although some of the marxist-leninist movements do not favour Québec's independence and would willingly join hands with their English-speaking counterparts in the rest of Canada), that it should dismiss the current political authorities, and radically change the whole regime. Since these nationalist spokesmen are well aware that the existing political system is unlikely to fulfill such "demands," they put forward the ground rules of an alternative political system which would meet their political, cultural, and economic requirements.

In the case of social-democratic nationalism, upheld by the Parti Québécois, the expectations are less clear cut. But, unless the Parti Québécois gives up basic parts of its platform, the express aim regarding the political community is its breakdown and subsequent replacement by a politically independent Québec. However, as one reads the party's program and manifestoes, or follows electoral debates such as the one during the October 1973 campaign and current discussions, it becomes evident that the scope, the form, and even the stages of this independence are still far from clear. (Some of the proposed approaches—most recently, Claude Morin's paper on the steps to political sovereignty in the event of the Parti Québécois' electoral victory—lead one to believe that the party's strategists lean but lightly on the people's pressing will "to make a choice," instead relying heavily upon the good will and the patience of the federal government and of English Canada!)

As to the political regime, it is also difficult to evaluate how far the Parti Québécois would push to replace the current neo-liberalism, should it gain the opportunity to implement its own brand of social democracy. One feels that, once in power, the party would continue along the welfare state lines that marked the best days of the Quiet Revolution, particularly if René Lévesque is still in power, after having led the Parti Québécois since its inception, and having been an influential minister in the Lesage government. Such a development seems more likely than do strictly socialist reforms, or even milder measures modelled after the British Labour party. The Parti Québécois' platform, as well as the declared intentions of its leaders, are particularly cautious as to reforms of the political regime. It would seem that Quebeckers are far more open to change in the political community than in the regime.

Finally, should social democracy come to power with the Parti Québécois, there would certainly be changes among political leaders, as happens whenever an opposition party replaces the ruling party; but it is doubtful whether this would involve extensive upheaval among elites. In the 1973 provincial election, the Parti Québécois candidates were personally, socially, and economically far more akin to Liberal candidates than in the 1970 election; and unless, as is always possible, a change occurs in the party line, these similarities are bound to be even more marked the next time around. Furthermore, the Parti Québécois' acceptance of current democratic institutions and rules, the importance its leaders attach to economic considerations, and the party's technocratic leanings, all suggest that its form of social democracy could be put into effect without introducing notable changes in the kinds of people who make up the establishment: whether legislators, civil servants, ministers, or judges.

Although the Parti Québécois' erosion of positive over-all support for the political system, particularly for the regime and the authorities, is far less marked than in the case of socialist nationalism, its extent is nevertheless quite significant. This erosion manifests itself by an "absence" of support, which certainly affects the rulers' ability to mobilize energies and resources and also has repercussions on how the Canadian political system functions as a whole. Thus, political authorities have to expend supplementary energy in order to compensate for lack of support, particularly among the intellectuals, notably by efforts to neutralize separatist influence by means of ubiquitous "pan-Canadian" counter-propaganda; by surveillance of separatist and socialist activities; by less pliability to demands from the rest of the country, to prevent any possible spread of the Québec "disease"; by repression of any attempts to radical opposition, and so on. Indeed, the political authorities may be tempted, as in fact happened in October 1970, to temper or even to renege on liberalism in order to save the Canadian political community as it now exists and also to maintain themselves in power.

It is not only the federal government which is affected by social-democratic and socialist nationalisms' absence of support for the Canadian political system. The repercussions of course also affect the Québec government. We see a significant trend among most Québec groups, from employers' associations, the Québec's Bishops' Conference, the Mouvement national des Québécois, through to labour unions and citizens' groups. In fact, all major forms of social organization in Québec tend more and more to fall back on the Québec government and, even though some of them strongly favour federalism, for practical purposes they consider Québec as their main if not only, political reference system. But while certain groups, such as Le Conseil du patronat (an employers' organization), and the Conference of Québec Bishops, support Canada's current political framework, others question it, and still others reject it.

The opposition of social-democratic nationalism and of socialist nationalism to the established political system is as much directed at the provincial as at the federal government; it may indeed prove, as foreshadowed in the October 1970 events, that the provincial government constitutes the weaker link in the chain. On the other hand, although the Parti Québécois' elected representatives sit in the National Assembly it does not necessarily follow that the party is being seduced into accepting the current political community; for its actions are largely governed by tactical considerations. It has, however, chosen to abide by the rules of democracy. It hopes one day to be able to take power under these rules. It would then be in a position to displace the current political system without wreaking havoc in the generally accepted rules of legitimacy; this would help to launch an independent State of Québec amid a people considerate of authority and order. As a recognized opposition party and a realistic contender for power, the Parti Québécois is a conditional and organic organization: organic, because it is officially recognized by the existing political authorities, and conditional, because it only operates within the system, hoping thus to gain a chance of dissolving it legitimately. Other organizations, such as many political action citizens' groups take much more negative positions towards the political system because they are unconditional and non-organic; that is, they are not officially recognized by the established political authorites and want to have no dealings with them.

This outline has, I hope, helped to bring out the great diversity of views covered by social-democratic and by socialist nationalisms. These views are indeed sometimes so contradictory that were it not for their common opposition to conservative nationalism, old and new, and to the liberal nationalism embodied in the Bourassa government, they could be viewed as belonging to opposite camps. Only the circumstances of the struggle have forced them or will force them to compromise with each other and to conclude tactical alliances. On the other hand, apart from the marxist-leninists, practically all left-wing groups accept the Parti Québécois as a temporary framework for action. This is in large measure due to the personality of René Lévesque, leader of the Parti Québécois from the time of its founding. He has managed to maintain stature and charisma, despite the inroads of time, and has, throughout, successfully balanced the conflicting claims of independence and of socialism, a balance expressed in the manifesto *Quand nous serons vraiment chez nous* (when we are really on our own). Thanks to the integrative approach and to the methods of action adopted by the Parti Québécois, it is now the only political organization able to rally around social democracy not only the relatively small group of progressives but also an appreciable part of Québec's population, that is of the "silent majority" from whom a ruling party must draw its strength.

Yet, it is at the same time quite true that intellectuals and left-wing organizations feel somewhat ill at ease in the Parti Québécois. They criticize it for sacrificing doctrine to electoralism. The Parti Québécois' tacticians answer that—to avoid falling back into the splendid isolation of unassailable doctrinal purity, which can never develop a praxis suitable for Québec—such radical support, if only temporary, of the Parti Québécois' efforts is indispensable. The Parti Québécois' policy makers also claim it to be the only party at present attractive to young people, to unionized labour, and to the many political action groups who feel less and less at home with Robert Bourassa's government, or who are openly struggling against it. They express the hope that Québec's left-wing intellectuals will soon learn to choose between positions beautifully elaborated on paper, and perhaps less coherent but definitely more practical approaches, of use in helping to introduce a new regime. The struggle for the survival of the French language, cultural development, mastery over the economy, political reform—all these tasks will, they claim, require a tough common stand by all the left-wing opposition forces. This is especially true if it is at the same time necessary to set up a new political community, and to reform the regime, despite the certainly tenacious resistance of the political authorities and of other leaders in every sphere of activity in Québec, in Canada, and even in the United States.

d. The political functions of social-democratic and of socialist nationalisms Both the older and some newer forms of conservative nationalism have roots in pre-industrial society. Liberal nationalism grew out of the industrial society which it blesses and upholds. As to social-democratic and socialist nationalisms, at any rate in their social aspects, I feel them to fit into the context of post-industrial society. Alain Touraine,[41] Daniel Bell,[42] and others have shown that post-industrial society is much more than the passage from a manufacturing economy to a service economy; it is at the same time, and primarily, the birth of a new culture, concerned with the quality of life rather than with economic growth.

If neither social-democratic nor socialist nationalisms were to provide the leaven for a new and improved synthesis of culture with economic and political activity, adapted to the requirements of a world thirsting for values, it would hardly seem worth-while to devote oneself to promoting their cause.

Yet it is obvious that this new nationalism of the left manages, in Guy Rocher's apt words, "to reverse the outlook in man's favour,"[43] and dares at last to cross the painful thresholds leading towards personal and collective self-determination, this great utopia of the contemporary world whose outlines I have sought to provide elsewhere.[44] In a self-determined society, everyone's participation in all activities that affect both individual and collective well-being will cease to be a simple electoral slogan, and will become deeply embodied in institutions, turning into a permanent datum of political life.

It seems difficult to challenge the social ideology component of social-democratic nationalism and particularly of socialist nationalism, even though the expressions "social democracy" and "socialism," invented to reflect nineteenth-century experience, may not provide a very adequate image of today's social reality. But the national-ideology component, independentism, presents more of a problem. In a context of world-wide interdependence, is not the time of natural sovereignties past, as many people claim? Would not Québec's push towards independence be a retrograde step? Would it run counter to history's unfolding?

"Interdependence" and "sovereignty" are fashionable expressions, descriptive of very real and long-lasting situations. However, having become labels, they may disguise unattractive truths. Not to mince words, I feel the same rejoinder applies in their instance, as does to the splendid label of "equality": in the great game of interdependence and of sovereignty, some are more interdependent and more sovereign than others.

The striking fact is that it is generally the most powerful nations who most willingly refer to interdependence, whereas the smaller nations fall back on sovereignty. What common measure is there between the United States' government, with its annual budget of more than $400 billion, and that of Haïti, whose national revenue lies far below that of the international corporations doing business in the little country? President Kennedy could check-mate for a time the American steel potentates because he had the means to do so; the Duvalier presidents of Haïti, father and son, though dictators at home, nevertheless behave obsequiously towards foreign investors who are the source of the country's bread-and-butter. Hence, when the United States speaks of interdependence, this in practice turns out to be a defence of their right to practise economic imperialism, and consequently political and cultural imperialism, towards smaller nations. And whenever these take a closer look at the realities masked by words, they soon come to realize that, in its full social and political context, the term "interdependence" for them means submission to the imperialism of the more powerful nations, while "sovereignty" represents little more than a set of symbols.

The arguments generally put forward in favour of the interdependence of nations carry little conviction to my mind.

Take the most frequently used argument, that of the integrative effects of technology. Since the impact of technological development is largely similar everywhere, on the surface at any rate, people hastily conclude that a world super-culture is developing, allegedly wiping out the diversity of particular national cultures. Referring to such "trends" with his usual impetuousity, Edgar Morin goes so far as to speak about the world "anthropolitics" or "anthrocosmopolitics," based upon the first "collective awareness of humanity ever experienced by human-kind." There is no doubt that, under the effect of science, technology, and innovation, people's ways of life are becoming more and more comfortable. Such similarities cannot however lead one to conclude that a world-wide super-culture is emerging, to swallow or annihilate individual cultures, political regimes, and economic entities. Other influences, stemming from culture, politics, and economics, may and indeed do run counter to the converging trends that admittedly do exist. There are today several dozen social indicators that facilitate comparisons between more than one hundred different countries. We see that these countries, close to each other when measured by the yardstick of several such indicators, nevertheless have radically different cultural, political, and economic systems. The impact of non-technological factors is also reflected in the fact that these countries, appreciably similar in terms of certain quantitative indices, are quite far apart in terms of indices that involve qualitative or cultural choices. Thus Japan and Spain in 1960 had roughly the same per-capita gross national income; however Spain's number of hospital beds per inhabitant was three times smaller than Japan's.

Such similarities and differences between civilizations and peoples retain a tinge of mystery. The more we uncover the secrets of ancient civilizations, the more we are amazed at their parallel achievements. And yet how could the men of these ancient civilizations, so remote in time and space, have established any contact with each other—short of methods of communication totally outside our ken? The parallels are not mere trifles; rather, they are productions of a complexity that does not cease to amaze us, despite our frequent claim to so-far unexcelled knowledge. Mummification existed not only in ancient Egypt, but also among the Aztecs and Ancient Chinese. Megalithic monuments, famous in Britain and Britanny, have even more striking counterparts in the Deccan, in Punjab, Pakistan, Ceylon, Korea, and the Easter Islands since they often take there the form of man-shaped stones.

Technology only partly accounts for man's achievements. The human mind's curiosity and ingenuity always outdo our expectations. Men of all time have always preferred health to disease, abundance to penury, virility to powerlessness, freedom to slavery, life to death. And it is to give these elementary preferences a shape meaningful in their own eyes and, it is hoped, in the eyes of all generations to come, that they created religions and engaged in astrology, mathematics, physics, biology, chemistry, and similar pursuits.

While ancient civilizations never cease to astound us by their similarities, it is today right and proper, in a world allegedly heading towards homogenization, to emphasize the still-extant and basic differences between peoples who constantly rub shoulders and who, by means of the worldwide tentacles of a common technology, are daily exchanging values, goods, and services of all kinds.

There is a second argument, based on the integrating effects of technology, being advanced in favour of the necessary interdependence of nations. I refer to the homogenizing effect of the modern way of life. Whether in culture, economics, or politics, each community that steps out onto the path to modernity ultimately gathers the same fruit, sometimes delicious, sometimes bitter. This homogenizing influence of modernity seems undeniable. And yet here again, I tend to believe that such obvious truths mislead one into false conclusions. While it is true that, today, all peoples tend to share the same problems, it is nevertheless up to each society, on the one hand to contribute to the joint work of finding internationally valid solutions to common problems, and on the other hand to invent its own solutions to the specific shapes that common problems adopt in different sets of circumstances—while at the same time also dealing with its own separate, specific problems, which still subsist even in our era of planetary interaction.

It is not only to offset prevailing ideas that I emphasize the similarities between ancient civilizations, and differences between current ones. I feel that a detached observation of fact—namely of the unifying effects of technology—has nevertheless produced a mistaken conclusion: the disappearance of differences between cultures and peoples. Bringing out these differences is absolutely essential. In fact, how else can the idea of sovereignty be justified, if not on the basis of lasting differences between peoples, differences felt to be worth-while despite the ever more numerous and stronger networks of links created by technology and by economic and cultural exchanges?

Here we touch on a crucial question: why in the world, in the Common-Market era, do France and Germany remain, and intend to remain, two separate nations and people? Why do some basic differences between the USSR, Japan, and the USA continue to grow, even though these countries' technology is becoming increasingly similar?

In order to account for such phenomena, I should like to examine the following hypothesis: the reason why the integrating effects of technology, of closer economic links, and more generally of modernity, leave room for fundamental differences between peoples, is that each national society has its own special ways of achieving a synthesis—or a symboisis—between culture, politics, and economics.[45]

Québec's premier, Robert Bourassa, has been making ambiguous statements about interdependence and sovereignty. On the one hand he finds it unthinkable that, in the North American context, Québec should claim any real political sovereignty, the networks of interdependence being as all-pervasive as the recent oil crisis showed once again. But at the same time, the premier advocates "cultural sovereignty" though it can only acquire real meaning if Québec becomes far more politically and economically independent than Mr. Bourassa would wish. Independentists, who desire cultural sovereignty no less or more than he does, believe that it can only be achieved in a politically independent Québec. They cannot in logic be denied, and as shown in my long digression on interdependence and sovereignty, neither history nor current trends can be used to invalidate their arguments.

In both of their ideological facets, the social and the national, the social-democratic and the socialist forms of nationalism thus seem to me capable of producing an appropriate definition of Quebeckers' current situation. This then may be the end-product of a long search for collective identity, still pursued today with so much heat if not lucidity. For example, we see our educated youngsters turning to "joual" (which Frère Untel, (Brother Anonymous), in the early 1960s, had wanted to vanquish once and for all) since they find in it a symbol of collective identification and a tool for communication between members of the same culture.[46] Among all the current socialist or social-democratic movements, it is still the Parti Québécois that seems most likely to bring this new culture to the light of day, a new culture adapted to the circumstances of post-industrial society, with its scientific research, its computers and electronics, its need for personal and collective security, its fearsome dangers of pollution, urban congestion, the depletion of non-renewable resources, the reign of super-bureaucracies, and so on—into which Québec is fast plunging, but in circumstances that are specifically its own.

However, the Parti Québécois will only be able to fulfil the difficult political mission which many of its supporters entrust to it, if it manages to become a popular party, democratic both at the leadership and at the grass roots level, and if it overcomes the technocratic leanings that are currently jeopardizing its usefulness. Should it fall into the gaping technocratic trap, it would at best amount to no more than another Liberal party, and at worst, would turn into "techno-demagoguery," an expression I first used in *Société et politique: La vie des groupes*. The fact that the Parti Québécois has become a significant political force in Québec does not mean the end to the struggle for national and social liberation. But it is a clarion call for the supporters of social-democratic nationalism as well as of socialist nationalism: the time has come to wake up and to act. If the tool does not fit the task ahead, then the time is ripe to fix it or to forge another.[47]

B. HYPOTHESES AND CONCLUSION

Nationalism has been associated with so many monstrous experiments over the last fifty years that discredit has fallen upon it. But such discredit in fact only touches the "old" nations where, between 1815 and 1945, nationalist fervour sometimes reached the pitch of a cult. It does not involve the "young" nations, which have fully awakened since 1945 and where nationalism thrives. In fact, the real question about nationalism is not so much that of its objective truth—an ideology does not lend itself to assessment by this criterion, which only fully applies to science—as that of its ability to reflect the situation of a community, which we call a people or a nation, and to give political shape to the hopes and the fears of individuals and of groups who, all together and in their multiple interactions, make up the body politic.

A nation may be considered as a community of communities. The nation is an organic entity of goals and resources. That is why a systematic study of any nationalism must go beyond the society's cultural facets and must symbiotically cover economics and politics as well. In fact every nationalism incorporates two ideological frameworks, different but closely intertwined: a basically national framework, incorporating the values related to the collective "we," and a social framework, incorporating the values related to the community's economic and political organization. This double framework of course fluctuates with time, depending upon circumstances and upon changes in institutions and outlooks.

In my analysis I have tried to provide a picture of Québec's nationalisms, rather than to develop a theoretical tool. But an embryonic tool did take shape as the analysis proceeded, and it proved highly useful along the way. It would, in concluding, be tempting to enlarge on my initial comments in the light of possible theoretical increments acquired in the writing; but I shall resist the impulse, and abide by my initial goal of bringing out some salient points and weighing their impact upon Québec's nationalisms. In this way, I shall first deal with the relations between Québec nationalisms and politics; then with the respective roles assigned to the elites and to the mass in experiencing and expressing nationalist ideologies; and finally, I shall attempt an evaluation of the over-all scope and importance of Québec nationalisms.

1.   Nationalisms and politics

The fact that Québec's nationalisms tend to be perceived as apolitical arises, I believe, from the use of criteria which inevitably limit study to the interactions between nationalism and the existing political system, whether federal or provincial. Seen in this way, Québec nationalisms only took on a truly political cast during the short periods between 1960 to 1964, and 1966 to 1968. Indeed, during these few years, identification occurred between the dominant nationalist representations and the established political system. On the other hand, from 1965 to 1966 and again from 1969 until the time of writing, our governments officially continued to abide by liberal nationalism. But the national dimension is waning, and the official liberalism is gradually turning into a new kind of conservatism, this shift being perhaps the most significant development on the current political scene in Québec. As demonstrated earlier, every nationalism consists of two ideologies, different but closely interwoven: a national and a social ideology. It is precisely the duality and the closeness of the ideologies which makes a study of the interaction between nationalism and politics at once so complex and so rewarding.

We have examined four expressions of Québec's nationalism: a conservative and traditionalist nationalism which, in most of its forms, is circumscribed by a qualified acceptance of the Canadian political community and is based on a pre-industrial society, giving a strongly corporatist tinge to the desired political regime; a liberal nationalism which also gives qualified support to the Canadian political community but fully commits itself to the welfare state concept and wholeheartedly endorses modern urban and industrial society; a social-democratic nationalism, whose national ideology favours independence and hence the rejection of the Canadian political community, and whose social ideology aims at the social and economic advancement of the entire Québec community; finally a socialist national-

ism which, broadly speaking, has the same national goals as social-democratic nationalism but which, in its social aspects, especially in its marxist-
leninist version, aims at thorough-going revolution.

It is difficult to evaluate the real measure of support these various forms
of nationalism have among the population. Even though conservative nationalism has given birth to many social movements, no political party has
ever adequately conveyed its ideas. Its disapproval of political factions left
little room for necessary compromise. Conservative nationalism is of
course correctly associated with Alexandre Taschereau's and Maurice Duplessis' long periods in power, even though both men approached politics
pragmatically rather than ideologically and even though they supported the
reigning laissez-faire in North America. But Taschereau, and Duplessis
after him, used the themes of conservative nationalism to their own advantage, often bending them to fit their needs, as happened in particular to the
themes of autonomism, clericalism, agriculturalism, and ethnocentrism.

Maxime Raymond's and André Laurendeau's Bloc Populaire drew upon
the national ideology of conservative nationalism, but went counter to its
social ideology in promoting a number of social-democratic ideas. At the
opposite pole, the Canadian Social Credit party never went along with the
national ideology of conservative nationalism, but became a lively pro-
moter of its social creed. The Québec Ralliement des Créditistes came
closer to the positions of conservative nationalism both in its national and
in its social ideologies, and Yvon Dupuis' failure to understand this de-
stroyed his chances in the 1973 provincial elections. However, in assessing
links between the Ralliement des Créditistes and conservative nationalism
we must remember that the party's ideology is directed at two specific con-
stituencies: the urban lower middle class, and farming communities. In
other words, the ideology of the Ralliement is associated with the second
and third strata of conservative nationalism's followers, namely the local
and regional "notables" and the mass of the people, and not with the intellectuals and the upper elite who created and who were the official spokesmen of conservative nationalism.

As to liberal nationalism, it was identified with Jean Lesage's government from 1960 to 1966 and with Daniel Johnson's government from 1966
to 1968. It is then that a symbiotic relationship, commonly called the Quiet
Revolution, developed between nationalism and politics. Québec's governments in that period went farthest in battling for Québec's claims, and
in pursuing the ideals of the neo-liberal welfare state. However, the symbiosis between liberal nationalism and politics started wearing thin during
the Lesage government's last year in office, while under Jean-Jacques Bertrand and Robert Bourassa it has dwindled to vanishing point. Under
Bourassa, the priority given to economics has stifled national aspirations,
the slogan of "cultural sovereignty within a profitable federalism" being
empty of real meaning; and so the autonomist leanings of men like Claude
Castonguay, minister of social affairs from 1971 to 1972, or like Jean-Paul

l'Allier, minister of communications since 1970, have been doomed to failure from the start.

Social-democratic nationalism (which for the time being also polarizes several other forms of socialism) has its own political party, the Parti Québécois. It rejects both the existing political community and the regime, and clearly defines itself in terms of an alternative political system. As long as the Parti Québécois remains a major political force in Québec (it collected 30 percent of the vote, including more than 40 percent of the French-Canadian vote, although it only managed to get six out of 110 seats in the National Assembly in the October 1973 provincial elections) one may assume it will continue to polarize most of the many splinter groups into which the spokesmen of socialist nationalism are divided. Its chances of one day taking power democratically cannot be set aside; and this would amount to a radical revolution, since, in principle at any rate, it would entail a break-up of the Canadian political system as well as adjustments in the liberal regime whose extent it is as yet difficult to gauge.

An attempt to weigh the electoral backing likely to be given to Québec nationalisms is no easy task. How can one know, for instance, whether a given form of nationalism can ever of itself assure the victory or the defeat of a political party? How a person votes is usually determined by a gamut of complex factors: the party label, the leader's personality, the circumstances, the platform, all of which barely border on ideology. And yet it is striking to notice how abundant nationalistic slogans have always been throughout Canada's political history.

The symbolism of a slogan such as "Duplessis gives to his Province, while the Liberals give to foreigners"—a slogan that served as one of the leitmotifs of the 1956 provincial campaign which brought Duplessis back to power with a crushing majority of seats—evokes a number of the typical themes of conservative nationalism: worship of the leader, ethnocentrism, autonomism. Nevertheless, it cannot be considered to have been instrumental in ensuring the Union Nationale's victory.[48] On the other hand, Bourassa's theme "cultural sovereignty within a profitable federalism," forged in December 1972, was for all practical purposes set aside during the October 1973 electoral campaign, because the party strategists felt this slogan could push Québec into the kind of "positive" autonomism which Bourassa had no intention of entertaining. Under different circumstances, Daniel Johnson had decided to downplay his slogan: "Independence if necessary, but not necessarily independence," because he realized the formula could lead Québec onto the slippery slope towards political independence, which he considered premature or impractical even though he sometimes felt personally drawn to it.

Partisan slogans are more than mere words intended to help mobilize potential voters. They reveal the tone of a political culture, they represent bridges between those who define the national situation and the men of action who must find the symbols and expressions required to maintain communication between the people and themselves. Both during and between electoral campaigns, political parties must try to keep their hold on people and to get support for their projects; and so must attempt, with varying degrees of success, to find among the stock of nationalist representations, the evidence, the justifications, and the lessons that will serve their ends. Whether we think of the Union Nationale until 1960 and, though differently, of the Parti Créditiste and the Ralliement des Créditistes with respect to conservative nationalism; whether we look at the Québec wing of the federal Liberal party or at the Québec Liberal party, or at the Union Nationale under Daniel Johnson, with respect to liberal nationalism; whether we consider the Parti Québécois in regard to social-democratic nationalism—all Québec's political parties broadly draw upon one or another form of nationalism in their platforms, their electoral slogans, and also in justifying their actions and decisions when they are in power. In any event, this is an assumption that deserves further critical study.

Whereas nationalism, which is a means of expressing people's expectations, has definite repercussions on a political system's legitimacy and on its ability to mobilize resources and to function effectively—that is not the sole contribution or hindrance it furnishes to a political system. National ideology also influences the way in which the members of the political system perceive that system, and consequently affects their attitudes towards it. Seen in this way, the various forms of Québec nationalism are as many ideological expressions of the efforts made by Quebeckers to adjust, whether positively or negatively, both to the Canadian political framework and to the liberal and capitalistic North-American context.

Hence autonomism may be recognized as a consistent factor in Québec's political history. There is a clear continuity between the slogans of Alexandre Taschereau and Maurice Duplessis: *Qu'Ottawa nous redonne notre butin,* Jean Lesage's Liberal motto, *Maîtres chez nous,* and René Lévesque's Parti Québécois slogan, *Quand nous serons vraiment chez nous.*[49] Similarly, on another level, there is continuity between the old doctrine of "a Confederative pact" enshrined in the 1956 Report of the Tremblay Constitutional Commission, the two-nations theory of the 1960s, and René Lévesque's idea of "sovereignty-association" in 1968. On the other hand, there tend to be sharp discontinuities between the official positions regarding the socio-political regime. Until 1960, these featured a rejection of industrialization and urbanization, and acceptance of laissez-faire; but since then they have firmly supported up-dating Québec to industrial and welfare state standards. However, this contrast between two ideological orientations concerning the regime betrays, through the very forms in which they are expressed, not only the ideological discontinuity itself, but also the deep, underlying historical continuity of Québec society.

The profound rift in time that split Québec nationalisms is thus not so much centred around national ideology (even though independentism is not just an extreme form of autonomism, as some would claim on the sole strength of the Parti Québécois, an example in some ways, atypical, as, rather, around social ideology). What common ground can there be between the motely collection of native socio-political laissez-faire views, enlivened by equally native corporatism in the 1930s and 1940s—and the Parti Québécois' form of social democracy which fully accepts modernity and the North American context? Not to mention the more or less radical forms of socialism propounded in the diverse marginal groups that mostly gravitate around the Parti Québécois?

Nationalism influences political systems through its impact upon political ends: authority, change, participation. It must of course be remembered that nationalism, as an ideology, both reflects conditions as they exist in actual fact in the various fields of social reality: ecology, demography, technology, economics, social stratification, culture, and politics—and also that it is a construct in its own right, in turn affecting the whole of the social fabric.

Thus, conservative nationalism, whose concept of authority derives as if from divine right, resists whatever change runs counter to tradition, and only accepts participation by members of the political system to the extent to which it confirms the dominance of the ruling elites. Unlike it, liberal nationalism employs a concept of change which accommodates the promises of modernity and which therefore also challenges the traditional notions of authority and participation. As to social-democratic and socialist nationalists, the ideal of participation may be expected to serve as a fulcrum for their activities. If successful, these would then reverse age-old ideas about the sacredness of personal authority, and would discredit the notion, dominant in Québec since 1960, that economic growth is the prime motor of change.

The ideological rifts revealed by comparing the four forms of Québec nationalism become even more distinct when we examine the reasoning processes and the standards of judgement underlying all political choice.[50]

The end-goals of conservative nationalism are primarily cultural. They mainly flow from French Canadians' will to survive as a specific ethnic group, with its own religion and ancestral traditions, which are seen as its distinctive features. Purely political goals, say in the context of parliamentary institutions, or the pursuit of economic goals are quite secondary, in comparison with the primary cultural goal. Frank Scott clearly expressed this when he wrote:

The English Canadian sees democracy as a form of government where the popular will is expressed in a Parliament elected periodically. He believes in universal suffrage, in equal rights for men and women, in freedom of speech and association, in a free press and in religious toleration. Democracy is for him . . . a method by which society may be constantly changed and improved. . . . The liberal tradition of the XIXth century has endowed him with a profound belief in civil liberties. . . . The French Canadians' experience with democracy has been quite different. He knew none of it under the old régime; what he learned of it came from his contact with the English; thus for him democracy became at once identified with his struggle to preserve his religion and his language. He used democracy as a tool rather than adhered to it as a doctrine. His Catholic upbringing made him more conscious of the duties and obligations of the individual than of his personal rights, and more ready to accept a hierarchical structure. He insists more strongly on group rights, in Canada called minority rights, than on individual liberties.[51]

Frank Scott's analysis is valid, provided it is taken as applying to a time largely past and provided one does not draw, as some people do, the conclusion that the "rehabilitation" of French Canadians must necessarily involve replacing their cultural end-goals, based on ancient values, by political end-goals imbued with the values of liberal democracy. Indeed it is towards this that many efforts were bent in the 1960s. Quebeckers then seemed on the way to acquiring a North-American approach to politics, one based on a democratic and liberal spirit strongly tinged with economic values. This has gone so far that it has today, under the Bourassa government, become a straightforward pursuit of economic goals, any left-over cultural goals apparently serving merely as window dressing. As to social end-goals, ever since Claude Castonguay's resignation, they seem virtually absent from any of the government's public pronouncements.

What we cannot know is the extent to which the economic viewpoint has become part and parcel of the thinking of the people and of community leaders in Québec. Support for this approach may be more apparent than real; it may be tied to Québec's relative economic prosperity since 1970, a prosperity which the Québec government attributes to its own "efficiency" and to the fact that it has given priority to economics over culture. But this is counting chickens before they are hatched. The culture of a people cannot be turned upside down in so short a span. Old values, like old habits, do not die overnight.

I thus wonder whether recent studies on Quebeckers' political culture, even John Meisel's important work,[52] do not fall victim to an optical illusion. Indeed, how can one adequately give an account of a political culture (not limited to a political party such as the Liberal party, for example), that is characteristic of all French Canadians if they are assessed in terms of the North American "civic culture" model—the very model which they explicitly rejected for so long while paying it the lip service required by their *de facto* integration into the Canadian political system? The "cultural vacuum," created in Québec since Trudeau's accession to power in Ottawa and Bourassa's in Québec, does not seem to me haphazard. I think it is due to the fact that there is no longer any official concern, as there was under Lesage and Johnson, to promote a native-born national and social ideology. Although such ideologies in the short run proved electorally disappointing, their real results could only have been gauged over the years. The hastily drawn conclusion was of the bread-and-circuses type—ruling by the carrot and the stick—on the assumption that today, as yesterday, people are undemanding about things social and cultural.

What emerges here is the potential importance of the Parti Québécois for French Canadians. A crucial task falls on its shoulders: will it contribute to giving a final political expression to Québeckers' own culture as we see it taking shape today among the songwriters, the artists, the trade unionists, the intellectuals, the citizens' groups, and the young people? That is the great, the only true challenge facing the Parti Québécois. Independence, social democracy, are only political reflections of the real problem, the problem that hinges on the will-to-be, the soul of a whole people. If this problem is to be answered in "liberal" terms, as the Parti Québécois sometimes seems tempted to do, it will first of all need to establish the economic advantages of independence for Quebeckers in accordance with "official" values and criteria, evidence of which cannot convincingly be mustered ahead of the event, as we were able to see during the October 1973 provincial elections.

The Parti Québécois must beware of the trap of "economism" and must not be ensnared by consideration of short-term electoral success. It must emphasize social end-goals, as expected of it by its more sophisticated supporters and as is proper for a society entering the post-industrial age.

2.   The role of the elites and the masses

The second point I consider it useful to raise is that of the relation between the elites and the masses in developing and promoting nationalism. The question of the nature of various nationalist beliefs, and of the changes they undergo from the time they are devised by intellectuals and acknowledged by elites, up to their dissemination throughout the various layers of society, raises a number of problems both epistemological and sociological, which philosophers have persistently raised since Plato's famous allegory of the cave, through Francis Bacon's theory of idols, up to the systematic examination of ideology as a particular mode of knowledge by Karl Marx, Karl Mannheim, and Robert K. Merton.

One of the most widespread ideas about French-Canadian or Québec nationalism concerns the elitism with which it is claimed to have been strongly imbued. This idea, so far based on rather vague assumptions, has now been more scientifically documented in Kenneth McRoberts' doctoral thesis, "Mass Acquisition of Nationalism: The Case of Québec Nationalism." McRoberts concludes from a series of surveys that, at least until the eve of the New Order in 1960, the masses were not very responsive to the autonomist messages of intellectual and political leaders. These autonomist messages provided a consistent thread running through conservative nationalism and subsequently, in a slightly different form, also through liberal nationalism. His logical conclusion is that Québec nationalism, at any rate until 1960, was largely characteristic of a relatively narrow elite, and that the masses remained apparently indifferent to all the ideological debates and federal-provincial political rivalries surrounding autonomism.

At the end of his thesis, McRoberts very relevantly wonders whether the analytical method he adopted, namely the study of surveys or polls, provides a tool capable of giving answers to the questions he raises. I would definitely claim it does not. On the one hand, the surveys used were not designed to bring out any of the interaction between the beliefs of the elites and those of the masses; on the other hand, his method of study led McRoberts to postulate a linear relationship between the beliefs held by the elite and those held by the people, as if the latter were necessarily an extension of the former, merely a bit watered-down. Now this may well not be the case. In the communications circuit linking elites and masses, and also in the process whereby the elite mobilizes the masses, ideology may undergo far-reaching changes, through rifts and breaks sufficiently serious to denature the ideology without altogether eliminating it. Similar phenomena of entropy appear in the communication of virtually every kind of knowledge from one stratum of society to another.

If political scientists used more sophisticated tools, we would doubtless far more clearly perceive, beyond changes in epistemological registers, the continuity that exists between ideologists' abstract formulations, interpretations by popularizers, and electoral slogans.

In an extensive study, Philip E. Converse showed on the one hand that ideologists only represent a minute part of the American public (some two percent) and, on the other hand, that the nature of beliefs undergoes changes in moving from the upper to the lower layers of society.[53] Similarly, the nature of the ideological support changes from one layer to another. Ideologists act upon their deeply-held beliefs. An intermediate layer of quasi-ideologists or popularizers, amounting to some ten percent of the public, expresses the ideologists' message and communicates it to the whole of the population; a third layer, some forty percent of the people, receives these messages as a result of belonging to various organizations; a fourth layer, some twenty-five percent, undergoes the influence of current events, whereas the remaining twenty-five percent seem to remain oblivious of all these currents and do not appear to react in any way to the ideologists.

It would appear that the mobilizing capacity of themes drawn from a particular form of nationalism depends, at any one time, upon the nature of the communication circuits, on the art of the communicators, and on the nature of the links between the various strata of society. As regards conservative nationalism, I earlier put forward the hypothesis that three-tiered communication circuits exist, namely that of the upper elite, that of the local and regional elites, and that of the masses. I also put forward the view that the local and regional elites, consisting of each small community's leading citizens, clerical and lay, represented the critical tier in the transfer or the communication of nationalist ideas. As regards liberal nationalism, social-democratic nationalism, and socialist nationalism, I hold the view that it is the secondary groups (labour unions, citizens' committees, employer organizations, political parties, and so on) which both relay and in their own way re-create ideology, thus constituting the critical tier in the dissemination of political culture. Thus, in our study of political cultures in Québec, we felt it appropriate to give special emphasis to this social stratum.

Those who seek, by surveys or otherwise, to determine the political culture of a national community on the basis of statistics and percentages drawn from individuals' answers, seem to me to be on the wrong track. Nationalism, like any pattern of symbolic representations, at any rate in its explicit structure, can only be meaningful to a minority of ideologists: philosophers, historians, sociologists, polemicists, political leaders, charismatic figures, and so on. The real questions that should then be asked concern the ways in which these ideas spread throughout the communication networks, from ideologists down to the mass of the people; this in turn requires an identification of the critical social strata in the process, and also an identification of the changes in the nature and the content of ideological themes at each stage. Further questions need to be asked about the mobility of elites in time and space, the incentives and constraints flowing from given institutions, and about the effects of fluctuations in prevailing living conditions.[54]

Thus the spread of social-democratic nationalism, and above all of socialist nationalism, seems to me to imply a far more people-based process than is true of liberal nationalism and particularly of conservative nationalism, both of which are essentially elite products. The basic ideology, the organizational framework as well as the real-life circumstances underlying some of the forms of socialist nationalism, if not necessarily the social-democratic nationalism embodied in the Parti Québécois, promote the creativity of individuals gathered together in grass-roots organizations such as citizens' committees, and backed up by the professional and ideological associations of which they are members; whereas in the case of liberal nationalism and still more in that of conservative nationalism, it is the political and intellectual elites which are the creators, promoters, and interpreters of nationalist ideas, transmitted to the people both by professional communicators, notably the mass media, and by the local and regional elites who watch over the people's welfare. However, in all cases (whether socialist nationalism or social-democratic nationalism, conservative or liberal nationalism) we observe both a committed minority and a more-or-less receptive majority; it is the sociological composition of the minority and majority that varies according to the type of nationalism considered.

3. The development of nationalisms

Finally, my last point deals with the nature and the extent of the influence Québec nationalisms have exercised upon society and politics. This influence cannot of course be quantitatively measured; but I have tried to arrive at a qualitative assessment. Here, I shall merely sumarize some of the key propositions drawn from my analysis, on the understanding that further work will still be required on them.

Both ancient and recent history show that, while it is always difficult to break up a political system, the task is by no means impossible. In counterpoint to the Biafra tragedy, we witnessed the splitting-up of Pakistan into two different countries, East Pakistan or Bangladesh, and West Pakistan. Since 1945, Germany, Korea, and Vietnam have also split from internal pressures and outside forces. It is, however, impossible to say *a priori* whether the break-up of a political system will enhance or deteriorate the quality of the life of persons and groups involved. The real question is how to determine the extent of the desire to separate within seceding areas, what efforts they are ready to make, and what sacrifices to accept in view of this goal. These cannot be guessed in advance.

Canada's survival, like that of any country, cannot be taken for granted. John Deutsch writes: "Among English-speaking Canadians, the attachment to a united Canada is primarily emotional; the discontents and fears are largely economic. Among French-speaking Canadians, the attachment to a united Canada is primarily economic; the discontents and fears are largely emotional."[55] Deutsch might have added that French Canadians, at any rate Quebeckers, only respond emotionally to their "patrie": the homeland, the land of their ancestors; and that for most of them, independentist or not, this homeland is Québec.

It is my hypothesis that of all Western liberal societies, it is Canada which is most threatened by break-up because of the internal contradictions it does not manage to solve. This view is based upon the direction in which Québec nationalism has been heading since 1940. Its influence was strongly integrative until 1960, and even the "separatist" trend in Québec conservative or traditionalist nationalism, for instance in Abbé Groulx's variety, never in actual fact followed through its logic to the very end, because of lack of self-confidence, and because of the far-reaching respect for established authority so characteristic of the followers of this brand of nationalism.

However, since 1960, the independentist wave has grown unremittingly; and it is the various forms of social-democratic and socialist nationalism which are the most outspoken vehicles of nationalism in present-day Québec. Even apart from the growing heaviness and complexity of government machinery and administrative procedures, it seems more difficult to govern Canada today than some fifty years ago. The development in Québec of a strong current of nationalism, which is at any rate in principle both independentist and socialist, will deprive the Canadian political system, both in Ottawa and in Québec, of part of the specific support and even of the diffuse support it has so far had among Quebeckers, save during times of crisis such as the Riel rebellion and the two conscription episodes.

Up to what point can the specific or the diffuse support of Quebeckers for the Canadian political system be thus reduced without precipitating the break-down of that system? The extent of this support was put to the test by the Parti Québécois in the July 1974 federal election, with results that seemed positive for the system, since the directive to spoil ballots was only followed by a tiny fraction of the voters. Quebeckers, independentists as well as others, continue to vote in federal elections, to pay their taxes, to take jobs in the federal civil service, in the RCMP, in the Canadian armed forces, and so on. Is it possible, in the North American context, to envisage a threshold of weariness, of disenchantment, or of anger beyond which a fair share of French-speaking Quebeckers might systematically engage in civil disobedience? The day may come when independentist leaders get a sizeable proportion of the citizens to share their view that Québec's integration in the Canadian political system leads to Francophone suicide (economic and political and not only cultural)[56] and when, at the same time, it will also appear increasingly improbable that Québec's separation could be achieved through the usual electoral channels.

The possible break-down of the Canadian political system could occur in several ways. It could arise out of Québec's political secession, or that of any other part of the country. It could also follow upon a serious crisis of the liberal regime in Canada, resulting, for instance, from an agreement between Québec socialists and those of other provinces, an agreement including the dismemberment of the Canadian political community. It might result from the play of electoral forces, but many other conditions might also cause such a break-down. A serious economic crisis, producing millions of discontented people, might trigger strong secessionist sentiments, the benefits accruing to the Parti Québécois. (Is it not after all one of the main arguments of federalists that the political status quo ensures the greatest measure of economic prosperity?) On the other hand, Quebeckers may come to wish for a new socio-political order. As Daniel Bell writes: "A new social system, contrary to Marx, does not arise necessarily within the shell of an old one but sometimes outside of it."[57]

But at the same time, and conversely, the capacity of the Canadian political system to resist inner stress is sometimes underrated. I do not believe that the reaction of the federal government and of the Québec government during the October 1970 crisis gives a reliable idea of the resilience of the Canadian political system. The soundness of a political system cannot be judged solely in terms of the quality of its instruments. The attitude of elites and of the people towards it must also be taken into account. In carefully reviewing distant and recent events, it seems to me that the will to maintain the Canadian political system is far stronger than most Québec independentists feel. However, all this still remains to be verified because so far, save for three major crisis, the Canadian political system has not yet had occasion to put the soundness of its various instruments to a real test, or to search the hearts and the inner soul of the people.

Another process, which I see as more significant than the previous ones, is under way. It consists of the growing polarization of political positions in Québec. The call to awareness (*branchisme*) and to commitment, addressed to individuals and to groups, urging them to choose whether they are federalists or independentists, represents a forerunner of such polarizations. Another forerunner may be seen in the demarkation, daily growing clearer, between liberals and socialists.

Underpinning such specific polarizations and encompassing them, we have since 1965 seen an ever-widening cleavage between the two great ideological modes that permanently subsist in politics: conservatism and progressivism. It is becoming ever more obvious that this last form of polarization is well under way and slowly but inexorably is leading Quebeckers into identifying themselves with one of two party lines. Indeed, Québec's Liberal party has gradually come to embody the conservative view, while the Parti Québécois alone seems capable of rallying progressives without forcing them to betray their convictions. (That, in fact, is the essential way in which the Parti Québécois seems to have fallen heir to the great era of the Quiet Revolution.)

The far-reaching changes in the Liberal party of Québec since 1965 would create a puzzle, if one were unaware of the fact that it is by mere force of circumstance that the party espoused liberal nationalism after the June 1960 provincial election. Already in 1965, national ideology was on the wane in the party, and since 1970, pragmatism and economic priorities have been the guiding light of its social ideology. Just like the Liberal party under Taschereau and the Union Nationale under Duplessis, Québec's Liberal party under Bourassa also seeks the unconditional support of the "silent majority." Jérôme Choquette was not mistaken when, on the eve of the October 1973 provincial election, he declared—perhaps unwittingly— that "Québec's Liberal Party from now on takes up the whole right."

There is, of course, no attempt by the Québec Liberal party to be conservative in the old style, as were the Taschereau and Duplessis regimes. It continues in general to abide by the principles of the welfare state, and still aims at consolidating and modernizing Québec. It is conservative, though, in the issues most closely touched by the great problems of the day: individual and collective security and justice, land use and rural and urban development, control over natural resources and over the main levers of the economy, education, and scientific research, the promotion of the French language, the Constitution, and so on. In these fields, the Liberal party generally favours the status quo, on the grounds that any change might be prejudicial to social peace, and particularly to the health of the economy which overrides all other considerations.[58]

For all sorts of reasons, tied to economics and to culture, a great conservative offensive has been unfurling in Québec since 1965. The repeated assaults of radical elements, of student youth in 1968, of the FLQ in October 1970, of the Common Labour Front in 1972, have one after the other broken up against the conservative wall, which they have on the other hand contributed to reinforcing well beyond the expectations of political agents—and notably of Premier Bourassa who thus finds himself perched on a slippery political slope, far more uncomfortable than he would have wished, since he sincerely wants to give a progressive image of himself and of his government and emphatically sees himself as a man of the left and his party as a ''social-democratically oriented one''!

This conservative offensive rests upon the support of the old liberal professions, of business leaders, and of the managers of small and middle-sized enterprise, of semi-skilled labour, and of farmers. The Liberal party has garnered practically all the benefits of this offensive. The Union Nationale, Québec's old conservative stronghold, has to all intents and purposes disappeared; Maurice Bellemare's return in the 29 August 1974 by-election in Johnson riding, even though significant for the man cannot be considered as a comeback for the party. As to the Ralliement des Créditistes, it has accumulated so many faux-pas that, if it did not exercise a very specific function of representing the views and needs of particular strata of society (a function which Vera Murray, following in Georges Lavau's footsteps, calls the *fonction tribunitienne*), (ombudsman function—for a fraction of the electorate only—of the MP), it would no longer even appear on the electoral map.[59]

A superficial glance at the situation might mislead one into believing that on the national as well as on the social fronts nothing has moved ahead in Québec since June 1972. Under the deceptively smooth surface, however, deep eddies show, in the hidden strata of society, that Québec is aboil. For the time being, the general impression is one of useless movement, so disparate and unco-ordinated do the forces of change seem. However, for reasons related to both economy and culture, progressive forces are willy-nilly more and more drawn into the wake of the Parti Québécois: students and teachers, journalists, artists, young professionals, the young managerial class, the trade-union leaders and officials, the under-privileged rural and urban groups, are all swept into the wake. In brief, even though the agents of change in the existing socio-political order are today opposed to each other in terms of interest and ideology, they no longer have any choice. Along among significant political parties, the Parti Québécois lends an ear to their clamour. Some would wish to see the party more radical. But its strategists, who legitimately pursue electoral goals, are trying to eliminate any ''leftism'' for fear of losing voters, a great majority of whom feel the influence of the conservative tide. Recent adjustments within the Parti Québécois have so affected it that one can no longer be sure that should this party one day come to power, it would resolutely pursue progressive policies. On the contrary, like the Québec Liberal party, it may also easily be drawn onto the slippery slope of neo-conservatism. However, for the time being at any rate, Québec progressives, whether federalist or independentist, liberal or socialist, have no other choice than to support the Parti Québécois if they want their desire for change to be expressed in political terms.

The political game in Québec today shapes up as follows. There is a Liberal party which officially stands by the creed of liberal nationalism, but unashamedly practises a form of electoral pragmatism that has thrown overboard the national or even social ideology which characterized it in 1960. The Union Nationale and the Ralliement des Créditistes maintain their marked autonomist leanings as well as a preference for the old-style conservatism whose electoral possibilities appear limited. The Parti Québécois shows sincerity in professing its brand of social-democratic nationalism, even though electoral pressures may lead it to adjustments in its national and in its social ideology whose extent is as yet unforeseeable.

If that is the way the cards continue to stack up, a decisive confrontation may shortly develop between conservative and progressive elements in Québec. The final victory of one side or the other depends upon then-prevailing circumstances which we cannot as yet know. Will we see a repeat of 1936 developments, when the provincial elections first brought to power the Union Nationale, born in 1935 of a coalition between the Action Libérale Nationale (a group of dissident Liberals under Paul Gouin) and Québec's Conservative party led since 1933 by Maurice Duplessis—an election won on a platform of liberal nationalism that Duplessis was to betray in less than a year? Or rather, shall we see a different-scale version of the events which followed the June 1960 election, bringing to power, again under the banner of liberal nationalism, the first progressive team Québec had ever had since Confederation? And should a progressive team again be victorious, will it be independentist and social-democratic, or on the contrary, will the Parti Québécois meanwhile have had to moderate its platform in order to gain the support of a sufficient number of voters?

History, it is said, never repeats itself, but if we examine the range of political ideologies conveyed by the current nationalisms—a traditionalist conservatism still rife, though weak in party support; a liberal nationalism empty of ideological élan but retaining a strong party base; a social-democratic nationalism conveyed by one party, the Parti Québécois, which has not yet firmly staked out its ideological territory, and a socialist nationalism still seeking a mode of expression suited to Québec society—we cannot fail to observe a marked polarization between the forces that broadly wish for a maintenance of the status quo, and the forces that want change in every field of activity. If such a polarization persists, as seems likely, are events in Québec in the short run likely to take any turn other than towards widespread confrontation?

But when all is said and done, what these many turn-abouts, breakaways, and possible new cross-roads for nationalism show, beyond real or apparent contradictions, is the perenniality of a people.

The coming revolution

The expression "the coming revolution" describes the direction of current socio-political processes. I wish I were able to offer a reassuring and comforting picture. But Québec, like most Western liberal societies, has in the last ten years been confronted with so many crises that a measure of pessimism is inevitable. Of course, the mere increase in the number of serious socio-political incidents cannot be considered proof that historical continuity will undergo a major and final break. A crisis marks a turning point in an uneasy situation. It is a warning. Either the faltering system will return to normal, or it will collapse.

The very way in which the problem is diagnosed could influence the turn of events. All my studies on the current situation in the West,[1] and particularly in Québec, lead me to conclude that the industrialized liberal societies are facing, not just a series of irritating, temporary ills, but rather a deep-seated, widespread and perhaps incurable malady. The symptoms can be seen in the economic and cultural areas, but in the political field they are especially arresting. For this reason, we may usefully focus our analysis on politics, going back to the root issues during the course of this exercise.

There are so many serious indications of the crisis that it is probably only from lack of foresight that contemporaries believe the revolution to be an unlikely event, or one still in the future, rather than already set in motion. Its true nature is still only vaguely grasped and its future path remains uncertain, yet the events already unfolding suggest a picture that may appropriately be described as the "coming revolution."

The prophets of the coming revolution are legion, as are the gods in whose name it is supposed to take place. But it has not yet found its own

language. It would seem that, like other historic upheavals such as the
French, the Russian, and the Chinese revolutions, it must be all-encom-
passing. Unlike these other revolutions, it may take place without blood-
shed, although the possibility of civil war cannot be ruled out everywhere.
Its agents come from a wide variety of social groups, but we do not yet
know which of these will most stand to gain from it. Although we can see
the general outline of the coming revolution, its direction remains obscure.
Final stands have not yet been taken. People can therefore, still manage to
direct its course, although preventing such a revolution altogether now
seems unlikely.

The coming revolution is taking place on a world-wide scale, at the very
least embracing the entire West. It is developing along similar lines in the
most diverse societies. In committing itself to joining the modern world,
Québec has caught the revolutionary virus. Having started late, with a
great deal of ''catching up'' to do, Quebeckers have unceremoniously jetti-
soned a number of vestiges of the French *ancien régime,* transplanted by
their forefathers to North America and passed on virtually intact for generations. The traditions preserved by Quebeckers, such as language, religion, and the rural way of life, are taking on a very different appearance as
they become grafted onto the new lifestyles that are being adopted here.

In speaking as I did in 1961 of the dawn of a new regime for Québec, I
had a premonition of the onset of a revolutionary process. Those who say,
as has become the fashion recently, that the Quiet Revolution was only a
collection of empty slogans, are closing their eyes to both the successes
and the failures of the early 1960s. In almost no time, the elite, if not the
whole population, seemed to take a new lease on life. Old dreams, long
cherished but carefully repressed, seemed for a while almost within
reach.

These great changes, however, sounded the death knell for old solidarities. Of course, all the elements of modern society had been present in
Québec for a long time—perhaps since 1920, certainly since 1940—but,
behind the pluralism of social roles and the polarity of ideologies characteristic of the modern world, the ancestral spirit still lived. Today we realize that it was a sort of instinct that led Quebeckers to keep Duplessis in office until his death. The results of the 1960 election clearly show that it was
neither unanimously, nor light-heartedly, that the people accepted their
adult status after the death of Duplessis and finally agreed to face their destiny without the strong hand of a ''chef.'' It is one of the ironies of fate that
this long breathing spell, instead of being beneficial, made their adaptation
to the modern world even more difficult.

Of course, this challenge to Western civilization—for that is what it
amounts to—has taken on specific features in Québec. Moreover, it came
at a time when the long-standing unresolved question of Québec's national
identity was pressing as never before. The subsequent second crisis enhanced the first and, because of its dramatic nature, has even tended to take

precedence in people's minds, overshadowing the more fundamental social crisis. Its specific direction does not stem from ignorance or from any congenital or acquired defect in Quebeckers. Rather, it is a quite natural consequence of the realization that, since their national identity is problematical it is a matter for them to raise and attempt to solve. In doing this, they risk overlooking urgent cultural, social, economic, and political problems. That, however, is a basic fact of life, arising out of their collective condition.

In acknowledging the two crises confronting Québec, we must not fall into the trap of thinking that nothing is right any longer, that those in government are inactive, that leaders in all areas of society are inept, and so on. But it would be just as wrong to relax into an unhealthy complacency. In many ways our societies are reaching heights never before known in history. It is precisely because of these achievements that we must turn to a serious examination of the evils that corrode such advances from within. If, however, as is undeniably the case in Western liberal societies, the sources of unrest multiply and deepen, and if, moreover, through ignorance or bad faith we refuse to tackle these problems seriously, or delay our efforts unduly, silencing our apprehensions, then we are becoming accomplices to regression.

In the realm of science, technology, and productive capacity, Western liberal societies have grown enormously, while their degree of social organization, in spite of certain outward appearances, has barely changed since the beginning of the nineteenth century. As a result, our societies have reached a stage of development where all kinds of distortions and contradictions appear and rapidly become intolerable to more and more kinds of people: the inequitable distribution of goods and services; the fight against poverty which is still based on the tradition of charity, with the government taking the place of private welfare institutions as the dispenser of alms; the inability to provide individuals and groups with the sense of dignity which they demand, and which they could acquire if permitted to earn their own living with their own hands and brains, without governmental big-brotherly attentions, and if allowed to participate actively in controlling their environment; the inability to formulate collective goals capable of creating a strong sense of confidence in and loyalty to the large administrative organizations, churches, governments, educational institutions, business firms, professions, and trade unions; powerlessness to change these vast organizations in a way that would make them responsive to the needs and aspirations of individuals and groups; and so on. Conditions can hardly become worse without creating irreparable damage somewhere in the social fabric.

This entire book has been dedicated to a thorough examination of the different aspects of Québec's twofold crisis. I think it would be useful, in conclusion, to review very briefly the chief dimensions of the crisis and to look at the likely outcome.

A.   THE CRISIS OF THE POLITICAL COMMUNITY

For Canada the danger of being torn apart by the interplay of internal contradictions is probably greater than it is for most western liberal societies.
The "two-nations theory" is a perfect illustration of the nature and depth
of these contradictions. When a Québec Francophone says that Canada is
made up of two nations, he means that the country consists of two distinct
societies, one French-speaking and the other English-speaking, that these
two societies are qualitatively equal in every way and that the Canadian
constitution should recognize this fact by giving special status to Francophones within federal political institutions and to Québec as a political
framework, since the overwhelming majority of Quebeckers are French-
speaking. I have hardly ever met an Anglophone who sees the two-nations
theory in just this way. Those Anglophones who support the two-nations
theory mean that Canada is made up of two main linguistic and cultural
groups, that the French-speaking group is concentrated mainly in Québec,
and that, consequently, it is appropriate that all Francophones in the
country be guaranteed the rights and conditions which would assure their
survival and that the Canadian political system be organized so as to give
Québec a good deal of cultural autonomy. There is a fundamental difference between these two views. Francophones begin with a dualistic conception of the Canadian political system which, in their opinion, is made
up of Québec on the one hand and the rest of the country on the other. Anglophones, for all their good will, are still bound by a unitary vision of Canada as a country stretching from the Atlantic to the Pacific, with a special
enclave called Québec.[2] These two views are irreconcilable, and there is
no doubt that until one of the partners adopts the other's point of view, no
substantial reworking of Canada's political order will be possible. This
conclusion is eloquently confirmed by the fruitless efforts made by Jean
Lesage in 1962-63, Daniel Johnson in 1967-68, Robert Bourassa in 1971,
Claude Castonguay in 1972, and Jean-Paul L'Allier in 1975, to reach practical compromises inclined towards the Québec point of view.

A number of people believe that the adoption of a pragmatic approach
would allow Québec to reap the greatest advantages in federal-provincial
affairs (which have for some time been known under the eloquent euphe-
mism of "intergovernmental affairs"). And as long as the questions are
strictly practical ones, I think that Québec could very well be content with
a polyarchic formula. As we know, this formula assumes the existence of a
system which does not set up permanent majorities or minorities in settling
particular questions. Consequently, if shrewd enough, each agent can,
through the clever manipulation of coalitions, manage to be on the side of
the majority a good deal of the time. On the other hand, because of a momentary lapse, or even in spite of the most inspired manoeuvring, he can
find himself in the minority.

Many instances may be cited to show that the eleven-part Canadian political system has behaved, and continues to behave, like a polyarchy. This

formula sometimes favours the federal government, at other times all or some of the provincial governments, depending on circumstances. The former has been dominant for the last few years, but the results of the 1972 and 1974 federal general elections could strengthen the movement towards provincial supremacy, a movement which seems to have been developing for some time. We see that, like British Columbia, Alberta, and even Ontario, the Québec government tries to create and exploit these tendencies, which could give a concrete meaning to its autonomistic slogans.

And yet we learn from observation that, whatever the circumstances, Québec cannot bring all her skill to bear in the high-stakes game of polyarchy because she must first examine each question to make sure it does not attack some value she considers essential to the French language and culture. If such a case were to arise, she could not, on principle, agree in advance to submit to a decision which could go against her. Consequently, polyarchy is not the appropriate formula for Canada. This conclusion may be deplorable, but it is inescapable. We could cite many cases of federal-provincial (or, to a lesser extent, interprovincial) negotiations which were inconclusive precisely because of this basic predicament of the Canadian situation.

We must look elsewhere for formulae of adjustment to the crisis in the Canadian political system. An example may be found in two Learned Societies, set up on a parallel but interrelated basis, the Société canadienne de science politique and the Canadian Political Science Association. They illustrate the kind of political device which could be acceptable to everyone, because all would feel at ease in their relationship with the other partners. The Société canadienne de science politique is officially a unilingual pan-Canadian French organization and, by constitution, fully independent from its sister organization. The latter is in practice, and should in all logic be, officially, a unilingual English body. A common journal is published in both French and English on a basis of perfect equality between the partners. There are bilingual conferences at which each individual can express his opinions in his mother tongue without constraint and without the risk of annoying anyone, and many other common activities are directed by a joint committee with equal representation from both organizations. In short, these two parallel and autonomous organizations work in an atmosphere which is favourable to the attainment of all the objectives that could bring together people involved in pursuing the same goals. One of the most remarkable aspects of this constitutional arrangement is that the members of the French organization, a good many of whom are politically separatists, not only are not in the least reluctant to build bridges and maintain contacts with the English organization, but frequently even take the initiative and always demonstrate a willingness to strengthen the ties between the two associations. For their part, the members of the English organization ask nothing better than to do the same. They are happy to work with their French-speaking colleagues, for once, rather than having to rely on token Francophone spokesmen as is so often the case in Canadian voluntary associations. Thus they avoid the risk of forgetting or misunderstanding their French colleagues' point of view, of having to be cautious in dealing with them, or of reaching the end of a long debate only to hear, "But we have forgotten the Francophones. Can anyone here tell us how they will react to the question under discussion?" etc.

What lessons for Canada's political system can be learned from this simple example of organically harmonious relations between French and English? I know we have to make allowance for the fact that these are two voluntary associations of relatively small size, with definite and limited goals. It will, of course, be more difficult to develop a corresponding formula in the larger, more complex, and more vital area of intergovernmental relations. Nevertheless, I think that this simple example can provide us with the basic principles for a possible concrete reworking of Canada's political community. In establishing a formula for remodelling Confederation, the very first thing that must be done is to ensure that Québec, as a political entity, has an adequate protective institutional framework. The rest, such as the distribution of specific areas of jurisdiction between the different levels of government, will follow naturally.

Aware that the collapse of the traditional rural way of life and the dissipation of ignorance have removed the bulwarks that had hitherto protected their language and culture, Quebeckers today feel the need for new protective structures and they expect to achieve them through a new or a revised constitution, or through an independent Québec. Should they no longer feel the constant threat of assimilation into the Anglophone world, their instinctive reluctance to maintain contacts with the latter would vanish. That, precisely, is the mainspring of the Québec separatist movement: in the absence of a major constitutional revision, independence offers the promise of a protective institutional framework. Once well sheltered behind political frontiers over which they have full control, Quebeckers would not only be willing, but eager, to renew contacts with their Anglophone environment.

The choices are becoming clearer and clearer to Québec's Francophones: affirm their nature as a separate nation within a new Confederation or through separation, or face inevitable disappearance as a distinctive community. The crisis of Canada's political community rests precisely upon the fact that Quebeckers seem unable to settle their long-standing internal debate. Let us ask the question: What prevents Quebeckers from opting for separation? Proposed reforms at the federal level? The improved position that Québec recently gained in Confederation? Not at all! Whether it is a question of the proportion of Francophones or the status of the French language in the federal civil service, the cultural effects of federal laws and policies, or intergovernmental relations, nothing has really changed in the last ten years. The decisions taken by the Pearson government in 1965 to promote bilingualism in the federal civil service and the 1970 Official Languages Act aroused only indifference among Quebeckers. These sincere but misguided efforts tax Anglophones' good will to no purpose, as the structural situation prevents such measures from making any perceptible improvement in the precarious position Francophones occupy in the Canadian context. And the federal machine is only likely to backtrack in the near future. There is but one way to bring about a real rectification of the Canadian situation—that is, the setting up of a protective framework that would lastingly guarantee Quebeckers' institutional security. This might happen through the emergence, at the federal level, of a great political leader—necessarily Anglophone—who would take up the work begun so sincerely, but too timidly, by Lester B. Pearson, and who could make the Anglophone majority across the country accept his plans. Considering the hesitancy that has prevailed during the last ten years, when Canada was supposed to be implementing bold new plans based on complete "equality between the two founding peoples," is it reasonable to place our hopes in the coming of a man of such stature? Scepticism to the contrary, the possibility cannot be ruled out.

But before this could occur, English Canadians would have to suffer a shock deep enough to make them realize the gravity of the situation. The Royal Commission on Bilingualism and Biculturalism tried to bring about this shock in 1965 when, following a series of regional meetings across the country, it published its *Preliminary Report* revealing the scope of the "Canadian crisis." At the time, English Canadians found the report "overly alarmist," while Quebeckers—to whom the message was not directed anyway—were unanimous in concluding that the document did not say anything they did not know already. Perhaps Jean Marchand was also trying to create this kind of shock with his speech of 12 January 1973, when he directed a stern warning—a warning that the very last chance was at hand—at those who continue to evoke the spectre of "French power," setting one part of the country against the other. If modern Québec's desires could be debated seriously and competently in the House of Commons it could produce a salutary shock through-out the country and force Anglophones to recognize the seriousness of the Canadian crisis. It is possible that this is the real service that Gérard Pelletier, Jean Marchand, and Pierre Elliott Trudeau, who were among those who contributed most to shaking Québec out of its torpor in the 1960s, can render Canada in the 1970s. But I feel that it will take more than speeches, even when those speeches are delivered in the House of Commons by prestigious federal ministers, to make Anglophones finally realize that their obstinate deafness is leading with increasing inevitability to the breakup of Canada. Such speeches, however, coming from the highest political tribune in the land, could begin the process of recuperation.

The federal general elections of July 1974 returned the Liberal party to power.[3] The party will have a comfortable majority in the House of Commons for the next few years. Will it profit from this favourable situation and begin a radical reform of the constitution to establish a "New Deal" for the provinces, and most particularly for Québec, a New Deal which would reconcile the desire for greater autonomy on the part of the provinces with the need to give the federal government the powers necessary to guarantee the fundamental unity of the country in conditions which have become very difficult? A number of the steps taken since September 1974 show that the federal government, strong in its majority, is trying to increase the Francophone presence in Ottawa. On 21 November 1974, Jean Chrétien, president of the Treasury Board, responsible for carrying out the Official Languages Act, revealed that the government intends to raise the proportion of bilingual jobs to 19 percent, instead of the 11 percent planned in 1972 (53,600 instead of 25,000 jobs) by 1978. The proportion of Francophone jobs will be raised to 13 percent (35,566 jobs) and the proportion of jobs that may be performed in either French or English will be 8 percent (22,938). The last-named category will apply mostly to executive positions. This program leans in the direction I suggested in 1971 before the Special Joint Commission of the Senate and of the House of Commons on the Constitution. It is certainly a bold decision, and its complete application would guarantee the Francophone presence right where it should first be felt, that is in the middle and higher levels of the federal civil service. If Quebeckers respond enthusiastically to this invitation and join the federal civil service in large numbers between now and 1978, federal policies as a whole would correspond much more closely to Québec's hopes and values than has been the case up to now. But this is not 1968, when such a policy should have been adopted. It is not even 1971, when there was still a good chance that it could have had a beneficial effect on Quebeckers' attitudes. In 1975, in evaluating the possible effect of the federal government's decision, one is tempted to say, as did André Laurendeau following the government's adoption of bilingual cheques, "Too little, too late." Even though the measures recently adopted are of considerable importance in themselves, and even if they were to be fully put into practice, which is doubtful, they might only exercise a limited effect on current tendencies in both Ottawa and Québec.

Furthermore, in spite of all the good will and energy expended by the present-day federal government, I very much doubt whether these policies will have any enduring effect, since the middle or intermediate tier of the federal civil service is particularly difficult to affect in terms of its language composition. As long as the Francophone presence is only increasingly felt at the upper echelons, as has been the case so far, the gains may be only temporary, since top civil servants may well be moved or replaced, as is customary when ministers come and go.

In Ottawa, the inflationary economic situation and, particularly, the problems created by the recent world energy crisis will oblige the federal government to observe very closely the political trends in provinces like Alberta, British Columbia, and even Ontario. Foci of political crisis will multiply in the next few years and the federal government will have to divert a fair share of the attention that has been riveted on Québec since 1959 to major sources of stress elsewhere. Moreover, it is obvious that the majority of the country's Anglophones and most of the other provincial governments, now as before, are going to use all kinds of pretexts to refuse to support any federal language policies that they feel limit "free competition" in access to the federal administration or could influence political decisions and actions in favour of the French culture.

In this context, why do Quebeckers not immediately embark on the road to separation? We must understand that it is not easy to decide to break ties such as those which link them to their fellow-citizens in other provinces, that such a stable political system as Canada's cannot be broken up as easily as one establishes or eliminates political borders between peoples who have never had their own country, such as certain African former colonies. In addition, we must realize that Quebeckers, in spite of what they say about themselves, form an economically prosperous community, often thanks to federal policies; that they already have a network of flourishing social and cultural institutions; and that, as a result, the alternative to separation weighs heavily in the balance. We must also take into account the patent generosity of the federal government towards individuals and communities as well as the ill-concealed blackmail practised by a number of Anglo-American and European firms and financial institutions. All this results in hesitation and understandable fears, the more so as worrying about linguistic questions or matters of cultural or national identity is of course limited to the upper strata of Québec society and hardly permeates the general population.

The Liberal party of Québec held its biennial convention on 23-24 November 1974. The atmosphere which prevailed throughout this meeting confirmed the fact that the party of reform had, since 1970, been transformed into a management-oriented party. It has become increasingly allergic to liberal nationalism as proclaimed in the early 1970s, and to any trend of social thought that is even the least bit reformist. At the same time, in keeping with the temperament of the premier, Robert Bourassa, the party encourages a policy of short-term economic expediency. The new president of the party, notary Claude Desrosiers, boldly and courageously warned the delegates against the increasingly intolerant conformity and intellectual and political asphyxia that threatened the Liberal party. He declared: "The party is giving the impression of being a spectator in the major discussions. I see a definite danger there, and I am certainly not the only one to see it. . . We are felt to be too close to the government, we have perhaps practised too much self-restraint in order not to harm the government . . . We must publicly take part in today's debates, or our party's existence and undertakings will not be able to attract those who can contribute to our cause today and those who will replace us in the future and whom we are failing to win." Will the boost that the new president means to give the party be enough to get it out of the conservative rut in which it has been since 1970, when it alienated most intellectuals, and to give it new intellectual vitality? I doubt it. On the contrary, I believe that the party's very successes, the necessary wear and tear of power, and especially the short-term bookkeeper mentality of its leader will cause the party to succumb to its characteristic lack of imagination, and political opportunism. In this way, it could, sooner or later, share the sad fate of the Union Nationale.

The Parti Québécois has not recovered from the disappointment caused by the results of the October 1973 elections, in which only six representatives were elected, with 30 percent of the popular vote, (out of a total of 110 seats); and it is attracting the same progressive elements that helped the Liberal party to power in 1960. At its convention in October 1974, the Parti Québécois showed, moreover, that it now has sufficiently sophisticated leaders and permanent staff to plan and implement strategies capable of bringing the party to power soon. The commitment to a referendum on Québec's independence then, was a political master stroke, if, as appears very likely, it becomes impossible to negotiate separation with the federal government and the other provinces. The Parti Québécois thus imperceptibly defuses the most hazardous features of its platform, from both the national and the social points of view, making it more acceptable to a population which has returned to a fundamentally conservative attitude as a result of certain undesirable effects of the reforms undertaken in the early 1960s, particularly in education, and the health and social welfare reforms of the early 1970s, as well as the tragic consequences of the FLQ's activities. If, moreover, René Lévesque's leadership is not challenged again before the next elections, as now seems probable, and if the radical factions in the right and left wings of the party are kept under control, as seems almost certain, the next provincial elections, considering the internal erosion taking place within the Liberal party, could very well turn to the advantage of the Parti Québécois. The latter is, in any case, the only party besides the Liberal party which seems capable of taking power in Québec. In these circumstances, a range of entirely novel possibilities are opened up to Canada's future.

Will the national impasse be resolved? If so, when? How? By whom? Any delay in finding some kind of solution to the national crisis could create the clear and immediate danger of violent confrontation.

The fourth annual report (1975) published by Keith Spicer, the federal Commissioner for Official Languages, as well as the clearly foreseeable signs of impotence and ineptitude building up around the July 1974 Québec legislation making French the official language of Québec, show once more, if indeed we needed any more proof, that in spite of sincere efforts by governments and many competent people, we have not yet begun to solve the problem of the official languages in either Canada as a whole or in Québec. I have arrived at the painful conclusion that since 1963, when the Royal Commission on Bilingualism and Biculturalism was formed, we have been looking at the language issue from the wrong angle. As long as Québec remains within the framework of federalism, concrete results can be achieved only by a federal law which officially establishes the French character of Québec and the English character of all the other provinces, a law which would also be able to make the present theoretical bilingualism in the federal civil service a practical reality within the next fifteen years, provided all Canadians are willing to honour it without reservation. Neither the federal government, nor Québec, nor New Brunswick, nor Ontario can, by their own means alone, resolve the linguistic conflict. Only by working together can they create an equitable protective status for the two official majorities and minorities. Quebeckers, both English- and French-speaking, as well as Francophones in New Brunswick and Ontario, would have the most to gain from a federal-provincial agreement on the official languages. As for other Canadians, once they understood and accepted action on the special linguistic conditions facing the federal government and those of Québec, Ontario, and New Brunswick, they would welcome a valid solution to the complex question of official languages that has plagued the country since 1963. In the autumn of 1975, Prime Minister Trudeau will probably encourage the provinces to recommence the negotiations broken off in 1971 at the Victoria Conference on the repatriation of the Constitution. That would be a perfect occasion to review the whole language question on a newer and much more promising basis, as well as to re-examine the broader questions of culture, science, communication, and immigration that are at the heart of conflicts which could, as things are going now, become the central elements of the most serious confrontations yet between Québec and Ottawa.

B.   THE CRISIS OF THE REGIME

Quebeckers did themselves a disservice in indiscriminately adhering to the liberal regime after Jean Lesage's victory in the 1960 elections. Today we can criticize their lack of foresight, but the unique circumstances existing in 1960 explain why they failed to separate the wheat from the chaff. It is nonetheless true that in throwing themselves so completely into the liberal orbit, they unwittingly created serious difficulties for themselves that a little insight might have avoided. At that very moment, in societies which had long adhered to the liberal creed, criticism of various aspects of the regime was becoming harsher each year. It is one of the ironies of fate that, at the moment when the liberal regime was at its height here, that is in 1963-1964, it was beginning to be seriously attacked elsewhere, especially in the United States. Today the liberal regime is undeniably facing a profound crisis almost everywhere, and Québec is no exception to the rule.

The crisis only makes sense if it is seen as a temporary situation which must be overcome one way or another. It will, one hopes, provoke a surge of reformist or revolutionary energy, opening the door to new forms of human relationships and new modes of collective organization.

The crisis of liberalism in Québec was dramatically demonstrated once more in March 1975 following the public hearings of the Cliche Commission, which picked up where the public hearings of Québec's Commission of Inquiry into Organized Crime left off. The Bourassa government itself set up these commissions, but we should not be too quick to take these magnanimous gestures at face value since the revelation of many scandals directly or indirectly involving members of the National Assembly and the civil service had to a certain extent forced the government into action.

One notable result of the commissions' uncovering of such disreputable activities is seen in the questions being raised about the quality of political leadership and, more generally, the state of health of democracy in Québec.[4] In spite of the limited means available for its own inquiries, the Cliche Commission found itself unintentionally crossing trails already laid by the Commission on Organized Crime. For example, it uncovered improprieties directly associated with the Pierre Laporte affair, raising sensitive issues that exceeded its original terms of reference.

The revelations of the Cliche Commission were a further demonstration of the fundamental deficiencies of the Liberal regime in Québec. Robert Bourassa did not create these deficiencies—they existed before he came to power. He can, however, be blamed for having done nothing, until very recently to correct them, and even perhaps for having indirectly aggravated them through lax leadership. It is sad to see irrefutable confirmation of the fact that the "efficient management" style which Bourassa boasted of having established in Québec since 1970 was nothing but a hollow façade. The premier seems to think that the public sector can be managed by methods appropriate to private enterprise, but what produces fruitful results in one sphere can prove to be a sterile approach elsewhere. The government's relations with the large secondary organizations, particularly the universities, business, professional associations, and trade unions, are deplorable. Its dealings with popular groups in the cities and outlying areas have been arrogant and show a scandalous lack of feeling for public sentiment. Public institutions and practices have remained cemented in their traditional moulds, and, over and above the small patronage that existed and continues to exist, we now have large-scale patronage, patterned upon the managerial style of the government, as a result of collusion between engineers, businessmen, trade-unionists, civil servants, and politicians, far more corrosive of public ethics and much more harmful to the common interest than the former, small-scale nepotism. We thus have contracts awarded without regular open bids, without precise cost quotations and containing secret clauses; while kickbacks and other kinds of misuse of public funds seem to be common currency. The conditions of the battle for the leadership of political parties force candidates to spend as much as $200,000 or more, which places those who have no private fortune in an impossible position. Because of the distorted results of the 1973 elections, the 102 Liberals who hold seats in the National Assembly (now "reduced" to 100) lost prestige and became particularly vulnerable to dubious pressures and temptations. The premier has not been able to satisfy this army of elected representatives: some have not received the ministerial appointments they had been "promised," others are ill-prepared for their role as MNAs inside and outside the National Assembly. The Liberal party itself has come under considerable criticism since Robert Bourassa took on its leadership. For the last four years, the party has been moving in low gear. The present attempt at regeneration under the current president, notary Claude Desrosiers, will be brief: he has just announced that, disillusioned, he will retire at the end of his one-year term; this will no doubt leave a bitter after-taste. Like other governments, that of Québec has made abundant use of political consultants, behind-the-scenes officials who are not part of the regular civil service and are therefore not subject to the same rules of conduct and routine controls as career officials. One thinks immediately of Paul Desrochers, who was until recently the premier's *éminence grise,* and who was frequently mentioned during the hearings of the Cliche Commission. This kind of parallel administration, no doubt made necessary by the shortcomings of the regular administration, involves obvious risks against which we should be on our guard. Resorting to empty slogans ("cultural sovereignty" for Québec, *federalisme rentable* (benefits of federalism), "a federal union within a common market," etc.) only masks the absence of political action. Ottawa can thus make hay while the Québec sun shines. All too often, Ottawa gets things done while Québec expends its energy upon generating noise—as for instance in the matter of "cultural sovereignty" over which there has been much Québec clamour. Similarly, the lack of any scientific and cultural policy elaborated by the Québec government makes nonsense of Québec's claim to an inalienable and unique responsibility for protecting and promoting the French language and culture in North America. Robert Bourassa's definition of his role as premier, seen as a mere manager of public affairs, has prevented his government from rising above everyday considerations and designing projects capable of exciting people's imagination and arousing a strong collective will to action. These are only a few of the problems that come to mind in this context.

It is clear, therefore, that the crisis of the liberal regime has taken on a rather special character in Québec. Québec has had a good many businessmen, professional men, and politicians who supported the liberal creed, but it never enjoyed the luxury of an original liberal thinker, or even a good commentator of liberal thought. In 1942, that is at the height of the war against fascism, among guest speakers invited to discuss democracy under the aegis of the church-supported, social movement called Semaines sociales du Canada, there were still a good many who (perhaps from personal conviction, perhaps to stay in the good graces of Cardinal Villeneuve, the honorary president of the meeting) energetically denounced liberalism in favour of the values of the old order and the social doctrine of the Church. Some, apparently forgetting the tragedy unfolding in Europe at the time, or having joined the Vichy camp, went so far as to suggest that democracy "here," in Québec, be based on corporatist principles.

It was only after 1959 that the liberal regime was able to take root firmly in Québec in politics as in all spheres of activity. Thus Québec liberals only held the reins of power unchallenged for less than ten peaceful years— since the liberal approach has been under attack, here as elsewhere, since

1968. We can even speculate whether, because of the very weakness of its roots in Québec, the liberal regime might not have been at bay here two or three years earlier than in societies where it lay entrenched for much longer. Jean Lesage, who was the herald of progress in 1960, began to say in 1965 that the forward movement would have to be slowed down, or even reversed for a while, to keep the rate of change in line with the population's capacity to absorb it. Or was he, as a good traditional leader, frightened by the changes that had taken place under his aegis within five years?

The crisis of the regime may be deeper in Québec than elsewhere, on the one hand, because the liberal creed only recently penetrated the political system, whose agents could consequently indulge in repressive measures with an easier conscience than if they had been more thorough-going liberals; and, on the other hand, because of the ever-present possibility of a reawakening of corporatism, which evoked nostalgia here and there and which left behind it certain unambiguous traces in, for example, the lack of inhibition with which businessmen, unionists, priests, politicians, and intellectuals speak of "intermediary bodies" (*corps intermédiaires*) when referring to the secondary organizations of society.

C. THE CRISIS OF POLITICAL INSTITUTIONS

The crisis of the liberal regime also involves the mechanisms that give them concrete form. Throughout this book, I have shown that these mechanisms suffer from many serious defects. These failings are particularly noticeable in Québec, partly as a result of the archaic nature of the political set-up, and partly because of the weakness of the social framework.

There is no need to repeat the indictment of our political parties, National Assembly, police, judiciary, and government. I have already in this work indicated their inadequacies and even, in some ways, their ineptness as a consequence of which the smooth functioning of modern society is hampered. As for Québec's civil service, although it is not very old in years, it demonstrates, in varying degrees, signs of the same unwieldiness and technocracy that are characteristic of older bureaucracies. The machine is not able to meet increasingly discordant and pressing demands or to deal with the problems that are becoming more numerous and more complex every day. It is in constant danger of jamming and overheating.

Business, particularly big business, does not nest well with Québec's social institutions, less dynamic here then elsewhere; and the increments it produces are neither sufficiently reinvested in Québec enterprise nor directed towards local social objectives. Big business escapes political control more easily in Québec than elsewhere, and almost effortlessly avoids being involved in public programs of social and economic development and regional planning. The proportion of available resources that it diverts from community objectives is larger in Québec than elsewhere, and its contempt for the environment and for men seems even more flagrant. The result is that here, more than anywhere else, there is a lack of essential publc goods and services, such as public parks, hospitals, mass transportation, truly low-cost housing, and so on. Under the circumstances, it is scarcely surprising that Quebeckers view bis business with so little enthusiasm.

Our universities and research centres are Québec-oriented, perhaps excessively so. Furthermore, even though they have not yet completed the process of "catching up," they are being subjected to an austerity program, and there is even talk of cutting their funds. People seem to have forgotten that the worst type of colonialism is intellectual colonialism. If the science, technology, and innovation that make our cities and industries possible and modernize our social structures come from elsewhere, then what is left for a Department of Cultural Affairs to do but make futile, extravagant gestures and spearhead the preservation of folkloric traditions and "historic" sites (and is that not an accurate description of what the Department has done to date)? The fact that our educational reforms were, in certain respects, badly oriented and expensive does not justify the reduction of the efforts undertaken in the last twelve years to give Quebeckers the training they must have in order to keep in step with modern society. The results already achieved, impressive as they are, fall far short of the objectives sought, that is a minimum of twelve years of regular schooling for all citizens, and a proportion of university graduates comparable to Ontario's.

The series of incidents centred around the labour unions in 1972 illustrate perfectly the crisis which grips Québec's secondary organizations. Labour unions have for a long time been essential organic supports for liberal regimes. Thus, the peacemaking action of the Confédération générale des travailleurs although it is a communist organization, enabled President De Gaulle to control the strikes and subversion that broke out in France in May 1968. But in publishing the manifestoes hostile to the "system," and in coming close to civil disobedience following the judicial injunction issued in reply to the strikes in the public and semi-public sectors in May 1972, Québec union leaders have adopted an attitude of open defiance towards the existing political regime. If such an attitude were to spread, the result would be either the political marginalization of unionized workers or the scuttling of the political order. And it would be dangerously short-sighted to rejoice over the dissension that has since arisen within the CNTU, or over the internal feuding among labour unions who used to present a united front. Business and government need strong union counterparts. The crumbling of unionism cannot but lead to anarchy in the vital labour sector.

There is no panacea for the crisis gripping the major socio-political institutions. How can we bring the arrogant and powerful technostructure to heel without destroying economic momentum? How can we allow universities and research centres to intensify their efforts while guaranteeing that they will pursue socially valuable goals and will not tax the community's resources unduly? What can we do to enable labour unions to continue their own particular review of the social aspects of work, its forms, the more equitable distribution of goods and services among different sectors of the population, the maintenance of human dignity through work, and workers' control of their own environment—while ensuring that this process does not lead them to radical rebellion against the existing socio-political order? The government has, more or less directly, ultimate responsibility for necessary reforms in various sectors. It is obvious, however, that the government cannot undertake the entire project of reform alone. Concerted action by the major socio-political organizations, involving the entire population, is necessary. First, the government itself must be emancipated from the control of the technostructure. Without this emancipation, how can we distribute goods and services according to the needs of the people rather than the demands of large private interests? But how is this emancipation to be made possible, except by reinvesting the elected representatives of the only true sovereign, the people, with their legislative prerogatives? Yet how can the people find representatives capable of assuming such an enormous responsibility? One question leads to another, and even when we try to find a starting point which might lead to a solution of the crisis of political institutions, the various facets of the crisis dance in front of our eyes, while we remain powerless to control their movements.

D.   THE CRISIS OF VALUES

Our efforts to repair or replace the socio-political institutions will be inadequate if they do not deal with the question of values, for the ramifications of the crisis also cover this area. I once wrote:

It is not just particular dysfunctions in the social and political systems, on the whole easily reparable, that are being called into question. The crisis involves the legitimacy of organizations and leaders, the integration of members into the political system, the involvement of members in the life of organizations, the rules and processes that determine the distribution of goods and services among individuals and groups. In short, it challenges the very finalities in man and society. The challenge involves the values themselves, their nature, institutionalization and internalization. Confrontations and conflicts are often awkward and brutal expressions of individual and collective anxieties in a world which has become strange and frightening. They also express desire for freedom, purification and creation. In the last analysis, all this is a reaching out towards a new humanism. The hippie, the drug user, the student who drops out of school, the mature man who abandons a successful career and takes refuge in early retirement, all are symptoms of confusion in a world that is losing its soul. The revolt against behaviorism and quantitative methods in American universities, the recent student swing towards religion courses, the great interest in ancient and exotic religions, the practise of the severest asceticism and mystic experiences of all kinds occurring in places which are officially considered disreputable, and, on the other hand, the sudden and apparently irreversible rise in reactionary and repressive impulses among those who only yesterday were the chief supporters of liberal values—these are all indisputable signs of both the depth of the cultural crisis and of its possibly disastrous outcome.[5]

Values are often treated with a casualness inappropriate to such a fundamental subject. People speak of "obsolete" or "outmoded" values, of casting aside "old" values and establishing "new" ones, as if changing values meant no more than trading in the old Ford for a new model. In fact, the values with which men are most concerned today are basically the same as those which prevailed at the dawn of civilization: security, freedom, justice, equality, happiness, truth, integrity. The periodic challenges are directed at the specific content of these values, which become closely linked with particular states of society. Of course, men can set new standards of excellence, establish new yardsticks. However, this is essentially a deepening of values rather than their replacement. It is sometimes said that this search, this meditation on values is an expression of a "crisis of conscience." Such a crisis arises during periods of structural and intellectual upheaval. We are at present experiencing one of the most troubled, if not the most troubled era in history. Should we be surprised at the anxieties our contemporaries feel over values?

An examination of the basic socio-political finalities—authority, change, and participation—can help us define the true dimensions of the contemporary crisis of values. The central significance of these three key concepts in an examination of values was discussed in earlier chapters. Each chapter discussed one or another of them, either as a central topic or as an element in the discussion of culture, the meaning of national identity, economics, politics, or modes and means of action. It would, no doubt, be appropriate to come back to each of these themes in the conclusion. I will, nevertheless, just highlight some particularly relevant aspects of the notion of authority, which has become so crucial to an understanding of contemporary views of life and of the world.

For twenty-five hundred years (if we limit our examination to Western civilization), human genius has been apparently carefully applied to the problem of making societies more governable. All this effort has not prevented individuals and communities from succumbing to the temptation of insubordination. Dormant for long periods, the spirit of rebellion occasionally awakens, often for obscure reasons, and there may be serious social unrest before it dies down. Our era has been marked by a radical challenge to the traditional supports of authority: religion and tradition. The collapse of religious convictions and of traditional ways of life in Québec since the Second World War has exposed and dried out the ancient roots of authority: belief and reverence. The present crisis of authority in Québec—and in varying degrees elsewhere—can be explained to a great extent by the fact that leaders in many fields of activity, particularly in religion and politics, were not able or willing to recognize the changes in circumstances and attitudes early enough. Had they been more alert, they could perhaps have allowed new bases for authority to become established gradually, without clashing with the ancient justifications. They are paying dearly for these omissions today.

It is not enough to say, as does Max Weber, that in modern societies, the foundations of authority are shifting, the law (or a rational-legal order) replacing tradition or the charisma of the chief. Besides the ideologies and the procedures, the symbols of authority have been replaced. The mystique of legal power does not rest on the same kind of signs or rituals as did traditional or charismatic power. Authority is no longer based on an association with divine power, where a halo of prestige around the person in authority resulted from his assumption of the status of father, priest, or moral leader. Authority is now based on competence in performing one's task and fulfilling one's social role.

When we say that in a democracy it is the people, as sovereign, from whom the legitimacy of the laws passed by their elected representatives is derived, we must beware of new myths creating a completely abstract and fictitious notion of the people, by means of such phrases as "the will of the people," "the common good," "the public interest." These terms are valuable in themselves, but they can easily serve as camouflage for positions taken by leaders in their own personal interest or on behalf of privileged private interests. The sole true criterion of the legitimacy of political decisions and actions in democratic societies is broad popular support, which is the only genuine manifestation of citizen consent. And citizen consent can only be enlightened if it conforms to these three principles: the principle of personal choice of participation; that of competence or full knowledge of all relevant elements; and that of economy or ability to evaluate the costs and benefits of all possible choices. One can judge the political maturity of a people by their ability to apply these three principles. Where do Quebeckers stand in this matter? If they are found wanting in their mastery of one or another of these principles, or even in all of them, who is to be held responsible?

If, following open discussion and negotiation, the people fail to reach a certain degree of unanimity, then the very legitimacy of law and government are open to challenge. What basis can we find for the necessary degree of unanimity in today's complex and pluralistic world? We must realize that, behind the defiance apparently aimed at the "powers that be," beyond the challenge to authority, lies a conflict between different cultural contents, and a confrontation between two opposing notions of rationality, one centred on economic criteria, the other based on social goals. The various "countercultures," Québec's new film industry (including its share of erotic films), socio-political quips of comedians and song-writers, the development of a "Québec" language, new forms of religious life—all these are collective manifestations offering a more or less direct challenge to the traditional concept of authority; and they prove the leaders' inability to rest their actions on bases rooted deeply enough in the environment to please the population as a whole, particularly today's marginal or underprivileged groups. When the social logic, expressed by a significant fraction of the population, begins to contradict the political logic, the leaders must bear the responsibility for the tragic situation, and it is up to them to redress it, not by repression in the name of law and order, but by contributing to a re-examination of values already undertaken by so many groups in Québec.

There is no doubt that both individuals and groups are less tolerant today than they were in 1960. And yet tolerance is the prime liberal virtue. Radicals have little use for this "virtue," which they feel is for people who lack faith in their plans and goals. While liberals believe that differences of opinion over ends and means within a society are healthy as long as everyone eventually accepts and supports the majority opinion, radicals feel they have a great deal to lose if their views are rejected. Thus, tolerance is a luxury they feel they cannot afford.

The increasingly intense polarization in Québec between federalists and separatists over national questions, and between conservatives and progressives over social questions, while helping to increase conflict between individuals and groups, does not merely destroy the old bases of solidarity. It forestalls the establishment of a broad enough basis for discussion to make the formation of a new consensus possible. The growing polarization of opinion is, in itself, only another symptom of the crisis which grips Québec, but it is particularly serious since it involves values.

These are demanding times. We must find a new way to reconcile the twin desires for security and freedom, aspirations which have long been considered contradictory. No state can be strong and stable if it is not able to guarantee the security of both people and property. But at the same time, at least in societies which adhere to the tenets of liberal democracy, there is a desire to secure the greatest freedom of expression and action for individuals and groups. In our pluralistic societies, it is believed that only open debate over ends and means can lead to the choice of the best alternatives, the ones capable of gaining broadest support among the citizens.

The speed and scope of technological change have shaken societies to their very foundations. While aggravating causes of conflict, they erode protective traditions. Until recently, Québec was seen as an oasis of peace in a troubled world. It is true that this peace was purchased at the price of a dormant democracy and a slow rate of social, economic, and cultural development. The Quiet Revolution brought about a brutal awakening to painful truth. While the rest of the world was moving into the post-industrial phase, Québec was fettered by a mixture of traditions that varied widely in quality, together with modern elements that had crept in unnoticed and had been indiscriminately accepted.

We went to work. We abolished our protective frameworks. We freed ourselves from the domination of the old hierarchies. We aroused new aspirations in various strata of the population. Certain patterns of thought and behaviour changed radically. Church attendance is a good example. Ten or fifteen years ago Québec had one of the highest rates in the western world, and today it has one of the lowest (dropping from around 80 to 90 per thousand in the period from 1950 to 1960, to about forty percent now).

Social structures (family, churches, elites) had, until the last few years, been solid and stable, and had long protected individuals and groups. They provided security. They were authoritarian, but paternalism (and the fact that the elites, which had patently risen from the ranks, remained close to the people) tempered the exercise of authority. Quebeckers were as mild and docile as the lamb they had chosen for a symbol. Respect for those in authority was taught from the pulpit, in the doctor's office, in the notary's chambers, as well as in the National Assembly and the schools. Democracy, except at the local level and in a number of large secondary organizations, was a mere abstraction. There was considerable practical freedom of action because the authorities seldom interfered and their subjects scarcely dreamed of escaping their domination.

The death of Duplessis in September 1959 and the Liberal victory in 1960 marked, in the political sphere, the end of the old order and the dawn of the new. Hesitantly at first, then rapidly, Quebeckers abolished the protective frameworks, proclaimed democracy among the people and eliminated the barriers to the free development of liberatarian aspirations which had found expression in a number of secondary organizations, magazines, and social movements during the 1950s. The high point of the ''revolution'' was the creation of the Department of Education in March 1964. This ended the domination of the Church in Québec and set in motion a great wave of democratization in education.[6]

The liberation movement has made itself felt everywhere, and has gained ground on all fronts. Even the family, church, and school have yielded. Almost unlimited freedom spread rapidly through universities, interest groups, and the mass media, replacing the old benevolent but rigid controls. The *Mouvement laïque de langue Française* died away for lack of real battle. In this general climate of libertarian euphoria, Québec separatism became an organized movement (1961-63). At another time, in another country, this movement would surely have been banned, as it openly aimed at shattering the Canadian political community. But in the special circumstances prevailing in a Québec that was dazzled and sure of itself, the movement was considered legitimate. Even the government toyed with the idea of separation between 1962 and 1964, and again between 1966 and 1968.

In contrast to the preceding decade, when all things seemed possible, the 1970s are proceeding under a lowering and stormy sky. On the one hand, the rate of growth in certain sectors in recent years has been disappointing, all the more so since the international situation is far from encouraging. On the other hand, people's aspirations have continued to rise. There is thus an ever-widening gap between real opportunities and individual and collective expectations.

Such a gap is in itself a source of difficulties for government leaders, but the prevailing social climate makes the situation infinitely more precarious.

The freedom that Quebeckers are enjoying was won only recently and with the greatest of ease. Like any sudden swing of the historical pendulum, it could easily run wild. Other peoples have had to fight hard for their freedom. They know better than we do what it cost, and perhaps they have more of the self-control necessary to protect it.

The situation is compounded by the fact that the libertarian movement in Québec coincided with the renewed outbreak of violence throughout the world. Post-industrial technology, the horror of modern wars, the advent of electronics and of broadcast media, and the rise in educational levels have accelerated violent thrusts in nations, groups, and individuals to the point where we ask whether even the most stress-resistant political system can contain them. The threshold of tolerance to violence may be reached well before dissident groups have set in motion all the possible modes and means of violence. In many countries, a great number of activities formerly considered unacceptable are now practised with impunity.

Nations are going through a cultural revolution whose principal tenets are the following: 1) The "system" or "establishment" is the real cause of violence; and 2), when dealing with "repressive" political and economic powers, is it right for individuals and groups to turn to psychological and physical violence and even to terrorism. And to young people socialized in such a climate, the all-out fight against the "system" and the "establishment" is considered natural. They acquire a political culture that in effect accepts violence as a positive value.

The tragic events of October 1970 and the crushing of the breath of revolt among the labour unions in May 1972 could prove so traumatic to Quebeckers that they may become completely apathetic or, on the contrary, openly rebellious. We must overcome fears and hesitations and demand freedom for all in the hope that they will be able to use it with the same wisdom that we must demand from governments in the exercise of their power of constraint.

E. DEVELOPMENTAL TRENDS

The diagnosis can be summed up as follows: Québec is caught up in a serious crisis involving the political community, the regime, the institutions, and finally its values. But crises are transient conditions, either resolved or ending in tragedy; and so is it possible to predict what main lines Québec's development is likely to follow?

Of course, we cannot know what turn domestic and international events will take. It would thus be pointless to try to measure all the cultural, economic, and political effects of, say, Québec's accession to independence, if one were merely to extrapolate from the current situation. But how can one gauge the precise scope of the handicaps, as well as the positive effects, resulting from Québec's possible separation from the rest of Canada? And how can we evaluate the impact on Québec of the third technological revolution, a revolution which is only beginning to be seen today?[7] How will objective constraints such as the ecological, economic, linguistic, and cultural environment, and so on, operate in varying contexts? How will the interpreters of the situation, the traditional and the new elites, as well as the masses, react to the new conditions? What convictions will spread among various groups, what causes of confrontation will arise, what new mobilizing forces, action strategies, and mechanisms of social control will emerge?

All these questions, and many like them, can be summed up as follows: how and in what form are social and political components likely to mesh in the future? In judging this to be the central question, I am leaving myself open to the charge that I give politics more importance than it really has in present society and more than it will probably have in the future. I believe that Québec's intellectuals do often assign much too large a role to politics, which they expect to be both the heart and brain of society, whereas politics are more often no more than a reflection of the causal factors, or at most a catalyst and an inspirer to action. It is the secondary organizations (parties, interest groups, business, workers', and ideological associations, various citizen groups) that most contribute to keeping society together. To the extent that these organizations are strong and dynamic, or weak and disorganized, society itself will be strong and dynamic, or weak and disorganized. In this book, I have shown that Québec can only count on a small number of strong and dynamic secondary organizations, and that these are too often poorly integrated into society. Among the indigenous institutions, only the labour unions and, to a much smaller degree, the universities, lately exhibit drive and adaptability. It is therefore hard to see how anyone who claims to be a good Quebecker can be glad of the difficulties these organizations face, even going so far as to favour cutting off their resources or breaking them up. Here more than elsewhere, governments are called upon to compensate for the chronic weakness of secondary organizations by means of direct aid to industry, by public works, public corporations, extensive (though not always wisely distributed) assistance to culture, education, telecommunications, health and welfare, housing, and so on. It is no doubt partly because of these special circumstances that politics too often become the principal object of the collective hopes and fears of Quebeckers.

Regardless of past intentions, in all liberal societies politics have, by force of circumstance, become the motive force of social change. The special circumstances prevailing in Québec parallel the basic trends operating everywhere and affecting the interaction between the social and the political spheres. I have named these possible general forms of interaction: techno-demagoguery, anarchy, and concertation. In one way or another, the forces that underlie current trends may be perceived at work in any crisis, at any point in the social structure, as well as during the intervening periods of calm; and each crisis may contribute to consolidating one or another of the three above forms.

By techno-demagoguery I mean a system in which the political leaders are in practice deprived of their prerogatives as official rulers in favour of civil servants who hold the real power by virtue of some specialized knowledge and who, at the same time, make one person, a new type of charismatic leader, the focus of the people's intense current longing for instinctiveness and spontaneity, a longing expressed now in supplication, now in anger. Techno-demagoguery is promoted by factors inherent in the growing complexity of societies moving into the post-industrial age, in which individuals and groups, despite the general rise in the level of education, become increasingly dependent on whoever offers to guide them through the complex ways and byways of organized social life. The comforting flamboyance of the demagogue provides a counterweight to the inhuman aspects of an omniscient technocracy. But the system may even dispense with the demagogue. With man's world transformed into a sleepy paradise, the mind itself can become dormant and passions can cool into nothingness. Such a pass, in which man may well find himself in the future—is he not already on his way?—was described by Albert Faucher when he coined the phrase "the tranquilizing revolution."[8]

To a large extent, the play of forces that promote the advent of techno-demagoguery also underlie tendencies towards anarchy. But even though anarchy is an anti-system, a plan for the anti-society or a parallel society, it is certainly not anti-political. Throughout the Western world, there is an undeniable weariness with politics, a weariness which, should it become stronger, may end in the rejection of politics as now practised by leaders and defined by political scientists. This trend was obvious in France in May 1968, it was certainly present in Nixon's United States, and it was one of the main forces behind the recent crises in Québec. People may stop expecting politics to provide a solution to all their problems because they will have learned that politics, so rich in compromise, are in the end quite poor in solutions. Even though the desire for anarchy can take the form of radicalism, terrorism, "dropping out," and apathy, these traits do not define its essential nature. Contemporary anarchistic tendencies are not a rejection of political organization as such, but rather a firm determination to escape completely from the grip of the existing systems. As far as it is possible to define anarchistic goals positively, these may be seen as a state of society in which citizens no longer organize themselves for action in the public arena (through parties, interest groups, etc.) but in small and often diffuse groups without immediate political aims, called on by force of circumstance to become centres for discussion and foci of political power, thus replacing whatever governmental arrangements are now in force. Anarchistic goals are, of course, utopian, at least in the sense that they rest on assumptions which not only go counter to the present situation but also appear altogether inprobable to actual leaders.

A third developmental trend (the one I would myself favour although, in view of mounting and widespread conflict, I fear that time is fast running out) is concertation, that is the organic co-operation of all the elements in society: individuals, as well as grass-roots groups, and the more powerful forces such as business, universities, labour unions, and government.

Such concertation would result from a synthesis between two current contradictory trends. It cannot be implemented exclusively from the top, that is, by a rapprochement among the leaders in each sphere of activity, for such a step would only serve to entrench the technostructure. Nor can it be accomplished from the bottom only, for this would border on anarchy and result in collective powerlessness. What kind of social and economic order could be achieved by a thousand citizen committees, a thousand "self-help projects" working alone, without the co-operation furnished by the main decision-making centres? It is just as impossible to draw up a plan for society without providing for its roots, as it is to envisage society standing upright without the support of solid secondary organizations, or to imagine development without the great social, cultural, economic, and political instruments that produce science, technology, and innovation and authoritative decisions and actions.

We know that the coming revolution is unavoidable. Its motive power comes from the hopes and fears, the loves and hates of people today. Thus it is men's enthusiastic, unfettered effort that contributes, largely beyond the ken of the actors themselves, to the advent of the revolution. Far from fearing it, they yearn obscurely for the day of its arrival. They hope then to see their individual and collective dreams unfold.

However, revolution means confusion. In this case, confusion arises from the fact that, depending on their temperaments and interests, men try to move toward the future by means of three different paths at the same time: techno-demagogy, anarchy, and concertation. This is why terms which supposedly describe points of view and outlooks, terms such as "right," "left," "reactionary," "radical," "consensus," "conflict," and so forth, are deeply ambiguous. The huge cacophony of schemes and actions is pinpointed in the manifold crises that are striking at Western liberal societies without warning.

Even so, man is far from helpless. On the contrary, he may, if he wishes, control the course of events, at least to some extent. Far from being reduced to resignation in awaiting some final cataclysm that will sooner or later seal his fate, there is a very great deal for him to do. He must reduce the material and human costs of the necessary transition period, and must help to smooth the process for as many people as possible—rich and poor, strong and weak, educated and ignorant, young and old.

Québec is bound up with the modern world. She has, however, her own appointment with history, one which she cannot avoid and which may turn out to be tragic. There is one issue Quebeckers must solve alone, for no-one else can solve it for them: the question of national identity. Here again, the chips are not all down. But, if they prolong the debate indefinitely, Quebeckers may run the risk of losing sight of other current stakes and of being bypassed by history.

Such is the dramatic situation which Quebeckers have been experiencing for more than a decade. They are driven strongly towards constructive action, but material and psychological obstacles weaken their momentum. The drive towards a great national plan is paralysed by the fear of an unknown future. The drive towards economic and social emancipation is immobilized by the enormous weight of the existing dominant structures. The drive towards a renovation of the political system is weakened by repeated disenchantments in the face of the negligible results obtained.

The whole problem facing Quebeckers can, in the end, be summed up in the following questions:

Will they succeed in creating an original synthesis of tradition and "progress" that will mark their coming of age as a people? Now that they have finally dared to make a commitment to the modern world, how will they reconcile it with their loyalty to their heritage?

EPILOGUE ... and the value of commitment

The cultural mutations experienced by Québec since 1940 are nothing short of astounding. Québec society has gone from rural and agricultural traditionalism to modernism and even to post-modernism, it has gone from monolithic Roman Catholicism to many forms of lay pluralism, from tribal corporatism to technocratic liberalism and socialism, from a somewhat hesitant federalism and a usually mild autonomism to various aggressive forms of autonomism and separatism, and the list could go on. One must also bear in mind the stress that these many shifts have caused both in institutions and in people's outlooks. These, then, are the movements, forward and back, reflected in the complex interaction between traditional-conservative, liberal, social-democratic, and socialist nationalism which I have attempted to describe in this book.

The above mutations took effect because, at each crucial moment in time, individuals and social movements stood at the ready: they did not view Québec with superb detachment, but rather attempted to sway its destinies one way or another. Whigs and Tories, independent Catholics and Ultramontanes, Montréal's "Nationalist School" of historians and Laval University's Faculty of Social Science; the movement of the Semaines Sociales and l'*Institut des Affaires Publiques*, l'*Action nationale* and *Cité libre*, *Cité libre* and *Parti pris*, trade unions and capitalist enterprise, the Union Nationale and the Liberal party, the Liberal party and the Parti Québécois, former as well as contemporary conservatisms and progressivisms. The mass of collusions and confrontations teeming between these various tendencies gave rise in the past, and is still giving rise today, to Québec nationalism.

Heading these movements were the men who, in various ways, left their stamp upon their times: Monsignor Bourget, Cardinal Villeneuve, Henri Bourassa, Lionel Groulx, Edouard Montpetit, Georges-Henri Lévesque, Alexandre Taschereau, Maurice Duplessis, Jean Lesage, Daniel Johnson, René Lévesque, Pierre Elliott Trudeau . . .

However, when we look at the impact of each of these figures, we feel that their historic mission was accomplished over a very short span of time. Once their essential task was fulfilled, those who persisted in trying to work became redundant, if not embarrassing. Henri Bourassa and Lionel Groulx were outstanding exceptions, but even their viewpoints had, in major ways, become anachronistic though still influential a number of years before the end of their active lives.

The responsibility for building a society or for undertaking its critique seems very rapidly to shift from one person or one movement to another. And for each movement or person who does leave a mark on the times, how many others, less talented or clearsighted, fail and fall into oblivion? History is shaped solely by those who have the ability to make the most of the right moment. Others, weaker, or shorter on intuition, leave little trace of their passing. The leading characters of history do not need to be right all their lives; they need not even be right at any one point. They must, rather, have the ability to take the right turning when the moment comes, and to stick to this chosen path with force and persistence enough to influence what is happening around them.

Thus, quite correctly, much is made of the influence of Laval University's Faculty of Social Science and that of its first Dean, Father Georges-Henri Lévesque. The early faculty members did indeed greatly contribute to demystifying some of Québec's long-rigidified or obsolete values and modes of behaviour. In so doing, and in opening up paths for the future, they had some rough clashes with the established clerical and lay leadership. But it is over a fifteen-year span at the very most, that is between 1937 and 1952, that the Faculty of Social Science accomplished its sizeable task of demystification. From 1952 to 1955, the faculty underwent profound change, and it is under a new leadership and with a new generation of teachers that it subsequently contributed to paving the way for the Quiet Revolution.

Until 1952, the faculty and its early teachers drew upon the philosophy of Thomas Aquinas, which by and large held the Catholic Church's stamp of approval, as well as upon the Church's social doctrine. In their struggle against Maurice Duplessis' ''realistic'' traditional-conservative nationalism, they upheld its opposite, pan-Canadianism. These were the kinds of ties that initially maintained the faculty in out-dated patterns of thought and behaviour, ties inimical to the full development of scholarly work of a kind that would subsequently attract the faculty's later teachers. It became their task, in turn, to base their teaching upon positive and critical theories, aimed at objectivity and universality; and, under the auspices of ACFAS (L'Association Canadienne-Française pour l'avancement des Sciences), which had so far only covered the natural sciences, they were to set up scholarly societies in collaboration with their more recently appointed colleagues at the University of Montreal. This was in turn to give rise to projects, symposia, and field-research, and to the publication of their results in a newly established scholarly journal, *Recherches sociographiques.* Thus, after 1952, the contribution of Laval University's Faculty of Social Science came to foster the spirit of liberal nationalism that became the official political formula after Jean Lesage's victory in June 1960; and this is also the faculty which trained many of the men who later put into effect the widespread reforms to which liberal nationalism gave rise.

Similarly, if we look at *Cité libre,* its period of social usefulness fits into a brief ten-year span. Even though the periodical emphatically stood up against the pan-Canadianism of the Faculty of Social Science; even though the editors no longer drew inspiration from Thomist philosophy, and were only moderately influenced by the Church's social doctrine, the *Cité libre* group nevertheless pursued the social struggle along the lines laid down by the faculty before 1952. However, from 1960 on, after the establishment of the liberal democratic regime for which it had fought with such strength, the periodical began an unsuccessful search for a new raison d'être. After 1960, the editors managed neither to grasp nor to bend the course of events, and it is a new generation of intellectuals who resoundingly broke away from *Cité libre* and founded *Parti pris* in 1963, contributing to the birth of new outlooks and paving the way for the newly-emerging forms of social-democratic and of socialist nationalism.

It may happen that the tides of circumstance bring the same man or the same movement to the fore more than once. Such a new lease on life or a new career may seem very different from the first, and Charles de Gaulle comes to mind as a prime example. Another example may be found in the many terrorist and revolutionary movements in Tsarist Russia which tirelessly repeated and improved on the scenario of the December 1815 revolt, right up to the successful October 1917 Revolution. Much the same applies to Gérard Pelletier, Jean Marchand, and Pierre Elliott Trudeau. Having been front-rank trade unionists or journalists between 1950 and 1963, they came to dissociate themselves from the Quiet Revolution's mainstream, but without being able to catalyze an opposition movement along the lines prevailing at the time outside official circles; and it seemed that they would no longer be able to play any major social role in Québec. The decision each of the three men took, in 1965, to enter the federal political scene, as Trudeau put it, to ''counter-balance'' a Québec that had in their eyes become too autonomist, opened up a second career which led them to the top posts in the Canadian federal government. Their ideas, no longer fitting

Québec's needs as defined by the official leadership or by the extra-parliamentary opposition movements, happened then to fit in with the situation of Anglophone Canada.

The list of such examples might be extended, but to no useful purpose as it would merely bolster the same conclusion: social movements and human beings are needed at history's turning points, but the time-span of their impact is short. It is not always easy for them to fade out of the political scene once their work is done. History very rapidly outdistances them.

To understand the value of commitment, it is important to look into this rough shoving aside of movements and of men who were for a time judged to be indispensable. An answer to the question must be sought in the very nature of values and in their relationship with the real-life situations in which value cycles are determined. The reason why movements and men succeed each other in Québec at so rapid a pace, and why the pace is quickening today as compared to yesterday, is that our society's rate of development and change has been a dizzying one over the past thirty-five years, and is still continuing to speed up.

A study of Québec nationalisms reveals, among the trend-setting formative values, a constant oscillation between the three different models of cultural patterns. Indeed, we find a constant state of tension between particularism and universalism, between conservatism and progressivism, and also between reformism and radicalism. Some forms of nationalism lean towards particularism and conservatism; others put more emphasis upon universalism and progressivism, while among the progressivists, reformists and radicals often clash with each other.

Somewhat similar tensions may, to a lesser extent, also exist within a single nationalist current. Thus, a look at the values underlying traditional-conservative nationalism shows that, between its coming into full sway in 1840 and its official demotion in 1960, particularism and conservatism were unconditionally preponderant. And while liberal rationalism is essentially progressive, the interplay of underlying values shows it not to be altogether immune to the conservative virus; moreover, while its support for modernity makes it lean towards universalism, its frequent falling back on Québec also introduces particularism. However, it is outspokenly reformist, and has little truck with any occasional leanings towards radicalism. As to social-democratic nationalism, like liberal nationalism, its operative values incline it to universalism and progressivism. However, since it favours Québec's independence rather than provincial autonomism, it finds it possible, at any rate in principle, to uphold universalism less ambiguously, whereas the tension between reformism and radicalism surges more forcefully. Finally, socialist nationalism's operative values are basically universalist, progressivist, and radical. However, it is very difficult to pin-point the exact nature of these tendencies, since this form of nationalism has not so far taken viable root in Québec in sufficiently broad and durable social organizations.

The value of a commitment always seems relative and impermanent because the attitudes of men and social movements towards this threefold cultural model can only produce an imperfect and provisional balance between the values they profess and the specific requirements of the action they promote. Thus, the circumstances of their time required Father Lévesque and his early faculty at Laval to side openly with the Church's social doctrine. Partly thanks to their activities, a shift in the social climate from 1952 on allowed a second-generation faculty, with the continuing collaboration of some of their elders, to choose to engage in thoroughly scholarly pursuits. At the same time, this new generation of teachers denounced the false universalism of the pan-Canadianism so far favoured by the Faculty of Social Science; and they thereby radically reoriented the process of demystifying traditional-conservative nationalism, a process spearheaded by the faculty since 1938.

Seeking to maintain a proper balance between values and operational requirements necessitates such periodical de-structurings and re-structurings of cultural representational models. Without these processes, frequently painful for the men most directly involved, the development of society would be impaired. Seen in this way, the extent of the upheaval in minds and in institutions in Québec since 1940 becomes striking. Here is a society in which particular value-patterns were long considered eternal within an immutable institutional framework. The society was suddenly shaken to its core by men who thus reverse the old balance, whereas they might normally have been expected to perpetuate it, inasmuch as they belonged to the traditional elites, as priests, journalists, and university teachers. The unusual thing about this truly revolutionary process is that the rate of change thus set off never reduced its momentum from the very beginning. But, side by side with the acceleration, two major phenomena radically modified the interplay of values and action: on the one hand, the ancient certainties, derived from religious faith or tradition, faded away one after the other without being replaced, so that today it is difficult to base operational values upon firm beliefs capable of enlisting the support of a sufficient number of people to keep a social movement alive. On the other hand, it is no longer possible to conceive of Québec while at the same time ignoring the rest of the world. Québec's accession to modernity, as well as the emergence of problems which Québec shares with other peoples and which require world-wide solutions, have made isolationism suicidal.

Ever since the cultural revolutions overtook the Western world around 1968, Québec shares the same basic concerns as neighbouring peoples. It shares in a civilization which may well be finite and which may, indeed, be hearing its death-knell.

Thus for example, in Québec as elsewhere, awareness is growing that the new requirements of social justice, expressed by spokesmen of underprivileged communities and groups, can no longer be met by measures aimed at alleviating poverty (charity, philanthropy, social welfare) as was the case so far, but that it is now imperative to eradicate the very causes of poverty. Similarly, the acute problems of world hunger, of environmental pollution, of the depletion of resources, and of energy scarcity, among others, are as pressing for Quebeckers as for other peoples. Searching for solutions to these problems implies that Quebeckers will devote as much energy to scientific research as may be expected from a people that, by world-wide standards, ranks among the most affluent. Since 1958, when, writing in *Cité libre,* I deplored the unenviable position of Québec's universities,[9] there has, it is true, been fantastic growth among Québec's institutions of higher learning. We must however note that masters and doctoral courses of study remain inadequate in most of the humanities and social sciences, and that the organization of scientific research remains rudimentary.

The effects of such shortcomings are felt in every area of activity. Formerly, operational values could be assessed in the light of recognized and broadly-acknowledged criteria. Thus in 1939, when Father Lévesque, prompted by his sociological studies and his Christian convictions, set up the Conseil supérieur de la coopération, his was a progressive and reformist action which so managed to balance universalism and particularism as to gain the approval of most of his contemporaries. But in 1951, at the conclusion of the work of the Royal Commission on the Arts of which he was vice-chairman, when he advocated pan-Canadianism and subsequently lauded the merits of "overlapping cultures," he was lagging behind the times.[10] He was sharply criticized, not only by autonomist nationalists (which fitted in with the old pattern of things), but also by the second-generation teachers at the Faculty of Social Science who, defending overriding standards of scholarship, considered his stand to be unduly tinged with traditionalist conservatism and pseudo-universalism.

What are the criteria, publicly accepted or potentially acceptable, by which one might today assess the relevance of the multitude of cultural patterns formulated by social movements and individuals to justify their operational values? Whichever of the main options open to Quebeckers one may examine, whether federalism, separatism, conservatism, liberalism, or socialism—can the deplorable sparseness of operational values escape one's attention? They are too abstract or too down-to-earth, too empirical or too doctrinaire, too prosaic or too idealistic; in short they fail to measure up to people's expectations.

These shortcomings are doubtless due to the great confusion that exists throughout the world with regard to values, and also to the great complexity of the problems assailing humanity. However, the confusion about values and the complexity of problems must be overcome in one way or another if social movements capable of solving them are to take shape. Quebeckers would be wrong to believe that, for good reason or bad, they are exempt from doing their share, together with Americans, Europeans, Africans, and Asians, in searching for viable solutions. Although values are fundamentally universal, it is of course up to each people to elaborate their own particularistic version and to apply it as circumstances permit.

It is, I believe, impossible to overrate the need for thoughtful research centred upon Québec as a field of study, but aimed at the overriding concerns of humankind. However, a hidden trap lies in wait for unwary researchers (and men of action) who use research data as their yardstick: science and technology are everywhere at the service of technocratic end-goals which, both in government and in the great corporations, are spinning out a soporific paradise in which no room is left for men's individual and collective creativity. In this new order, which is being introduced throughout Western societies with the glib connivance of politicians and businessmen, whoever wishes to escape the totalitarianism of the new ideology (striving to draw status from science itself) will have to start listening to society's humblest and most under-privileged ranks: the pioneer farmers of the Lower Saint-Lawrence and the Gaspé Peninsula, clinging to their wood-lots and their rocky soil, the people of the forgotten slums of Montréal, Québec, and other cities. It still remains, of course, important to know what the leaders of the day are saying and doing. But, just as in Ancient Greece the culture of the slaves and not that of the masters carried the day in giving rise to the Stoic values upon which Roman civilization and subsequently Western civilizations were largely built, so today we must look towards the poor for pointers to the values that may guide us in choosing sound commitments.

NOTES

CHAPTER 1 TRADITION AND PROGRESS (pp. 1-30)

1. The use of this expression carries implications which, although not expressed explicitly, are so important that they deserve careful attention.

2. It is significant that, of the four most influential members of the Lesage cabinet, three (Lapalme, Lévesque, Gérin-Lajoie) also come from the Montréal area, and that one of them (Lévesque) was also very much a member of the intellectual elite.

3. It is under the "old regime" that the intellectuals got their education and acquired their skill in the use of the mass media. It would be interesting to examine to what extent they themselves contributed to the downfall of the Duplessis system. On the other hand, precisely because of their mastery of the mass media, acquired under the old regime, they are now the best-equipped and also the most self-confident men in the public eye, in these, the early days of the new regime.

4. Reference to this will be found in my essay, "Opinion publique et systèmes idéologiques" in *Ecrits du Canada Français,* xii (1962), 10-172, where the United States and the USSR media are compared.

5. This survey was based on a questionnaire. See *Cahiers de L'ICEA* (Institut Canadien d'éducation des adultes), no. 2, 1958.

6. See my study "Bill 60 et les publics," *Cahiers de l'ICEA,* no. 1, 1966; in 1967 my book, *Le Bill 60 et la société Québécoise,* was published by HMH, Montreal, 1967.

7. I realize that these are relative concepts whose meaning varies from one society to another and from one period to another. The use of these expressions immediately gives rise to questions such as, conservatism and progressivism in relation to whom? In terms of what? Up to what point? Thus, specific ideological orientations must necessarily be taken into account. The same political system may seem to be shockingly conservative to a socialist and dangerously progressive to a reactionary. Moreover a political system may be conservative in certain fields and progressive in others. Finally, the degree of a system's conservatism or progressivism may vary in particular instances. Seen in this way the two concepts may be regarded as the opposite poles of a continuum, current political systems lying at some point or other between the two extremes. An answer to the above questions will thus require an analysis of specific cases in the light of predefined criteria. This is not the purpose of the present chapter, which attempts to describe outlooks rather than situations. I shall therefore not attach any practical content to the concepts of conservatism and progressivism, except to say that by conservatists I mean those who are change resisters and by progressivists those who are change agents. I shall examine the image po-

litical authorities have of their own power, as well as the overall impression created by the attitudes and behaviour of governments; and will also take into account the related views of intellectuals and of leaders influential in the major fields of thought and of social activity.

8. The concept of ''authorities'' has been hotly debated among political scientists. The expression is of course often used lightly and improperly. Authorities are commonly understood to be centres of power: political, religious, economic. I have no objection to this usage provided it is merely an abbreviated and non-operative description of a complex phenomenon, and not a magic formula implying that quasi-personal powers arise within society, to which human beings are blindly subjected. In this chapter, the expression ''authority'' is used synthetically. When I use it as an operative concept, authority is taken as an attribute of political or social agents and becomes one of the three components of ''influence,'' the other two being power (or resources) and prestige.

9. See my two articles: ''Le libéralisme du statu-quo: l'idéologie protectrice,'' *Recherches sociographiques* 1, no. 4 (October-December 1960): 435-65; and ''Le libéralisme du statu-quo: le droit protecteur,'' ibid, 2, no. 1 (January-March 1961): 69-100.

10. The most outstanding study along these lines, even though it is still preliminary, is that by Fernand Dumont, ''Structure d'une idéologie religieuse,'' *Recherches sociographiques* 1, no. 2, (April-June 1960): 161-89. Researchers for some years have carried out extensive surveys of religious practices, but the primary aim of such surveys has not been sociological.

11. This is not an attempt to deny the legitimacy of the great political options as such in the Canadian context. Their very existence is evidence of their importance. Indeed, the crisis of Canadian federalism is one of today's major problems. However I deplore the frivolity with which a number of political figures and intellectuals discuss so serious a question.

12. Since the writing of this section, Maurice Pinard, Michael Stein, and Vincent Lemieux have published work on the ascent of Social Credit.

13. I have nothing against these slogans in themselves. They may be considered as rallying cries geared to action. However, it must be recognized that they do not go beyond a rather elementary level of conceptualisation and that their power to generate enthusiasm is likely to be short-lived. Probably, myth related to the general goals of the community rather than to the daily tasks of the government, would do better.

14. The clash of ideologies produced by Bill 60 shows the lack of realism among those who hope the voluntary associations will harmoniously and unanimously exercise a controlling and necessary influence, braking or accelerating the application of government programs. But voluntary associations cannot be turned into ''intermediate bodies'' otherwise than through persistent governmental action. Left to their own devices, if they pursue political goals, they will turn into pressure groups. And the circumstances of political struggle will then lead them not so much into common courses of action, as into opposing each other in the pursuit of divergent interests and aspirations. As I see it, the development of so-called participatory democracy will depend far more upon how well the members of voluntary associations learn the methods of political pressure, than upon associations' becoming tools to convey or promote governmental objectives with the assistance of political agents cooperating with intellectuals and social leaders. The doctrine of ''intermediate bodies,'' as it is often advanced, in itself bears the seeds that may destroy the ideological spontaneity of associations and social groups. Not only does it not increase the influence of social agents upon the action of governments, but the full application of the doctrine may cause the loss of the voluntary groups' ideological spontaneity and their take-over by the power-structure.

15. The overthrow of conservatism by progressivism has certainly changed the temperament of ideologies. Thus, the essentially negative nationalism which had long paralyzed political action is now replaced by a positive nationalism, aimed at inspiring formulae and programs of action. One may thus wonder whether the reversal of political dynamics, in ad-

dition to influencing the temperament of ideologies has given rise to the development of new ideologies. That is a complex question to which I cannot give any certain answer. However, I believe that recent efforts to introduce here ideologies invented elsewhere— for instance those arising out of colonial situations or decolonization—have so far met with little success among the mass of the people.

16. BAEQ (Bureau d'aménagement de l'Est du Québec) [The Eastern-Québec Development Office] was established in June 1961 under a federal-provincial agreement, within the framework of the Agricultural and Rural Development Act (ARDA). The BAEQ researchers, mostly young university graduates in their twenties, in addition to carrying out extensive socio-economic studies of the area, became deeply involved in community mobilization.

17. The *Opérations-dignité* represent protest movements, led by local dignitaries, particularly village parish priests, against what they considered inhuman treatment of the inhabitants of "marginal" parishes in the backwoods, to whom the government proposed financial compensation if they left their farms and moved into the cities, where they would almost inevitably swell the number of the unemployed and of low-income neighbourhoods.

CHAPTER 2   NATIONAL IDENTITY (pp. 31-51)

1. The present paper does not intend to take sides. I do not propose to examine the extent to which nationalism, that is the definitions which French Canadians give of themselves when they think of themselves as a group, faithfully mirrors reality. I shall rather consider nationalism as a social fact, which it is, in that it constitutes at least one of the aspects of that reality. More precisely, I shall concentrate upon the description of the main tendencies of nationalism as they appeared on the eve of the "quiet revolution."

CHAPTER 3   ECONOMIC ASPECTS (pp. 53-72)

1. Many such instances are reported in my two articles: "Le libéralisme du statu-quo: l'idéologie protectrice" and "Le libéralisme du statu-quo: le droit protecteur," *Recherches sociographiques* 1, no. 4 (1960): 435-65 and 2, no. 1 (1961): 71-100.

2. A recent American study concludes that, of all North Americans, it is the blacks and the French Canadians who have attitudes and ways of life least compatible with business. This curious association, which brings to mind the title of a well-known book by Pierre Vallières (*White Negroes of America*) raises questions which a number of people would doubtless prefer to ignore.

3. Fernand Martin, André Raynault, "Les choix urbains et régionaux dans le Québec des années 70" (Urban and regional choices in Québec in the seventies), *Le Québec d'aujourd'hui*, ed., Jean-Luc Migué (Montréal: HMH, 1971), pp. 195-208. By comparison with American industry, Canadian industry in general so lacks vitality that Maurice Lamontagne considers it to be ailing. See Maurice Lamontagne's "The Sickness of Canadian industry," *Canadian Forum*, June 1972, pp. 18-21.

4. Jean-Luc Migué, "L'industrialisation et la participation des Québécois au progrès économique," *Le Québec d'aujourd'hui*, pp. 227-51.

5. This was written before the break-away from the CNTU, in June 1972, of the group which formed the CSD (Confédération des Syndicats Démocratiques), a break-away which had been in the making for some three years.

6. See Ralph Miliband, *The State in Capitalist Society: An Analysis of the Western System of Power* (London: Weidenfeld and Nicolson, 1969).

7. Jean-Luc Migué, "Le nationalisme, l'unité nationale et la théorie économique de l'infor-

mation,'' *Revue canadienne d'économique,* III, no. 2, 1970; and ''L'industrialisation et la participation des Québécois au progrès économique,'' *Le Québec d'aujourd'hui.*

8. Among the difficulties to be overcome, one of the first to come to mind is that of French-Canadians' attitudes (shown both in the work of Gilles Auclair and in a recent American study to be poorly attuned to business). But these unsuitable attitudes are largely due to the situation in which French Canadians have been operating, and may be corrected by business experience. Another difficulty is the inadequate number of qualified French Canadians. This is doubtless true for the time being, but it can be corrected relatively rapidly. Yet another is the required recognition of French as a working language in every sphere of business activity. And why not? The resultant French-Canadian economic elite would be a capitalistic one. This, needless to say, would not enchant the advocates of socialism. But it would entail the disappearance of a great many incongruities, now caused by the fact that big business in Québec is headed by non Francophones.

9. It is of paramount importance that business should contribute to maintaining strong trade-unionism in Québec and should correctly understand recent trends in Québec's labour unions. Business needs a sound partner, adequately reflecting the work-force. Consequently, for their own good, neither business nor government should rejoice at current rifts in the labour movement, especially since these divisions are ideological. Ideological polarizations—for example, between a view of trade-unionism as limited to the place of work, and a view of trade-unionism as a spokesman in the defence of over-all social and political interests—will first of all intensify radicalism among some of the workers, and will represent a continuing threat of union conflict and socio-political disruption. Secondly, such polarization would provide built-in channels for expressing many socio-political protest movements in Québec, whose present weakness lies in their dispersion rather than in the lack of response among the under-privileged classes of society and among intellectuals. In fact, such response is very strong and is likely to be all the more durable as the government of Québec, by its sins of commission and omission, sometimes seems to be deliberately encouraging it. On the other hand, ideological polarization will become inevitable if the labour unions manage to cover, as they are often encouraged to do, at least sixty percent of the workers who are currently non-unionized. Of these, most come from the underprivileged groups whose living conditions are far removed from those of the qualified workers—technicians, office employees, and professionals—who today make up the main strength of Québec's labour unions.

CHAPTER 4   POLITICAL LIFE (pp. 73-103)

1. Margaret Atwood, *Survival: A Thematic Guide to Canadian Literature,* (Toronto: Anansi, 1972).

2. See the amazing revelations in the Fantus Report, a study carried out by the American firm, Fantus, in May 1972, for the Department of Industry and Commerce. The government tried to keep the report secret, but the Québec daily, *Le Soleil,* published large excerpts.

3. It is widely known that the claimed superiority of Francophones in the fields of classical humanism, arts and letters, has little basis in real fact. Community colleges and McGill University in no way lagged behind classical colleges or French-speaking universities. But at the same time, English-speaking education was attaching a great deal of importance to science, engineering, business management, and administration, unlike the French-speaking educational institutions which concentrated almost exclusively on classical humanistic training. In fact, surveys have shown that Francophones have less regard than Anglophones for careers oriented towards the arts, letters, or ''things of the mind.'' (Even the Roman Catholic clergy rank higher on the professional prestige scale among Anglophones than Francophones!) As the less affluent of the two, French Canadians have very naturally taken to the professions they see as financially most rewarding. It is the Jews and the Anglophones, less obsessed by day-to-day survival, their material needs

having been amply met, who may by preference turn towards intellectual or artistic pursuits. See J. Porter and P. C. Pineo, *French-English Differences in the Evaluation of Occupations, Industries, Ethnicities and Religions in the Montréal Metropolitan Area* (Royal Commission on Bilingualism and Biculturalism, 1966). It then becomes clearer why, as soon as they were permitted to do so, Francophone program directors, teachers, and students so joyfully and promptly abandoned Greek and Latin studies and most of the humanities: they had no great attachment for these subjects (any more than they did for rocky farmland).

4. Having brought out the fact that, in Québec, dignitaries and politicians were given to proclaiming that all sovereign authority comes from God, and that hence citizens (or subjects) own Him unconditional obedience ("Think about it carefully before you go to vote," parish priests used to admonish at the lectern) Trudeau went on to say the following about the responsibility of the federal liberal party:

But power entails responsibilities; and there is no doubt that the Liberals tragically failed to shoulder theirs. A party cannot have the approval of a majority of the electorate for well over half a century without accepting much of the blame for that electorate's political immaturity.

If French Canadians even today have learnt so little about democracy, if they twist its rules so shockingly, if they are constantly tempted by authoritarianism, it is to a large degree because the Liberal Party has been miserably remiss in its simple political duty. Instead of educating the French-speaking electorate to believe in democracy, the Liberals seemed content to cultivate the ignorance and the prejudices of that electorate. I should not like to apportion blame between French- and English-speaking Liberals in this regard. The gravest faults no doubt fall squarely on the former. It is they who have failed to inject valid democratic concepts into the innumerable campaigns waged during the present century. On the contrary, forgetful of the common weal, they have always encouraged Quebeckers to continue using their voting bloc as an instrument of racial defense, or of personal gain.

From "Some Obstacles to Democracy in Québec," *Canadian Journal of Economics and Political Science,* 24, no. 3, 1958. Translation by Pierre Vadeboncoeur and published in French in Pierre Elliott Trudeau, *Le fédéralisme et la société canadienne française* (Montréal: HMH, 1967.)

It is to be noted that, in the federal general elections of 1968, 1972, and particularly 1974, Québec's Liberals, under Trudeau's wing, unashamedly appealed to the French-speaking electorate's ethnic feelings. This tactic gave the Liberal party some of the best showings in terms of French-Canadian votes ever recorded since Confederation.

CHAPTER 5   POLITICS AND NATIONALISM IN QUEBEC (pp. 105-176)

1. Ferdinand Toennies, *Gemeinschaft und Gesellschaft,* 1887, translated into French by J. Leif, *Communauté et société* (Paris: Presses Universitaires de France, 1944), translated by Charles Loomis, *Fundamental Concepts of Sociology* (New York: American Book Company, 1940); Karl W. Deutsch, *Nationalism and Social Communications* (Cambridge: M.I.T. Press, 1953), and *Nationalism and Its Alternatives* (New York: Alfred A. Knopf, 1969); Louis Hartz, *The Founding of New Societies* (Cambridge: Harvard University Press, 1965) (translated into French, *Les enfants de l'Europe* (Paris: Editions du Seuil, 1968); Martin Seymour Lipset, *The First New Nation* (New York: Basic Books, 1963). For an excellent study of Hartz's and Lipset's theoretical contribution to the analysis of Canadian political culture, see David V. J. Bell, "Methodological Problems in the Study of Canadian Political Culture," paper delivered at the June, 1974 meeting of the Canadian Political Science Association (unpublished).

2. David Easton, *A Systems Analysis of Political Life* (New York: John Wiley, 1965). In

two unpublished papers, "Theoretical Approaches to Political Support" and "A Re-Assessment of the Concept of Political Support," Easton goes into the crucial concept of "political support." Léon Dion, *Société et politique: la vie des groupes,* vol. 1: *Fondements de la société libérale;* vol. 2: *Dyamique de la société libérale* (Québec: Les Presses de l'Université Laval, 1971, 1972) An English translation is forthcoming (University of Toronto Press, 1977).

3. André J. Bélanger, *L'apolitisme des idéologies québécoises: Le grand tournant de 1934 à 1936* (Québec: Les Presses de l'Université Laval, 1974).

4. Karl W. Deutsch, *Nationalism and Its Alternatives,* p. 125.

5. Anthony D. Smith, *Theories of Nationalism* (New York: Harper and Row, 1971).

6. On Groulx's separatism, see Jean-Pierre Gaboury, *Le nationalisme de Lionel Groulx, Aspects idéologiques* (Ottawa: l'Université d'Ottawa, 1970), 153-60.

7. Michel Brunet, "The French Canadians' Search for a Fatherland," in *Nationalism in Canada,* ed. Peter Russell (Toronto: McGraw-Hill, 1966), 47-61.

8. Ramsay Cook, *Canada and the French Canadian Question* (Toronto: Macmillan, 1966).

9. See John Trent, "Considerations for the Study of the Estates General of French Canada," Queen's University, 1970 (unpublished), and "Participation in the Estates General of French Canada," Annual meeting of the Canadian Political Science Association, University of Alberta, June 1975 (unpublished).

10. See my article "Le nationalisme pessimiste. Sa cource, sa signification, sa validité," *Cité libre,* November 1957, 3-18. English translation in *French-Canadian Nationalism,* ed. Ramsay Cook (Toronto: Macmillan, 1969), 294-304. For a similar viewpoint, see Jean Blain, "Economie et société en Nouvelle-France: l'historiographie des années 1950 à 1960. Guy Frégault et l'école de Montréal," *Revue d'histoire de l'Amérique française* 28; no. 2 (1974): 163-87.

11. *La grève de l'amiante,* ed. Pierre Elliott Trudeau (Montréal: les éditions Cité libre, 1956), 1-92.

12. "Some Obstacles to Democracy in Québec," *Canadian Journal of Economics and Political Science* 24: 3 (1958): 297-311 (translated into French by Pierre Vadeboncoeur, and reproduced in Pierre Elliott Trudeau, *Le fédéralisme et la société canadienne-française* (Montréal: HMH, 1967), 107-28).

13. Edouard Cloutier, "Les fondements micro-économiques du nationalisme canadien-français: une hypothèse," *Revue canadienne des études sur le nationalisme* 2, no. 1 (1975). On the basis of surveys, Maurice Pinard and Raymond Breton believe on the contrary that there is no difference in the economic attitudes of Francophones and Anglophones. See Maurice Pinard, "Ethnic Loyalty, Constitutional Options and Support for Independentist Parties in Québec; Some Basic Dimensions," 1974 (unpublished); Maurice Pinard and Richard Hamilton, "The Recent Québec Elections: an Analysis of the Electorate," 1974 (unpublished), and "Separatism and the Polarization of the Québec Electorate: the 1973 Provincial Elections," 1974 (unpublished); Raymond Breton, "Etude sur la satisfaction au travail," 1972.

14. Norman Ward and David Hoffman, *Bilingualism in the House of Commons,* Royal Commission on Bilingualism and Biculturalism, Ottawa 1968; Alan Kornberg, *Canadian Legislative Behavior* (New York: Holt, Rinehart and Winston, 1967). Also see R. Manzer, *Canada: A Socio-Political Report* (Toronto: McGraw-Hill, Ryerson, 1974), 187-263; Normand Duern, "Cohesion and Factionalism in Federal Political Parties," M.A. thesis, McGill University, 1969. See also: Charles-Michel d'Inumberry De Salaberry, "Culture and Nationalism in Québec Politics," M.A. thesis, Queen's University, 1972.

15. Kenneth McRoberts, "Mass Acquisition of Nationalism: The Case for Québec Autonomism," Ph.D. Thesis, University of Chicago, 1974.

16. Fernand Dumont, ''Un socialisme pour le Québec'' in *La vigile du Québec. Octobre 1970: L'impasse?* (Montreal: HMH, 1971), 145-55.

17. Jean-Paul Bernard, *Les rouges. Libéralisme, nationalisme et anti-cléricalisme au milieu du XIXème siècle* (Montréal: Les Presses de l'Université du Québec, 1971. Also see the special issue devoted to: *Idéologies au Canada français: 1850-1900* in *Recherches sociographiques,* 10, nos. 2 and 3 (1969).

18. Jean-René Suratteau, *L'idée nationale de la révolution à nos jours* (Paris: Presses Universitaires de France, S.U.P., 1972).

19. Anthony D. Smith, *Theories of Nationalism,* 15. Also, Elie Kedourie, *Nationalism* (London: Hutchinson, 1960).

20. Georges-Emile Lapalme, *Mémoires,* 3 vols. (Montréal: Leméac, 1969-73). I refer to vol. 1, *Le bruit des choses éveillées.*

21. *Cahier d'éducation des adultes,* Vol. 2, November 1958. This issue also includes my text: ''L'esprit démocratique chez les Canadiens de langue française,'' 34-43.

22. Marcel Rioux, *La question québécoise* (Paris: Seghers, 1969), 103.

23. Edwin R. Black, *Divided Loyalties: Canadian Concepts of Federalism* (Montreal: McGill-Queen's University Press, 1975). For an English view of the ''pact'' and the ''two-nations'' theories, see R. M. Burns, ed., *One Country or Two?* (Montreal: McGill-Queen's University Press, 1971).

24. Falardeau, Jean-Charles, *L'essor des sciences sociales au Canada français* (Québec: Ministère des affaires culturelles, 1964); ''La génération de la Relève,'' *Recherches sociographiques* 6, no 2 (1965): 123-33; ''Léon Gérin: une introduction à la lecture de son oeuvre,'' *Recherches sociographiques* 1, no 2 (1960): 123-60. For more on this period, see Fernand Dumont and others, *Idéologues au Canada Francais,* vol. 1: 1850-1900, and vol. 2: 1900-1923 (Québec: Presses de l'Université Laval, 1971 and 1975).

25. Jean-Louis Roy, *Québec 1945-1960: la transition,* to be published in 1976.

26. Léon Dion, *Le bill 60 et la société québécoise* (Montréal: HMH, 1967).

27. Léon Dion, ''La polarité des idéologies: conservatisme et progressisme,'' *Recherches sociographiques* 7, nos. 1 and 2 (1966), reproduced in *La prochaine révolution* (Montréal: Leméac, 1973), pp. 28-44.

28. Claude Morin, *Le pouvoir québécois . . . en négociation* (Montréal: Boréal Express, 1972).

29. Karl W. Deutsch, ''Between Sovereignty and Integration: Conclusion'' in *Between Sovereignty and Integration,* ed. Ghita Ionescu (London: Croom Helm, 1974), 186-87.

30. André D'Allemagne, *Le R.I.N. et les débuts du mouvement indépendantiste québécois,* (Montréal: Editions l'Etincelle, 1974). Also, François-Pierre Gingras, ''L'engagement indépendantiste au Québec,'' Ph.D. thesis, Université René Descartes, Paris 1971.

31. Jacques Hamel, ''Le mouvement national des Québécois à la recherche de la modernité,'' *Recherches sociographiques,* 15, no. 3 (1973), 341-63. As to the unofficial organ of the Parti Québécois, the daily *Le Jour,* while its nationalist stance is clearly an independentist one there seems to be an absence of any social ideology.

32. André Potvin, *L'allié-nation. De l'idéologie nationaliste de la revue Parti Pris, ou pour comprendre le nationalisme québécois,* M.A. thesis, University of Ottawa, 1970. On the various social-democratic and socialist nationalist movements, see S. H. and H. Milner, *The Decolonization of Québec: An Analysis of Left-Wing Nationalism,* (Toronto: McClelland and Stewart, 1973).

33. Louis-Marie Tremblay, *Le syndicalisme québécois. Idéologies de la C.S.N. et de la F.T.Q., 1940 to 1970* (Montréal: Les Presses de l'Université de Montréal, 1972). In the framework of the study of Québec political cultures at present conducted by Micheline de

Sève, Jacques Hamel, and myself, four papers are devoted to the main trade-union organizers: Raymond Hudon (Confederation of National Trade Unions), Carol Levasseur (Québec Federation of Labour), Louise Laliberté (Corporation of Québec Teachers) and Gabriel Gaudette (Confederation of Democratic Trade Unions).

34. Léon Dion and Micheline De Sève, "Québec: Interest Groups and the Search for an Alternative Political System," *The Annals of the American Academy of Political and Social Science,* Vol. 413, May 1974, 124-44.

35. Kari Levitt, *Silent Surrender* (Toronto: MacMillan, 1970).

36. Malcolm Reid, *The Shouting Signpainters. A Literary and Political Account of Québec Revolutionary Nationalism* (Toronto: McClelland and Stewart, 1972).

37. Marc Laurendeau, *Les Québécois violents. Une étude sur les causes et la rentabilité de la violence d'inspiration politique au Québec* (Montréal: Boréal Express, 1974).

38. For a description of the October 1970 events, see: Jean-Claude Trait, *F.L.Q. 70: Offensive d'automne* (Montréal: Les éditions de l'Homme, 1970).

39. Guy Rocher, *Le Québec en mutation,* (Montréal: HMH, 1973), p. 56.

40. Ramsay Cook, *Canada and the French-Canadian Question.*

41. Alain Touraine, *La société post-industrielle,* (Paris: Denoël, 1969).

42. Daniel Bell, *The Coming of Post-industrial Society: A venture in Social Forecasting,* (New York: Basic Books, 1973).

43. Guy Rocher, *Le Québec en mutation.*

44. Léon Dion, "Vers une conscience autodéterministe," *Revue de l'Association canadienne d'éducation de langue française,* 1 no 1 (1971), 4-11. Reproduced in *La prochaine révolution,* pp. 260-74.

45. Contrary to the claim of the impatient advocates of the growing interdependence of peoples, it would appear that since the end of the Second World War, there has been a strengthening of people's will to use national states to satisfy their individual and collective needs. Thus, the volume of international trade transactions has decreased as compared to intra-national transactions. Communications between leaders have regularly increased since the end of the Second World War, but we see no reduction in the nationalism of the various states' citizens. So, instead of being an anachronism in the contemporary world, nationalism remains very much alive. See Karl W. Deutsch, and others, *France, Germany and the Western Alliance,* (New York: Charles Scribner's Sons, 1967), and Richard Rosecrance, with Arthur Stein, "Interdependence: Myth or Realty," *World Politics,* 1973, 1-27.

46. Jean Marcel, *Le joual de Troie* (Montréal: Editions du Jour, 1973).

47. On the choices the Parti Québécois must make, see André Larocque, *Défis du Parti québécois* (Montréal: Editions du Jour, 1971). The book reports on the debates in the Parti Québécois over the last three years, debates which still continue. Guy Joron (P.Q. member of the National Assembly) wrote the preface.

48. Gérard Dion and Louis O'Neil, "Lendemain d'élection" in *Ad Usum Sacredotum,* 11, nos. 9-10, (1956), 198-204, reproduced in pamphlet form by the Ligne d'action civique, Montréal 1956; Herbert F. Quinn, *The Union Nationale: A Study in Québec Nationalism* (Toronto: University of Toronto Press, 1963), pp. 131-51.

49. "Let Ottawa hand over the loot," "Masters in our own home," and "When we are really on our own."

50. In the theoretical working paper entitled "Cultures politiques au Québec" (Québec, 1972), 263-64, Micheline de Sève and I postulate four different types of "nationalistés" (end-goals), defined as follows: *economic end-goals,* whereby the values of a group or or a person are concentrated on accumulating wealth or putting it to optimum use. Essentially *political end-goals,* wherein a people's or a leader's most dearly-held values centre around the search for power, where it can in turn influence the community's objectives in line with "the general will" or the "common good"; *Social end-goals,* where satisfying

the aspirations of the members of a community is related to their well-being as they them-selves define it, as opposed to an "ideal" or imposed determination of the common good or the general interest, overriding considerations of cost, order, or even ethics; *Cultural end-goals* where "transcendental" values become the crux of a person's "value sys-tem."

51. Frank Scott, "Canada et Canada français," an issue of the periodical *Esprit,* devoted to French Canada, August-September 1952, 185.

52. In his vast survey on the 1968 general election, John Meisel has carried out a number of studies that touch on the issues discussed here. See "Some Bases of Party Support in the 1968 Election;" "Party Images in Canada: A Report on Work in Progress;" and " 'Can-cel Out and Pass On' ": A View of Canada's Present Options"—all in John Meisel, *Working Papers on Canadian Politics* (Montreal: McGill-Queen's University Press, 1975). See also John Meisel, "Cleavages, Parties, and Values in Canada," Sage Profes-sional Paper in Contemporary Political Sociology, 1, 06003 (London and Beverly Hills: Sage Publications, 1974). See also John Meisel, with Philip E. Converse and Georges Dupeux, "Continuities in Popular Political Culture: French and Anglo-Saxon Contrasts in Canada," a paper prepared for the International Conference on Comparative Electoral Behavior, Survey Research Center of the University of Michigan, April 1967 (unpub-lished). The tendency to try to fit Québec political culture into the North American liberal democratic framework, which I seem to perceive in John Meisel's work, becomes strik-ing in other authors, less sensitive and qualified than he. Thus, in his thesis "Culture and Nationalism in Québec Politics" (1972), Charles-Michel de Salaberry unhesitatingly ca-tegorizes Québec political culture in line with Almond and Verba's *Civic Culture.* In the area studied, Hull County, he finds few "citizens," many "subjects," and a good many "parochials." Like Trudeau, de Salaberry concludes that this is a case of "democracy subverted by nationalism."

53. Philip E. Converse, "The Nature of Belief Systems in Mass Publics," in *Ideology and Discontent* ed. David E. Apter (Glencoe, N.Y.: The Free Press, 1964), 206-61.

54. This is the approach that, under the influence of Neil Smelser, John Trent appears to be following in his research upon the methods whereby nationalism spreads. See "The Poli-tics of Nationalist Movements: A Reconsideration," *Canadian Revue of Studies in Na-tionalism* 2, no. 3, Annual Meeting of the Canadian Political Science Association (1975).

55. John Deutsch, in Introduction, *One Country or Two,* ed. R. M. Burns, 14.

56. For a similar viewpoint, see Karl W. Deutsch, *Nationalism and Its Alternatives,* p. 173. It seems to me unlikely that separation could be decided upon for purely cultural reasons. Economic and political reasons will also have to come into play. As things stand, the "evidence" brought forward by independentists seems far-fetched to many people.

57. Daniel Bell, *The Coming of Post-Industrial Society,* p. 378.

58. An exception to the largely conservative approach of the Bourassa government may be found in the "socialist" measures of former Minister Claude Castonguay, adopted by the federal government and continued by his successor Claude Forget in the field of social af-fairs, and particularly of public health. The English-speaking reader may find it strange that I consider Québec's Liberal party to be maintaining the status quo in language mat-ters. In a number of English-speaking circles, Bill 22 on "French as the official lan-guage" introduced by Minister François Cloutier and adopted by the National Assembly in July 1974, is perceived as a radical measure. However that is not how the great major-ity of Francophones, whether federalists or independentists, liberal or socialist, see this legislation. They considered it as one-of-a-kind with Bill 63 which it replaces and which merely entrenched the status quo, unfairly favouring the Anglophones. The premier of New Brunswick decided to challenge the constitutionality of this legislation before the Supreme Court. Once again, failing substance, Québec will do battle over a "symbol."

59. Vera Murray, "La culture politique du Ralliement des créditistes," Laval University re-search report (unpublished), 1974.

CHAPTER 6   THE COMING REVOLUTION (pp. 177-207)

1. See my *Société et politique, la vie des groupes,* vol. 1: *Fondement de la société libérale;* vol. 2: *Dynamique de la société libérale,* (Quebec: Presses universitaires de Laval, 1971-1972). See also my presidential address to the Canadian Political Science Association: ''The Political Uses of Political Sciences,'' *Canadian Journal of Political Science* 8, no 3, (September 1975).

2. Of the two main transcendental categories of understanding, space and time, Anglo-phones lay the greatest emphasis upon space, and Francophones upon time. In this respect, the former are typically North American. Their patriotism, which is underplayed but deeper than Francophones realize, is based on the size, the ''great open spaces'' and the wild beauty of the land. Many of them, even as far away as the prairies or British Columbia, declare proudly that Québec is the finest jewel in this vast country. Pierre Elliott Trudeau, like many Canadian politicians before him, is trying to base national unity on this dream of a ''vast, beautiful Canada.'' French Canadians see themselves primarily in relation to time. They are still experiencing the consequences of a traumatic event that took place during their childhood as a nation, that is, their defeat at the hands of the English. If there is a ''people without a history'' in Canada, it is the English Canadians. The French Canadians, richer in terms of time, have hardly yet begun to tap the immense possibilities of space. More than 80 percent of them huddled shiveringly, fearfully, lovingly along the banks of the Saint Lawrence.

3. The rest of this chapter, save for one paragraph, has not been published before.

4. For more on this subject, see my article, ''La crise du leadership. Un autre défi redoutable pour Robert Bourassa: assainir le climat politique au Québec,'' *Le Devoir,* Tuesday, 11 March 1975.

5. *Société et politique: la vie des groupes,* vol. 2: *Dynamique de la société libérale* (Québec: Presses de l'Université Laval, 1972), 1469-70.

6. See my book *Le Bill 60 et la société québécois* (Montréal: HMH, 1967), on the impassioned debate set off by this legislation.

7. If, however, one judges by initial indications, the effects might tend to be unfavourable for Québec, as indeed for the rest of the country. In the field of natural resources, hydro-electric power (which was for eighty years Canada's principal attraction in the eyes of industrial investors) has dropped to second place in importance, coming after nuclear energy. The market for industrial goods and services is small, Canada being practically alone, among advanced industrial countries, in having a domestic market of fewer than one hundred million people. Our immense natural resources are threatened by the growing number of synthetic products (plastics, synthetic fibres in paper manufacturing, synthetic foods, etc.). On the social and human level, union demands are higher than those of our future competitors, the African and Asian peoples. The Canadian economy lacks vigour, dominated as it is by the American economy. There is a lack of ambition and innovative ability among engineers, and a poorly developed sense of management among executive personnel. Finally, on the political level, governments sin by inefficiency, incompetence, and sheer carelessness in economic and scientific policy. On this subject, besides the points made throughout this book, see the Report of the Special Senate Committee on Science Policy, *Science Policy for Canada,* vols. 1 and 2, Information Canada, 1971-72.

8. Albert Faucher, ''La révolution tranquillisante,'' *Revue canadienne de science politique/Canadian Journal of Political Science,* 5, no. 1 (1973).

9. See my article: ''Aspects de la condition du professeur d'université dans la société canadienne-française,'' *Cité libre,* July 1958, 7-30.

10. ''Chevauchement des cultures,'' the title of a paper delivered before the Institut des affaires publiques, 1955.